Picking Your Battles

ALSO BY BONNIE MASLIN, PH.D.

Loving Men for All the Right Reasons: Women's Patterns of Intimacy
Not Quite Paradise: Making Marriage Work
The Angry Marriage: Overcoming the Rage, Reclaiming the Love

Picking
Your Battles

Winning Strategies for

Raising Well-Behaved Kids

Bonnie Maslin, Ph.D.

S ⟨...⟩ w York

www.stmartins.com

Library of Congress Cataloging-in-Publication Data

Maslin, Bonnie.
    Picking your battles : winning strategies for raising well-behaved kids / Bonnie Maslin.
        p. cm.
    ISBN 0-312-26378-3
    EAN 978-0312-26378-2
    1. Child rearing. I. Title.

HQ769.M346 2004
649'.1—dc22   2003058772

First Edition: June 2004

1   3   5   7   9   10   8   6   4   2

This book is dedicated to

the blessed memory of Amy Elisabeth Rothholz,

beloved daughter of Paula Trachtman

and cherished stepdaughter of Edward Butscher.

Contents

Preface

Truth in Packaging

Bookstore shelves groan under the weight of the many books written on parenting, and a significant number of these well-stocked shelves are packed with a wide variety of "How to Discipline Your Child" manuals. Some are good, some are excellent, and a few are genuinely indispensable. (My indispensable favorites are listed at the end of this preface.)

Each author's background invariably brings a worthwhile point of view that can make raising a well-behaved child easier. My perspective is informed by my experience as a teacher; scientist; teacher trainer; educational consultant; author of books on relationships, marriage, and family; school psychologist; psychologist in clinical practice; mother; stepmother; and grandmother (thanks to my stepchildren). You will find my approach to discipline to be very practical, but I always base my down-to-earth recommendations on a serious understanding of the child. With my background, I do not have it in me to give simplistic advice. What's more, I firmly believe that only discipline methods, techniques, strategies, tactics, or tips based on serious knowledge help you succeed.

While the ideas come from professional knowledge, they also come from hard-won experience—I am a parent. I did not write *Picking Your*

Battles from the lofty perch of parenting pundit. Mine is not the "I'm so perfect, so you'll be so perfect" approach to child rearing. While I am a psychologist with over twenty-five years of experience working with families and children, flawless parenting is not my stock-in-trade. The vantage point of *Picking Your Battles* is the trenches, not the exalted heights. I wrote this book because I made every mistake in it and fortunately learned from it. From this humbling experience, I know what every one of my readers knows: parenting is one tough job, and we can *all* use help.

These days, more than ever, busy, overworked, thoughtful parents want and need to be more effective. Why is it so crucial to be effective and in charge? Parents have all too little family time to spend it battling kids. They need to know how to pick their battles to ensure that the time

---

INDISPENSABLE PARENTING BOOKS

The Beast in the Nursery or any of the other books about children by psychologist Adam Phillips. This is a challenging read, as are all his books, but very much worth it.

Touchpoints—a series of books by the sensitive pediatrician T. Berry Brazelton.

The Mother's Almanac and *The Mother's Almanac Goes to School* by Marguerite Kelly and illustrated by Katy Kelly: books that do a wonderful job of describing children's development from birth to eleven years.

Your Child, an excellent book on child development issued by the American Academy of Child and Adolescent Psychiatry.

The Magic Years: this classic by Selma Fraiberg is a bit dated but marvelous for getting into the mind of your baby and pre-schooler.

Any good **teacher's manual**, especially one intended for new teachers; teachers' manuals are a great source of information about children and are chock-full of creative ideas on discipline. A good one is *The New Teacher's Handbook: What All Good Teachers Need to Know*, by Gary Garfield.

Between Parent and Child and all other books by Haim Ginott. Written by this teacher, principal, psychologist in the 1960s but timeless in its advice on communicating with your child.

they do share with their children is not marred by unnecessary discord and conflict, but rather marked by peace and joy. I trust that the wisdom you will find in the pages of this book will make you an effective, in-charge parent, which will create the possibility of this greater peace and joy for you and for your family.

Acknowledgments

Tis book made a long journey from conception to completion, and I am grateful that it found a welcoming home at St. Martin's Press, in the competent hands of my editor Jennifer Weis. My agent and friend, Carla Glasser, was mother to this project and the driving force behind this book. My first reader was, as always, my dearest friend Themis Dimon. Her insatiable curiosity about the human mind and soul fuels all of her ventures in life, including assisting me with my first drafts. Additional editorial help also came from my circle of close friends. Jackie Hord was an astute editor as well as a pal in the dark winter days at the beach where I wrote most of this book. The final shaping of the manuscript was in the talented hands of Paula Trachtman, who offered a home-cooked meal and a warm embrace every time we traded chapters. To all of these women I offer abundant thanks.

My husband, Yehuda Nir, my children Sarah and David, and stepchildren Aaron, Satoko, Dan, and Jill were, as always, a source of support, as they are in all my ventures. My grandkids Phoebe, Sophie, and the latest arrival, Jonah Miyake, have helped me stay deeply and lovingly connected to the wonder and delight of "kids under construction." I deeply appreciate the patience of family and all my dear friends, especially Beverly

Moore, Andrew Alloy, and Marcia Richards, who kept my life running during the long and sometimes entirely absorbing process of crafting this book.

Thanks, also, to Dr. Ruth Resch, Dr. Paul Fink, Barbara Sassoon, Amira Trattner, and Dr. Edward Hartmann for their invaluable assistance.

I am indebted to many scholars in the field of psychology who have shaped my understanding of the human heart and mind, in particular Donald Winnicott, Haim Ginott, Lawrence Kohlberg, Jean Piaget, Selma Fraiberg, and Louise Bates Ames.

I am, as always, deeply grateful to my patients. My work is informed by the knowledge I have gained through knowing them and I thank them for the privilege of their trust.

Above all, I thank my own mother, who wrote the book on generosity, goodness, and love, which is why I am able to do all that I do in life, including writing this book.

Picking Your Battles

Introduction

....

It's 7:59 A.M. Do You Know Where Your Sanity Is?

If you don't put on those pants in one second, you can get on that school bus naked!" When you read these words, you should immediately imagine a mother or, more precisely, a woman who was a mother before the blood in her veins started to seethe, before the eyes in her head began to bulge, before her voice cracked the sound barrier, before she morphed into a deranged I-have-got-to-get-this-kid-into-pants-or-he'll-miss-the-bus-and-I'll-be-late-for-work-and-my-boss-will-have-a-fit lunatic rather than the good-natured mom she usually is.

It is 7:59 A.M., and she has spotted the large, banana-yellow vehicle rounding the corner toward the house. For the last hour, besides making breakfast, finding school-lunch money, grabbing clean socks out of the dryer, locating misplaced school books, signing permission slips, and trying to get ready for her own job, she has been unsuccessfully trying to get the pants on her youngest son.

Forget the pants! Suddenly, with the bus driver honking his final I-am-fed-up-waiting-again honk, dragging the lovable tyke onto the bus in his Barney-Fruit-of-the-Looms seems like a mighty real possibility. What a way to start the day! It isn't even eight A.M., and she is already fried to a crisp.

Can you conjure up this vision of "former mom?" No? Then save your money and put this book back on the shelf.

Now, for the rest of us . . . Even if the scenario is not precisely yours, any real parent can easily picture this scene, because at one time or another everyone has turned into a parental lunatic. We battle with our toddlers, skirmish with our preschoolers, clash with our preteens, and wage war with our adolescents. And no matter when or where the combat takes place, the results are invariably the same: aggravation, irritation, frustration, and exasperation.

Kids, bless them all, seem to have an extraordinary capacity for finding endless ways to drive parents to distraction. And it is teeth-gritting, jaw-clenching, muscle-tensing episodes like this that make life as a parent difficult and trying. *But it doesn't have to be that way!*

This is a book about making life as a parent easier. It is about learning to pick your battles. It is about developing a strategy for addressing these inevitable conflicts with children—successfully. Not all battles are well waged or worthwhile. More often than not, battles resolve little they seem intended to address and instead get endlessly replayed. All too often they make things worse. But picking your battles is not the same as advocating a free-for-all. It is not about throwing out the rules or throwing in the towel. Rather it is about understanding which battles are necessary and how to wage them adaptively. It is a way to make anger work for, rather than against, you and your child. It is a way to raise healthy, happy, and decent children, while at the same time retaining your sanity.

Everyone Morphs: What Sends You Over the Top?

Parents battle with children, all of us. If it isn't getting pants on your child's bottom that currently sends you over the top, for sure it is something else.

No, you cannot have another glass of water.
Look at that closet; what do you mean you have nothing to wear?
Those toys will go to some child who will really appreciate them;
    not some spoiled brat like you.
This room should be condemned by the Board of Health.
Do you think money grows on trees?

Get out of bed this instant.

Oh my gosh, you did what on the new living-room wallpaper?

If you don't brush your hair, I'll take scissors and cut it all off.

I don't care if everyone in the whole world is doing it. No child of mine is going to school dressed like that.

This is the worst report card I've ever seen. You just don't live up to your potential.

For the last time, keep your fingers away from that socket or you'll electrocute yourself!

That telephone (television, computer, CD player, etc.) is going out the window.

It's ten P.M., and now you're telling me this science project is due tomorrow?

Your teeth will fall out of your head if you eat those cookies for breakfast.

Fine. Don't walk the dog. I'm giving it to the pound.

I don't care who started it. Stop fighting or you'll both get it!

Quit whining. You are too big to be carried.

If you can't play nicely and share, I'm sending your friend home this instant.

Do you know what time it is? Couldn't you at least have had the decency to call us?

Go ahead, have a tantrum; you're still not getting it.

If you're not hungry enough to eat broccoli, you are certainly not hungry enough to get dessert.

Sound familiar? Of course, it does. It has happened to you. It has happened to all of us: The Battle Royal, the all-out war between you and your child. True, you are not proud of it. This was not your finest hour. But trust me, there isn't anyone who hasn't gone over the top with kids. No one. Now, not all parents lose it at the very same spot. Some go breezing through toddlerhood as if it were a freeway with no potholes. Then they turn the corner only to find a preteen who makes them feel as if the road they are navigating is pocked with one chassis-cracking crater after another. On the other hand, it could just as easily go the other way: Preteens may seem a piece of cake while it is the little tykes that undo you. When it comes to the magnitude of frustration, size does not count. Many a four-year-old getting ready for school has brought a Wall Street titan to his or her knees, while more than one otherwise self-possessed parent has dragged a screaming, kicking toddler out of Toys "R" Us, hoping they won't be mistakenly charged with child abuse. Our battle scenes may vary, but conflict is unavoidable, and, invariably, they are repeat performances without happy endings. Fortunately, life with kids does not ever have to be this wearing, and parenting can actually become easier and a lot more pleasurable.

What This Book Offers: How to Have an Almost Hassle-free Home

I have two critical and, I believe, enormously useful objectives in writing this book. I would like to help you become a take-charge parent 1) skilled at preventing parent/child battles *and* 2) expert at successfully resolving conflicts when (not *if*, but *when*) they do occur. This is a parenting guide for encouraging cooperation and self-discipline in kids as well as for effectively dealing with their misbehavior. With this dual approach— avoiding *and* surviving parent/child fights—instead of morphing into a frenzied parent, you might actually make it through most days in charge *and* relatively aggravation-free.

Throughout these pages, to help this dual process, I will offer you advice distilled into sayings that I call **Picking Your Battles (PYB) Words of Wisdom.** These highlighted maxims are intended to reinforce many of the important parenting ideas that make advice, strategies, and tactics effective. You may find it useful to jot down some of these **PYB Words of Wisdom.** Pay close attention to them. If you have principles and knowledge behind your discipline strategies, they will not be hollow words, and the transformation will be real and lasting.

I offer something else that I believe can be invaluable; actual concrete examples, right down to the very words you might say to your children when you are navigating through a discipline problem. This may surprise you, but my goal *is* to put words in your mouth so that you can constructively communicate with your children. Every study shows, and every child or family therapist will tell you, that healthy communication between parents and children is the number-one factor in positive parenting and raising good kids. And this book will most certainly give you *and* your children the words.

A Brief Look at What's to Come

Part One: Preventing Unnecessary Battles

You will learn the four key steps that go into prevention:

1. Setting **reasonable expectations** about conduct, based on an understanding of your child's developmental stage
2. Developing a common sense **parenting philosophy**
3. Creating thoughtful and practical **family policy**
4. Adopting a **positive pattern of discipline by eliminating self-defeating "No-win Discipline Reactions"**

Step 1. Becoming a Kidology Expert: Setting Developmentally Reasonable Expectations

You wouldn't ask your eight-year-old to drive you to work and then grow angry with her when she runs the Jeep through the garage door. It wouldn't be developmentally appropriate. There'd be no argument, because you would never create such an unreasonable expectation of your child. All too often, however unwittingly, we parents make requests of our children that are beyond them. Then we, and they, get irritated when they can't measure up.

Kidology—practical child-development know-how—is key to effective discipline strategies. It allows you to understand developmental readiness—what kids can do and when they can do it—enabling you to tailor discipline to your child's developmental stage.

There are four behavioral stages every child goes through on his or her way to preadolescence:

• Infant (the first twelve months)
• Toddler (thirteen months to three years)
• Preschool (nursery to kindergarten)
• Grade school (first to sixth grade)

Every few years development shifts so dramatically that you actually have a very different creature inhabiting your home at each of these four ages/stages. You may be surprised to see how easily this information can be used to make life with your child at her particular stage aggravation-free and much more fun.

Step 2. Developing a Commonsense Parenting Philosophy

The single most powerful determinant in raising decent, respectful, and cooperative kids is a sound parenting point of view, a philosophy of child rearing. This philosophy is essentially your notion of what it means to be a parent; the role you see yourself playing in the life of your child. Think of it as your parental job description. Fortunately, once you have a firm grasp on the common sense parenting philosophy offered in these pages, countless unnecessary battles will all but evaporate.

Step 3. Creating Family Policy

> *Please, ma, just five more minutes.*
> *But everyone else's parents lets them.*
> *I don't wanna.*
> *Why do I have tuh?*
> *No fair.*

These are the sounds of the daily skirmishes of family life. Yes, big battles are very taxing, but it is the daily skirmishes that wear us out and whittle us down. Establishing family policy with rules and guidelines governing family life seriously reduces endless discussions, debates, and threats about a kid's conduct. A clear family policy sets children straight on what is expected of them so that it doesn't have to be rehashed time and again. Just imagine dinner, bedtime, bath, and homework with no more tears, either yours or theirs! But there is more good news; establishing routines and rituals creates a stable family life, which is key to raising good and decent kids.

Step 4. Adopting a Positive Pattern of Discipline

When it comes to discipline, many well-meaning parents repeatedly try to get kids to behave in ways that just don't work. You have probably even noticed this thinking: "She always lets her kids get away with murder";

"He's constantly yelling but it never makes a dent in his child's behavior"; "No matter how poorly they behave, he acts like his kids can do no wrong. I think he's making them into spoiled brats." After years of observing parents and children, I've identified eight most common, predictable, and completely self-sabotaging patterns: No-win Discipline Styles. These are the eight ways we try to do right with our kids but, regrettably, mishandle our anger and get discipline wrong. Parents, unwittingly caught in a no-win discipline style:

- furiously forecast or threaten punishment that never comes
- have angry resolve, initially insisting a child "behaves himself," but then capitulate—or "cave in"—in the face of a protesting, unhappy, or resistant child
- shift or displace anger and responsibility for discipline onto others so that they are never in direct conflict with their child
- have a short fuse and react impatiently and instantly to a child's behavior, flying off the handle at the slightest infraction with a volley of reprimands
- do a "slow burn," tolerating misbehavior far too long before finally reaching the last straw and then—and only then—going ballistic
- angrily find fault, detecting trouble even when it may not exist, and are hypervigilant about their child's misbehavior
- erupt with fury, erratically meting out punishment unpredictably and inconsistently
- disconnect from anger, denying or burying rage so that they do not have to feel it, or know it exists

These overused no-win approaches, which **never** make our kids more cooperative or well-behaved, invariably have a long history springing from our very own childhood. Even as we try to be the new and improved version of our own parents, they often deeply and adversely influence our discipline reactions. We unwittingly drag baggage from the past into our present parenting, but, with help, you can break these bad emotional habits, remnants of the past, and stop them from interfering with raising your children in peace.

Part Two. Surviving Hassles and Headaches: Strategies and Tactics

This second section focuses more directly on strategies and tactics for managing the everyday headaches and hassles of child rearing, as well as the more serious transgressions.

Strategies

Here are the Six Fundamental Strategies for Effective Discipline that you will learn to implement:

- **Setting Limits and Boundaries:** creating the basic guidelines needed to answer the all-important question, "Is this a battle worth fighting? Do I go to the mat for this one or give it a pass?" (chapter 5)
- **Developing Your Child's Capacity for Self-discipline:** creating the critical capacity for good judgment in your child, so that discipline comes from the inside out (chapters 6 and 7)
- **Developing Your Child's Moral Compass:** assuring that your child develops a conscience, so that she becomes ethical, honest, and acts with decency (chapter 8)
- **Encouraging Compassion and Respect:** developing your child's capacity for empathy, the bedrock of cooperation and good citizenship (chapter 9)
- **Getting Good at Getting Angry:** transforming anger—yours and your child's—into a positive force that resolves conflict and eliminates misbehavior for good (chapter 10)
- **Implementing No-Nonsense Discipline:** learning to use the effective strategy of "cost and consequences," which puts a stop to even the most serious misbehavior (chapter 11).

Tactics

You can also count on becoming well versed in many practical and winning tactics that will make everything (from strapping your toddler into a car seat to ensuring your grade-schooler keeps his seat at the dinner table) a relatively peaceful undertaking:

- **The Structured Choice:** making a request of your child so that "yes" is the only possible answer:

- **Step-by-Step:** gaining cooperation from kids by breaking requests down into a series of smaller tasks
- **Joining, Not Fighting:** deflating defiance by constructively joining in on your child's actions and ideas instead of opposing them
- **Staying in the Groove:** getting kids to stop whining, and gaining cooperation by uncompromising repetition of your requests and/or decisions
- **Positive Reframing:** recasting your child's behavior in a positive light in order to defuse tension
- **Giving Notice:** assisting your child in making changes and transitions, which ensures compliance
- **Practice Tactics:** using pretend play, visitation, rehearsing, and role-playing to help kids develop more mature and accommodating behavior

Tools, Not Talk

I want to emphasize a point that is absolutely central to my approach to practical and sensible discipline: *I don't subscribe to the quick fix.* Many books on this subject race through scenario after scenario, offering instant recipes for gaining your child's cooperation. Some even whisk through every potential conflict from A to Z, offering simplistic advice on every possible misstep a child can make. This book doesn't. I am giving you tools, not rhetoric. In addition to the fact that they actually work, the greatest advantage is that real tools can be used on various discipline jobs. *One thoughtful strategy will go a long way to resolving many battles.* As you gain knowledge of these versatile tactics and strategies, each will spark your imagination and creativity, making you a more effective parent and, most important, your *own* expert on keeping the peace.

How to Get the Most Out of This Book

Good parenting builds on itself. Don't make the error of thinking that there are parts of this book you can do without. For example, don't jump over a section on toddlers just because you have a preschooler. Your preschooler was also a toddler, and what you know and understand about that earlier stage influences every other that follows. Reading about a later stage and ignoring earlier development is a lot like walking into a building thinking that you can take an elevator from the fifth story, without starting your ascent at the ground floor.

But here is the good news, the very good news: Put in the time, and improvement of your family life will astonish you. There are ideas in these pages that can turn your child around, making a troublemaker into someone far closer to angelic, and making a good kid into a stellar one. This is a promise that can be delivered on, because there is nothing more powerful than a new idea, and this book is full of them.* Be open to the knowledge in these pages, and there is more than a good possibility that the life of your child and your family can be transformed from tense to tranquil.

> ▶ **PYB Words of Wisdom:** *Becoming good at discipline is not an event, it's a process. Get your grounding.*

---

*Many ideas in these pages are original. For example, the concept of kidology and joining not fighting are concepts that I have developed out of my clinical experience. However, many of the ideas in Picking Your Battles build on principles developed in the field of psychology, child development, and education that are in general use. For instance, limits, empathy, and resilience are widely used concepts. The idea of Family Commandments are derived from my experience as a classroom teacher. Reframing is a concept developed in the field of cognitive psychology, while structured choice is an idea based on the work of psychologist Hiam Ginott. When the ideas derive from a particular individual's work, I will cite it as a basis.

Part I

Preventing
Unnecessary Battles

Chapter 1

A Crash Course
in Child Development

Getting the Kids to Get It Together

Get ready. Get washed. Get here. Get settled. Get up. Get down. Get moving. Get dressed. And, for goodness sake, get that macaroni out of your nose!

Would you ever have imagined that you, a grown person of otherwise sound mind, might be sitting across a dinner table from another, much smaller, human being, imploring her to extract tiny tubes of pasta from her nostrils? While once it might have been beyond your imagination, these days, thanks to the offspring, it's your life we're talking about. And what a life it is! If you are a parent, no day passes without having to prod an uncooperative offspring into much-hoped-for but not-always-achieved compliance. If compliance was always achieved, your pediatrician would not be so adept at removing noodles from noses. It's a job and a half.

Children can turn us into full-time nagging machines. When we aren't nagging, we're scolding. Be quiet. Stop fighting. Quit dawdling. Sit still. Don't touch. Watch out. And, for the tenth time, put that candy back on the rack. (How can I reprimand you? Let me count the ways.) Fortunately, there is a sure-fire way to cut down on this need for nagging and especially the repertoire of reprimands. It is not all that difficult. All you need is a Ph.D. in kidology, a practical understanding of your child's development.

Knowing the Beast in the Nursery

The key to smooth sailing is to understand the world from your child's perspective, which is *not* at all the same as an adult's. But don't be fooled even if your child is the "spitting image" of you; it will be quite a few years—nearly two decades—before she is capable of thinking and behaving like a full-fledged grown up; despite bearing a striking resemblance to a person, children are ***not*** miniature versions of adults. How many adults do you know who think that sitting in a metal shopping cart and snatching packages from grocery shelves is an indoor sport?

Kids are born developmentally unfinished—from birth, they may have all their parts, but it takes time before everything is fully operational physically and mentally: Each and every one of them is a work in progress. In fact, as they grow and mature, because of their changing bodies and minds, children are not always the same little "beast in the nursery." In the early years (from birth to eleven), they change into at least *four* distinct creatures along the way to becoming a human adult. Once you understand that each child is a parade of ever-changing little beings, you will get a better handle on the capabilities and limitations of your offspring, and you will have far less conflict.

> ▶ **PYB Words of Wisdom:** *When you look at your growing child, think "Person Under Construction," and adjust your expectations accordingly.*

Knowing what makes your child tick and how he sees the world as he journeys through these developmental stages makes you a *kidologist*, a real-life expert on your own child's growth and maturation. Parents who possess this knowledge know what to expect, and they can wisely judge what to accept as appropriate behavior. They also come to understand when the demands they make are beyond a child's developmental reach, and, most important, discover what discipline approach can work with kids and what won't make a dent in behavior. By recognizing these phases and making accurate behavioral assessments, you will more deftly and calmly navigate the challenges that each stage invariably brings.

Kids on Parade

Here are the four stages in the parade:

Infant	the first twelve months
Toddler	thirteen months to three years
Preschooler	three to five years (nursery to kindergarten)
Grade-schooler	six to eleven years (first to sixth grade)

At each stop in this parade, you will actually discover a very different sort of child—physically, emotionally, cognitively, and socially—living under your roof. Understanding these phases and the age-appropriate behavior that go with each will help you set reasonable, appropriate, and, most important, *achievable* goals and standards for your child. Expectations in sync with your child's *behavioral readiness* make compliance possible and children a lot less impossible.

> ▶ **PYB Words of Wisdom:** *Misbehavior often results from expectations that unwittingly misfit your child's developmental stage and behavioral readiness. A good fit makes for good kids.*

THE CANDY GRAB

An All-Too-Common Example of a Developmental Misunderstanding

Asking a toddler to get past the Gummy Bears on the supermarket checkout line without the infamous "candy grab" is demanding the near impossible. All the warnings, threats, and reprimands are useless. Whether you sweetly cajole or shriek at the top of your lungs, the words "don't touch" are incomprehensible to your toddler.

(continued on next page)

Words don't and can't make an immediate dent in your child's behavior, because kids at this stage are developmentally wired to *touch* and *clutch*, but not yet wired to reason. They are not being bad, willful, or dishonest. The capacity to reason doesn't start to emerge until three or four years of age. Toddlers are not yet able to understand an abstract concept like "Thou shalt not steal" or "You are driving me nuts by pulling that unhealthy junk off the rack."

Developmentally, you are talking to a wall, though you may feel as if you are butting your head against one. But you are *not* being ignored. This is *not* misbehavior. It is an easily remedied misunderstanding of a child's mental and physical equipment that doesn't yet work through language and ideas. *Remember: Children are good, but not always that good at obeying because of their developmental age/stage.*

Kidology Enables Parents to Be Prepared

Kidology provides a *sneak preview* of what you can expect from your child at a particular stage, and this can make life a whole lot easier. You will probably find yourself less reactive and angry about a behavior that you know is challenging but developmentally expectable. Your patience for a nine-month-old intentionally dropping his food from his high chair will expand as you discover that it is *not* an activity designed to drive you mad but actually a measure of his cognitive maturity. He is no smart aleck; he is trying to become smart.

As surprising as it sounds, you may well find endearing a behavior that could have otherwise made you hit the roof or cry your eyes out. This happened to Julia, mother of nine-year-old Robyn, who knew in advance that every grade-school child goes through a "Mommy, you are so mean" phase.

"I didn't let Robyn know it, but her first 'You are so unfair, I hate you' was a milestone that touched me. Robyn had such a heartfelt sense of injustice written across her face. It was impossible not to be sympathetic to her tragic plight of having such a 'terrible' mother. I recall saying to myself and then out loud to her, 'Well, the two of us are going to live through this, aren't we?' And we did!"

▶ **PYB Words of Wisdom:** *A dose of kidology inoculates you against overreacting. When you expect a behavior, and it feels developmentally on target, you are far more patient and less likely to be thrown by it.*

KIDS ON PARADE

At each of the four stages of development, from birth to age eleven, there is virtually a different being inhabiting your home. To get a flavor of each stage, it may be useful to keep these different creatures in mind:

Infant: A small, squawking, hungry little **bird,** all mouth and unable to fly on its own

Toddler: A curious **monkey,** a veritable natural scientist bent on actively exploring his world

Early Childhood/Preschooler: A fanciful, talkative **sprite,** whose sense of the world is magical more than logical

Middle Childhood/Grade-schooler: A busy and industrious **beaver,** who leaves home to join others at school, to learn and to discover who she is and how she fits into the world outside her family

---

1. Your Baby: First Twelve Months

The Parade Begins: Your Baby

Bundles of tension waiting for release, newborn infants are hungry bodies full of physical cravings long before they are reasoning minds. They are "can't-wait" beings that notice no one and nothing—not because they are selfish but because they have yet to discover that they are "a self," let alone discover that a world outside of them exists. They are driven by what they need and, especially at the beginning, they need almost everything ASAP. Like newly hatched birds in a nest, infants make a racket and need you to fly to their aid.

Born so poorly equipped for survival on their own, infants are dependent, powerless, helpless, vulnerable, and needy beings. Fortunately, nature has seen to it that with these profound limitations, human infants are born into another's embrace, a caregiver who can make up for the faculties and abilities a baby so sorely lacks.

For his very survival, every baby depends on a bigger, stronger, more capable person coming to his aid—you! Initially, parenting *is* a one-way street, because of this. You give, because as an adult you have the faculties; babies receive, because they don't. So here is the most important point about expectations: When it comes to parenting an infant, especially in the very beginning, everything is expected of you and virtually nothing can be expected of your baby.

This means that, in the beginning, you *cannot* expect a tiny one to:

- wait and be patient
- keep safe
- be regular, regulated, predictable, or maintain a schedule
- be calm and quiet
- know that *you* have needs
- be appreciative
- be reasonable (they are driven by their bodily urges, not their reasoning minds).

If you find yourself demanding behaviors that require these capacities, you are heading for trouble. Take waiting, for example: Your baby can't manage it. It is beyond behavioral readiness. Practically speaking, you surely will be aggravated if you settle down expecting an uninterrupted viewing of your favorite four-hour video when your infant feeds every three hours. Your tiny one *cannot wait* for the hero's final farewell as her empty stomach growls. You will have to do the waiting, not she. The video has a pause button, your infant doesn't.

Infants do not stay helpless creatures oblivious of others forever. With time and maturity, the street starts to go both ways, and children discover the world outside themselves and their own needs. Think of this developmental process—finding out that other people exist in the world (and discovering that those others have needs)—as "hatching." Yes, in the beginning your infant does not know you exist as a person.

It might sound strange, since this baby is so at the center of your life. Yet, despite your devotion to her, your newborn does not have the faculties to feel the same about you. It takes time for that understanding to kick in. Babies are naturally self-absorbed, in the beginning.

The work of parents is to assist in transforming an infant's powerlessness into possibilities, to help an infant become regulated, reasonable, able, to manage urges, and, with time, to recognize others and their needs. With your guidance it does happen, but in the beginning your baby is in total need of you!

What to Expect of Your Newborn Infant

Expect Your Newborn to Be Sensitive

While newborn babies don't make sense of the world the way adults do, they are **very** sensitive to their surroundings. They see, hear, smell, taste, and feel their way in the world. And they are particularly sensitive to the perception of their own body position, movement, and muscular tension, which makes them reactive to their own bodily sensations and tensions, as well as to how they are touched, held, and moved by you. That is why your being gently responsive is essential to their well-being. Your smile, the sound of your voice, your embrace, your odor, the touch of your skin, and your feeding, form the foundation of sensory experience from which they will grow and mature into calm, well-balanced children.

Gentle responsiveness is the basis for bonding with your infant. Sensitively tuning in to your baby creates a sturdy and secure attachment, laying the foundation for calm, loving, and peaceful relations between you and your child.

> ▶ **PYB Words of Wisdom:** *As a parent, you are your infant's first teacher in how to become lovingly connected to another human being. You are also your baby's pupil as he works his magic and makes you fall in love with him. Teach him and learn from him. Guide him and let him guide you.*

APPLY KIDOLOGY TO AVOID AGGRAVATION

To Calm an Infant, Take Your Cues from the Womb

A fetus spends nine months bobbing in a warm bath. To cut down on aggravation, create a similar environment for your baby. Gentle and rhythmic rocking, swinging, and swaying soothe babies. Cooing, humming, and singing will also have a calming effect. (Some researchers think those noises resemble the muffled sounds your baby heard in the womb.)

- A car ride or a walk in a stroller can be calming for an inconsolable baby.
- Sound machines or tapes that simulate heart or ocean sounds soothe.
- Try a rocking chair, swing, or cradle.
- With your baby in your arms, gently dance and sway to soft music.

Gentle rocking is not shaking. Never shake a baby—it is extremely dangerous.

Expect Your Newborn to Have an "Alarming" Cry

Helpless babies come with one piece of equipment that works very well—their lungs! From the very first moments, babies are well equipped to cry, because their lives depend on it! A baby's cry is nature's alarm system that succeeds in getting capable parents where they belong—at their baby's side, to care for him. In fact, to ensure that this alarm system works as it should, a newborn's cry is especially high-pitched so that it cannot easily be ignored. Don't despair, after the first month or so, an infant's cry gets lower pitched and less noxious, and, in eight to twelve weeks, their stomachs start to hold more, enabling them to become more regulated. You will get more sleep, so hold on; there is a light at the end of this tunnel.

Your baby's cry may feel painful, especially if you are a first-time parent. It may feel like an accusation—"You are not making me happy." Then, when you can't come up with anything to stop the crying right away, tension soars. The dreaded "Yikes, I don't know what I am doing" jitters take over, which, of course, makes you even more tense. This feeling is at its worst if you are breast-feeding and your milk is coming in slowly, or if your baby does not take to the breast easily, or if your baby is colicky (which is common). To prevent crying from escalating into stress and strain, and from making you feel at odds with your little one, understand this **very** important kidology point about your newborn's cry:

Your new infant is **not** crying the way you might from unhappiness and sadness. This is not the emotionally laden crying of an adult. In fact, you will see that your newborn does not even cry with tears until she is several weeks old. Crying is just the way your baby signals that she is experiencing bodily tension, as well as the way she releases tension to help restore bodily balance. In the beginning, this is a baby's main work. An infant's full-time job, with your loving assistance, is to practice feeling bodily discomfort and then discovering that a calm and steady bodily state can and does follow. She feels the discomfort of hunger, gets fed, and achieves balance. This shift from tension to relaxation is absolutely normal and keeps on rapidly cycling in those first weeks of life, getting more rhythmic with time—which is why your baby will cry less with time, and why sleep and feeding will also become more rhythmic.

> ▶ **PYB Words of Wisdom:** *Don't mistakenly misread your baby's normal cycles of tension and release as "cranky" or "difficult." This mislabeling risks setting up attitudes that put child and parents at odds from the beginning.*

EXPECT A LOT OF CRYING IN THE BEGINNING

Newborns spend from one to three hours each day vigorously crying, often for fifteen-minute jags. Since they sleep so much, it may seem as if all they do is cry. While crying is related to discomfort from hunger or cold, it can periodically be nonspecific and unexplained. So, if you have done everything that can be done, it may just be a bout of unexplained crying, which will pass.

Apply Kidology to Diminish Tension: Measure Your Baby's Actual Crying Output Since crying can seem unending, try logging your baby's crying time. You will find that he is developmentally on target, which may at least calm you down.

If your child has long periods of unexplained crying, especially if she seems in acute distress, consult your doctor.

Crying is also your baby's language, and it is the way she can tell you what she needs. By three months, an infant starts to "hatch" and discovers the world, and she will spend less time crying. By eight months, this "language" gets easier to understand, since at this stage babies cry in different ways to communicate that they are hurt, wet, hungry, lonely, or just trying to unwind and let off tension. As your baby gets older, try to tune into these differences; it will make your life a lot less hectic if you do.

> ▶ **PYB Words of Wisdom:** *When you answer your baby's cry, you are creating the second miracle of life— love. Loving attachment and trust comes from your attentive responses to your little one. It is the basis for creating a life with a contented child.*

RECOGNIZING DIFFERENT CRIES

To help you recognize the communication of your infant's cry and reduce tension, write down the different types of cries you hear:

1. How many are there?
2. Describe what each one sounds like: Are they long and piercing, short and fretful, or bleating?
3. When do you hear each of them?
4. What action quiets them—rocking, cooing, singing, patting, changing, feeding?

Paying attention will help you decode your child's "language" and will let you feel more in charge and less anxious.

Making Life Peaceful with Your Newborn: Establishing Rhythm

Expect Your Newborn Not to Know Night from Day (but Work to Establish Sleep Patterns Early)

When you arrive home with your bundle of joy, he lands in your arms with an infant form of jet lag—he doesn't know what time zone he is in, day and night are interchangeable, and some babies may even spend more time awake at night than during the day. This topsy-turvy day just happens, so don't think that your baby is "difficult" or that you are doing anything wrong; it's just luck of the draw. It will be about two weeks before your infant begins to show signs of adjusting to anything that even vaguely resembles a schedule, so, to avoid aggravation and total exhaustion, whenever possible, sleep when he sleeps. Feel free to ask anyone near at hand to take over so you can rest. Learn to nap but expect to be bone-tired for a while.

It takes a good few months for sleeping and wakefulness to get into any rhythm that is similar to the patterns that make up your family's day, but to do this, your baby needs your support. What's more, establishing this rhythm is vital for you *and* your baby in order to keep bedtime from becoming a long-term combat zone of childhood.

Sleep for a young infant is uneven. Your baby will cry when you put him down, move about in his sleep, and frequently awaken for a few moments when sleeping. For the most part, if you give your child a bit of time, he will comfort himself and fall asleep or go back to sleep unaided. Giving your baby a chance to do this *self-soothing* early is critical in helping him develop a regular sleep schedule and helping you to resume getting something that comes close to being called a good night's sleep. At around **three months**, you will be well served if your baby is on the way to some regularity. Getting this rhythm down nice and early is an important step, because at around **four to six months** babies become aware of separation and protest a parent's leave-taking, which, in turn, can make getting your baby to sleep much more challenging (this protest period is more fully explained later in the book).

All this said, here is what can happen: You lovingly put your infant to bed, and, instead of peacefully drifting off to dreamland, she cries. This is a trying moment for any parent, especially a new one. Sometimes it may feel too painful to deny a child your parental comfort, so some parents become oversolicitous and overreactive, running to every nighttime whimper. Establishing this reactive style makes things go from bad to worse, since overattentiveness backfires; a child invariably awakens often and demands more, not less attentiveness. Research shows that such frequent periods of heightened alertness actually ***prevent*** a long sleep cycle from taking hold, making a child a light sleeper, restless and more likely to awaken. Beleaguered parents faced with such continual middle-of-the-night demands suffer exhaustion and anger—at each other, at themselves, and at their child. Regrettably, they get hooked and keep responding to nighttime crying, but now they do it with the added aggravation that exhaustion brings, which a child *always* senses and finds less soothing, so he just cries that much more. What a predicament! This sets the stage for a demanding child who cannot soothe himself, which can become a torturous cycle that keeps everyone miserable for a *very* long time. As he gets older, this child may cry for comfort *long* after he needs it, require and get numerous nighttime visits, and/or be routinely taken to his parent's bed making sleep a family nightmare.

> ▶ **PYB Words of Wisdom:** *Always respond to a baby in distress. If crying is piercing and continual, attend to your child. Never leave a child in a crib if he is hurting himself, e.g., with head banging. Helping a baby learn to sleep should never include letting a child suffer. Consult your doctor if this is happening.*

APPLY KIDOLOGY TO AVERT EXHAUSTION

Both babies and parents need a good night's sleep, and **gently shaping** the sleep cycle is a critical and central role for parents of infants. To get a feel for this process, keep these touchstones in mind: 70 percent of American babies can sleep eight hours by **three months**, more than 80 percent have it down by **six months**, and about 90 percent are managing this feat by **one year**. To get on track, try this:

1. Start actively shaping sleep cycles once your child reaches the weight of about **eight or nine pounds,** the weight at which a child is physically ready to sleep longer. Your child's stomach holds more food now, which contributes to making longer sleep intervals possible.
2. If you have yet to do it, consider moving the baby out of your room by the time she is about **four months old.** This can help reduce your sensitivity to normal nighttime stirrings. If your child is close by, you have your door ajar, and you can't hear her cries, she is probably OK

and just having normal nighttime arousal that you don't want to turn into wakefulness.

3. If hearing your baby cry is always too painful for you, remind yourself that you have done all that needs to be done for her and say this mantra: "My baby is just releasing the tensions of her stimulating day." Over the course of a few weeks, increase the length of the time you say this to yourself without running to your child.

4. If you must go in, don't reward or encourage awakening. If needed, soothe your child and calmly say, "Now is sleep time." Try your level best not to give in to the temptation to pick her up if there is no acute distress.

5. Babies advancing through a milestone, like learning to crawl or walk, may become restless at night during these periods. Some researchers theorize that the onset of dreams **at about eight to ten months** also increases restlessness. At these stages of advancement, expect awakenings but resist the urge to go in and rouse your child when these start to occur: her nervous system is just discharging energy and excitement aroused by these new milestones.

6. With your older infant, breaking into her sleep cycle by waking her before you go to bed at ten or eleven o'clock seems to lessen the possibility that she will have a middle-of-the-night awakening. (Suggested by pediatrician T. Berry Brazelton in his book series *Touchpoints*). Waking a small infant for a feeding at that time may also prolong a sleep interval.

Breast-feeding Can Be Challenging: Do What Works for You and Your Baby

Despite some mothers' falling deliriously in love with breast-feeding, many find it daunting, especially the first go round. It may be hard to get the knack of getting your baby to grab hold of your nipple, your baby might take time becoming a hearty sucker, and/or your milk may be slow in coming in. It can also be difficult to judge how much you have provided your child, as you do not have the reassurance of seeing the ounces of formula disappear from a bottle. New mothers often doubt that they are adequately supplying their newborn, which results in anxiety and tension that may make breast-feeding more difficult. Sensing that you are "failing" at this maternal task can create anxiety, disappointment, and frustration. Especially if you have put a great deal of stock in breast-feeding, you have read books, taken a lactation course, bought a breast pump, and come to believe it is the ultimate sign of being maternal, you may feel like you are letting your baby down, or feel annoyed with your infant for not making it easier on you.

APPLY KIDOLOGY TO AVOID TENSION
OVER BREAST-FEEDING

- Be patient, most moms are doing a lot better than they give themselves credit for. Listen to your pediatrician, who will no doubt confirm this when he sees your healthy baby in the office and shows you that your baby is gaining weight.
- You can find reassurance in wet diapers, babies who are feeding well have a lot of them.
- Lactation consultants can make a home visit and assist you in getting comfortable with breast-feeding.
- Just before breast-feeding, briefly use a breast pump to stimulate milk flow.
- Just prior to breast-feeding, place your index finger in your baby's mouth to stimulate her sucking reflex. You will probably be surprised to find that your baby has a hearty sucking reflex, which can make you feel more confident about her getting what she needs from you.
- Don't be afraid to place your entire nipple area in your baby's mouth, and gently but firmly hold her head while doing this. You are not forcing her but guiding her with a sure hand; babies are meant to plug in. If you are reluctant to be gentle and firm with your tiny baby, think about how babies like the solid feel of being swaddled.
- Experience and time usually get mothers over the hump, so do your best to hang in there while you gain both. Give yourself and your baby a chance. After all, it is a completely new venture for the both of you.

If you can't get the hang of breast-feeding, don't beat yourself up for "failing." Don't be a slave to expectations, your own or society's. There is no shame in sitting back and admitting that this just doesn't work for you and your infant. Breast-feeding has its benefits but it is not a determinant of a good mother or an indispensable ingredient in the recipe for raising a good child. It is your loving attachment that is emotionally nourishing, feeding a child for the rest of his life. Ask around; once you say that you have not breast-fed, you will be surprised to find that many mothers such as yourself opt for the bottle. Whether an infant gets the bottle or the breast takes a back seat to contentment; happy mothers raise happy babies. And be patient: you may simply discover that you prefer mothering an older and bigger child rather than a younger, very tiny and dependent one.

> ▶ **PYB Words of Wisdom:** *Remember, you have choices about feeding. If breast-feeding is interfering with joy and your goodwill toward your baby, consider switching to a bottle. The most important organ that needs to be full and overflowing is your heart.*

What to Expect of Your Maturing Infant

Expect the First Cries of Protest at About Four to Six Months*

Babies are born with all their senses operating, but in the very beginning these senses appear to work only to keep them aware of their surroundings. By about **four to six months**, this changes, and actual recognition sets in. The great news is that your baby now recognizes mom and dad, and smiles at you to prove it (before this, babies smile at any face that smiles at them). But this also means that your baby can now tell people apart, distinguishing between familiar people and strangers.

Because of these cognitive changes, babies at this stage become more attached to their mothers, and unhappily protest, sometimes vehemently, when mom leaves them. By about **eight or nine months**, this capacity for recognizing their mother as special also makes them wary of strangers. Put them in the arms of a baby-sitter or even your best friend, and they are not pleased. They will wail. This separation anxiety usually

*All ages of developmental milestones are approximate, since babies mature at different rates.

peaks at about **eighteen to twenty-four months**. Your baby is not being impolite or difficult. Hatching out of her natural and normal narcissism, *she is falling in love with you.* Protest is a sign that your baby is learning to become attached to other human beings, which is a critical ingredient to becoming a good person. Find joy in becoming special to your baby and realize that your baby's protest and cries is a marker of this wondrous connection called love.

> ▶ **PYB Words of Wisdom:** *A child with secure and sturdy attachments to others is bound to grow up feeling confident, cared for, and calm. To ensure this healthy connection, respond warmly, sensitively, and consistently to your baby's body language, facial expressions, and cries; pick her up and give her soothing words when you "read" that she wants to be held or needs comforting. This will get you both through separation development without a struggle, and will set in place your baby's good relationship to you and to her world.*

APPLY *KIDOLOGY* TO MANAGE YOUR INFANT'S PROTEST OVER SEPARATION OR STRANGERS

Separation protest is *not* a problem. It is a marker of the healthy development of your baby's mind and heart. Here is what you may do to sensitively advance this development:

1. Stay with your baby if an unfamiliar person needs to come near.
2. Slowly introduce unfamiliar people, like a baby-sitter or even a grandparent (your baby only recognizes people whom she sees constantly).
3. Put a baby in a position to see you when you cannot be directly available. Face an infant seat toward you while you work in the kitchen.
4. Play disappearing/reappearing games like peek-a-boo to develop your baby's capacity to hold on to a visual memory.
5. Make sure to say good-bye to your baby when leaving. **Never sneak out.** Coming and going reliably—even if it provokes crying—is the best way to help your baby see that you "disappear" but will reappear, which is calming. When she cries, kiss her good-bye, adding a sing-song

phrase of reassurance, such as *"Mommy goes, Mommy comes, but Mommy's love is always with you."*

▶ **PYB Words of Wisdom:** *Every time you gently and sensitively come and go, it is very good practice for strengthening your baby's memory and giving her another tool with which she can soothe herself. Always remember: A self-soother is an easier child to raise.*

APPLY KIDOLOGY: KNOW
WHEN TO EXPECT PROTEST

At about six months, ask yourself, how does my infant respond when things disappear from his view? Answering "yes" to several of these questions indicates that your infant's memory has matured to the point where he can remember things that are out of sight. In effect, he now has the cognitive capacity to picture things in his mind's eye. Once this develops, separation- and stranger-protest are sure to follow.

• Does your baby look for things he drops?
• Does she put a toy down and then "remember" to go back to it?
• If you slowly cover with a cloth an object he's viewing, does he try to uncover it?
• If you hide an object in your closed fist, does he try and open it?
• Does he delight in playing peek-a-boo?

Expect to Be on the Move from About Five Months

Babies have a burst of energy at **five months.** They seem to be moving all the time, rolling, wiggling, and undoubtedly squirming if you try to hold them. In another month or two, they are also trying to stand and even sit up. Many babies begin to crawl at about **nine months**, and, shortly after, begin to pull themselves up to stand but cry to be rescued, because they may not necessarily know how to get back down. By about **ten or eleven months**, kids are climbing on furniture, and then, once they get stable, stand on their legs, cruising around the house holding on to the nearest chair or coffee table. Some infants naturally bypass crawling and head straight to standing. Babies like standing so much that they may refuse to sit or lie down, so you may find yourself challenged by such feats as "the vertical diaper change." This does not last long, so go with it. Strapping a one-year-old into a car seat may become a real challenge.

APPLY *KIDOLOGY* TO AVOID AGGRAVATION ONCE YOUR INFANT IS ON THE MOVE

- Limit your baby's access to certain areas of your home (install door and gate locks).
- Babyproof your house.
- Use a playpen, but only on a very limited basis, when you must.
- Keep a special toy for diapering.
- If you have the option, don't take your child to the mall or supermarket— especially if you are harried.
- If creative distractions fail, resign yourself to cries of protest when your infant must sit in a car seat, high chair, or grocery cart. Firmly but gently say, "I know you don't like being strapped in the seat right now, but it keeps you safe, and protecting you is my most important job as your parent." Get this parenting motto down from the very beginning: *Safety never takes a back seat to pleasing your child, which is reassuring and calming to her in the long run.*

Food Tossing and Toy Dropping: How to Have More Patience with Your Suddenly "Annoying" Nine-Month-Old

Is your nine-month-old intentionally making a game of dropping food on the floor from his high chair? Does she throw her toys out of the crib, playpen, or stroller? This may be wearing for you but it is actually an extraordinary cognitive exercise. She is developing her visual memory by playing the exciting disappearing/reappearing game. She makes an object vanish, and you make it materialize. Think of this as a short stint of baby's cognitive aerobics: She is doing exercises to mature her memory. This maturing memory means that she will also balk if you take her toy away. She is not being difficult. She is just feeling startled at its disappearance but not yet up to understanding that her toy still exists even if it is not at hand.

APPLY *KIDOLOGY* TO AVOID AGGRAVATION OVER TOSSING

- Place a plastic cloth under her high chair
- Give her sponges and Nerf balls she can drop harmlessly and without a mess while eating
- Place a container on her high chair and have her do "the dropping game" into it rather than the floor
- Fix a toy activity box to the side of the crib
- Fasten a toy onto the stroller bar (these are commercially available)

Do not tie toys to the crib, playpen, stroller, or highchair to prevent dropping, because it can be dangerous and cause strangulation.

Making Life Peaceful with Your Maturing Infant: Learning the Difference Between Adapting and Enslavement

If you understand your infant, you will come to realize that picking your battles, at this stage, really amounts to recognizing that *there aren't any to pick.* In the beginning, go with the flow. As your infant becomes more competent, you will gradually require more of him, but in the beginning, join, don't fight. *Adapt to your infant.* Tune into the needs of your little one. Do not strictly force him into situations that require waiting, regularity, reason, ability, neatness, and control of urges.

This sounds so simple, doesn't it? Start by going along for the ride and then progressively get your child on board. Do not be fooled. Particularly the first time around it is hard to get this down pat. You have to be quite artful to nudge this transformation along. Believe me, having a few kids under your belt helps. For better or worse, your first infant, bless her tiny soul, is practice. Because it is not a snap, and because getting off to a wrong start can have some sticky consequences and lay the groundwork for *endless* future battles, let me give you some indispensable words of wisdom.

In the beginning, your baby demands and you supply. This is not something to resist. Not only must you attend to all his bodily needs but you also *must* shower a baby with affection. Your infant needs to be hugged, kissed, caressed, picked up, rocked, sung to, and warmly fussed over. Babies need to be babied. Now, do not get confused. I am telling you to adapt, and I am certainly suggesting that you lovingly tune into your child's needs then react and reply with sensitive assistance. This is being responsive, which is **not** the same thing as being captive to your child's needs. Responsive is reacting out of awareness of his utter dependence on you and respect for your infant's needs and for his inability to take care of them on his own. Captive is acting as if your child's needs were the only ones that exist in the entire universe. The former is a reaction meant to make the frustrations of life manageable for your helpless infant. The latter is a reaction meant to eliminate the frustrations of life for your infant, and that does more harm than good for your baby and for you.

Adapting **does not** mean enslavement. You need to *accommodate, not capitulate.* If you grow to be captive to your child, then you are not getting the point. While a newborn absolutely does need you to forgo your own life for a while, *completely* sacrificing yourself to your maturing child's every need weighs in on the side of overgratification. How can you tell if you may be on the path to overdoing it? There may be early warning signs. If you never leave home so that you can whip off your shirt to breast-feed every time your older infant whimpers, or if your husband has given up sex for the duration and is sleeping in your baby's room every night "in case she cries and needs me," the two of you might be confusing responsiveness with the beginnings of servitude.

There are other possible hints: If you tear up a flight of stairs as if the house is on fire rather than sensitively respond to your baby's normal cry, you may be running into trouble. If your baby monitor has replaced your phone as an indispensable device, and you have permanently dispensed with calling friends, start monitoring yourself. You may have a tendency toward overinvolvement. If you establish *a pattern* of running to take care of a child's every need the instant she fusses, in the hope of eradicating frustration, you may raise an excessively demanding child, one who can't learn to soothe herself. Make your full-time job one of completely eliminating the discomfort and yowls of your baby and you will be the one screaming before long.

First-time parents always tend to overdo it. *This is to be expected.* It takes time to figure out how to read a baby's cries, to distinguish a howl of distress from a whimper of discomfort. Modify my warning if you are a new parent. You overdo it simply because you are doing it all for the very first time. As you gain confidence in your parenting ministrations, you will learn to tune into your baby's needs, to be appropriately and lovingly responsive to her demands, and to pace yourself.

Just pay attention to your motives and your reactions, and you will be able to judge what is going on.

▶ **PYB Words of Wisdom:** *As your infant matures, make sure to be adaptive, not captive to your child's needs.*

Putting in a Good Word for Frustration

This may surprise you, but moderate frustration is good for your child, and it makes her better behaved. Here is the paradox: *Frustration feels bad, but it makes good kids.* Let me explain. Your infant has yet to find out, but she will discover as she matures what all adults come to know— *life is a team sport.*

Your newborn does not, and should not be expected to, have the slightest inkling about this fact of life—at first. Recognition that life cannot and will not be a one-way street forever needs to develop little by little. While she is a helpless baby, you care for her as if only her needs existed. For her own good as she matures, that must change, but she needs to be let down gently. Gradually, as her parent, you will lovingly let her in on the news—she will not always be the center of the universe in the way she is and should be as a newborn.

Slowly she will start waiting longer intervals between feedings, and she will be frustrated. She will cry out but "discover" that she and you can survive the delay. With time she will also determine that she has to sleep through the night because you need your forty winks and you cannot be on call 24-7 for the rest of her life. Do not fall apart at the prospect of being a source of frustration to your child, and do not retreat.

The capacity to tolerate frustration is a required life skill. Make sure to give your child this indispensable capacity so that she can negotiate life smoothly. An ability to manage frustration will enable your child to pursue life without requiring things to always and exactly go her way. As she becomes more capable, your child will develop these and many other qualities of acceptance that will let her successfully "join the team."

The capacity to tolerate frustration will make her reasonable, able to adapt, responsive, resilient, and well behaved. Take my advice: Gradually and lovingly allow frustration into your infant's experience and you will have a much more loving and far less frustrating experience throughout parenting.

And remember: If you don't show her how to cope with frustration, who will? Your love is a cushion to soften the blows of discovering that the world does not revolve around her. What better way for a soft landing into such a harsh, but altogether necessary, reality than cushioned by your love and good intentions?

> **PYB Words of Wisdom:** *Gently developing a child's capacity to tolerate frustration is a gift parents bestow on their child and themselves. An infant reasonably frustrated becomes a child who is reasonable when frustrated.*

It *Can* Get a Lot Worse Than a Cranky Kid: Preventing Emotional Terrorism

For your good and the good of your progeny, to say nothing of our civilized world, I am telling you to get this distinction forever engraved into your parental soul. Repeat after me: responsiveness, yes; indulgence, no; adapting, adjustment, yes; enslavement, servitude, no; managing frustrations, yes; eliminating frustrations, no. If you do not grasp this difference, I am issuing a *stern* warning. One day in the not too distant future you could be in danger of tearing your hair out, to say nothing of tearing off to the county jail to post bail for your errant child.

How and why could this happen? Overindulgence is the fertile breeding ground for some dicey defects of character that go well beyond the headaches of a demanding, foul-tempered child. Try, for starters, incapacity to tolerate and manage life's frustrations (and, boy, does life come with frustrations that need to be tolerated and managed!) or give lifelong helplessness a spin. Slavishly ministering to a child is a path to creating a dependent, infantile personality, the child who never grows up.

▶ **PYB Words of Wisdom:** *Run as fast as your legs can carry you to serve a child's every want and need—and risk raising one who can't stand on his own two feet. Overindulgence can breed permanent helplessness and crippling dependence, which is so very taxing.*

At its unfortunate worst, overgratification may create extreme self-centeredness. This can lead to arrogance and disrespect for others, which does not, among other things, make your offspring a great addition to your family or the civilized world. Do you need further convincing? I promise you, there is nothing that will ratchet up the battling and wipe the smile off your face faster than a child who develops any of these character flaws. The moral of this parenting tale is: to avoid waking up one morning to find that one of these emotional terrorists has taken residence under your roof, just don't let it go beyond adapting.

▶ **PYB Words of Wisdom:** *If your child learns to fall in step, he is less likely to trample over you or anyone else. Then you will have a child of good character at home and a good citizen in the world, and we certainly need those!*

Avoiding Another Battleground: The Unattached Child

Do not confuse this advice with the "I'll just let him wait until I am good and ready" approach to infant care. ***To suggest that a caretaker ever deny a baby a timely and sensitive response would be criminal.*** Asking an infant to "tough it out" is *always* wrong. It makes a helpless creature suffer overwhelming frustration. Studies of babies left unattended show the heartbreaking effects.* They suffer a sort of *emotional starvation*. Not responded to, they may become unresponsive,

*Rene Spitz was a researcher who, in the 1950s, conducted these landmark studies of infants separated from their mothers through hospitalizations.

listless; they seem to lose their spark. In the extreme, as they mature, these children find great difficulty making meaningful attachments to other people. Without the sense of attachment to others, a child is lost, sometimes forever.

The risk here can be serious. The unattached child may grow into an adult without the ability to care about and for others or about or for himself. He may become the detached, unfeeling, delinquent adolescent, because he is missing the emotional capacity for deep sentiments of care and concern. He may also lack the all-important capacity for empathy and end up treating others badly. This defect in personality can mean trouble—and big battles—for all.

> ▶ **PYB Words of Wisdom:** *Loving responsiveness does not spoil children, but failing to regularly and responsively satisfy them does put them at risk. Cooperation, independence, resilience, achievement, emotional well-being, as well as good and responsible behavior patterns, develop if you adequately fulfill the needs of your young infant.*

What to Do if Your Newborn Baby Is Really Ruffling Your Feathers

For a new parent, patience is a requirement exceeded in importance only by the need for stamina. Running back and forth is tiring, so getting frazzled is understandable and expected. Yes, you will occasionally feel annoyed by the demands of your infant and then feel guilty for feeling that way, which increases the misery. Periodically you might even have thoughts like "Is there a way I can drop this child off somewhere until after he is housebroken?" If your feelings do not stop here, and you begin to feel that your baby is giving you a hard time *purposely*, in order to make you miserable, remember this: ***There are no mean babies.*** Babies are not constructed with the capacity to make you mad intentionally or drive you crazy on purpose.

If you find your frustration unbearable, and particularly if you start believing that your baby hates you or that you hate your baby, this may be a more serious issue than mismatched expectations with your child. You may actually be struggling with postpartum depression,

which can be wrongly mistaken for "having a rough time with a difficult baby."*

If, as a new mother, you think of yourself as a failure, this may also
be a sign of depression. You may be angry or disappointed with yourself, not your baby. While the anger is self-directed, the problem
remains the same—postpartum depression.

This may seem like bad news, but, fortunately, it is quite the opposite. There is very good news: with professional help, postpartum
depression is very manageable. You and your baby do not have to start
life battling and feeling mutually miserable. Many things can work to
reduce intense frustration and anger. Talk to your doctor about these
feelings and get help. If this frustration has spilled over into any behaviors, such as shaking your baby, you need to stop this behavior now and
get help—*immediately*. You and your little one deserve better. And it
can get better!

> ▶ **PYB Words of Wisdom:** *Babies may be trying, but
> they are never trying to make you miserable. If you are
> battling with your infant, you may actually be battling
> with depression. Get help immediately to defeat the real
> enemy—postpartum depression.*

Take Time to Be Good to Yourself

When you are parent to an infant, the most useful aggravation-avoidance
strategy of all is **cutting yourself some slack.** This stuff of tending to a
baby makes for wear and tear. So, be nice—to yourself. Lighten your
load: do less than you would ordinarily do, try paper plates, forget the
food groups. Bathe your bigger kids a little less often. A dingy kid is not a
health hazard. Learn to procrastinate, bag refinishing that antique pine
dresser, ignore those dust balls (they will wait for you, trust me!), go easy,
allow yourself to say "no" to anything that is not critical, essential, or

*It may surprise you to know that depression is a **very** underdiagnosed problem. Therefore,
women suffering from postpartum depression frequently go untreated, which causes some parents and babies get off to a bad start—unnecessarily. If you don't like your baby, or you don't like
yourself as a mother, check out the possibility that these sentiments are the result of depression
and insist on getting help.

urgent. The fewer nonessential things you do the more resources you have for parenting. Make do, and everyone will do quite all right.

There is one person who is genuinely entitled to more than a tad of indulgence—you—a new parent. Doctor's orders: Be very nice, kind, and generous to yourself. Gently request that anyone within shouting distance of you kindly do the same. Call that friend who owes you a favor and ask her to baby-sit. Splurge on a dinner out, grab that nap, spring for a new pair of shoes, get that manicure. Make sure to "sleep in" if it is remotely possible. Why are you encouraged to think of and even indulge yourself? Parents and *especially* new mothers are nonstop giving machines, giving sustenance, security, protection, time, attention, energy, concern, and love. To adequately get the picture of a mom as a "giving machine," just stop and think about breast-feeding. At a moment's notice, baby "plugs into" mom, and voilà, "dinner is served," food on demand. The maternal feeding machine is expected to be in service more hours than the local all-night diner. No one can keep this up with a smile on her face without being recharged, physically and emotionally. If you are always giving and not replenished, you risk feeling depleted, used up, and worn down. Your baby and you will have fewer bad patches if you give him and yourself plenty of TLC.

> ▶ **PYB Words of Wisdom:** *Take as good care of you as you do of your baby. Every new parent, especially a mother, needs and deserves mothering.*

How to Nip Potential Conflicts in the Bud: Consider Your Child's Temperament

Particularly if you have more than one child, you are probably aware that even kids from the same set of parents can be as different as night and day. Your full-of-beans daughter may be an active and eager explorer, while your placid son, more the observer, takes time to warm up to new situations. When you think back on it, these are differences that you may have seen early on. True to form, your daughter may have readily taken to your breast from day one, while your son was more tentative about feeding. What you are seeing is that from the beginning children exhibit markedly different levels of activity and approach. This difference in activity levels and approach says ***nothing*** about the personalities, talents, intelligence, or cooperativeness of these or any children for that matter. It only indicates the way a child takes on the world, which is called *temperament*.

Temperament is the behavioral style of a child, the natural and predictable way a child reacts in a given situation. Scientists believe temperament is a behavioral disposition that is present at birth, which stays constant through life. This means that your child will more or less maintain this constant behavioral approach, or style, throughout each developmental stage. In studying temperament, researchers have found that 40 percent of all children are immediate responders (adaptable, low-intensity, regular); 15 percent take time to warm up (reserved, cautious); 10 percent are "spirited" or challenging (high-intensity, active, slow-adapting, easily frustrated, irregular), while the rest are a combination of temperament traits.

Knowing about these natural differences can make parenting far more relaxed. Parents who understand their child's temperament are more likely to respect differences and, most important, to **not** mislabel their child, calling a slow-to-warm-up child "uncooperative" or an active child "unruly." Unwittingly mislabeling a child can end up evolving into real headaches and hassles. Negative labels in particular are very corrosive to parent/child relationships. Often they stick like glue to children, so that they begin to believe that they are uncooperative or unruly and act accordingly. What's more, labels invariably follow a child out of the home and into school, which can cause no end of problems.

Not realizing differences in temperament may also trap parents in feelings of disappointment. ***This is especially true when a parent's own temperament does not match his child's behavioral style.*** A parent—let's say a wheeling-dealing entrepreneur who values eagerness over contemplation—may feel dissatisfied with a child who is more the observer than the go-getter. Or a reflective, contemplative parent—let's say a scholarly researcher—may feel at a loss with a very physically on-the-go child who doesn't sit still for a minute, taking to sports rather than books. Because nature is random, these "mismatches" are bound to happen. It can help enormously if parents who differ temperamentally from their children don't take these differences personally or try to push children to be different but instead see them for what they are—natural differences in disposition. Try to avoid falling into these traps, because there is far less tension in a home where parents accept the style of a child rather than fight it or try to fashion a child in their own image.

▶ **PYB Words of Wisdom:** *Knowing your child for who they are, not what you want them to be, is one of the very, very best ways to avert a future of conflict. "I love you for being you" are the words you need to say to your child— and mean them.*

Understanding Temperament to Make Life with Your Child Peaceful

Use the Temperament Questionnaire, below, to figure out your child's behavioral disposition so you do not fight your child's natural disposition or mistake your child's natural behavioral style for lack of cooperation, or defiance.

KNOW YOUR CHILD'S TEMPERAMENT*

Temperament may be defined by the following nine categories. Answering these questions about each will help you determine your child's behavioral style and avoid the hassles that arise from misunderstanding your child's natural tendencies.

1. **Adaptability** How does he deal with change? Easily or does he find it hard to adjust? Is he quickly frustrated or easygoing? Are transitions challenging or uneventful?

2. **Activity** During usual or daily routines, what is your child's level of physical activity? Does she sit still or move around? Is she quiet or lively, active or passive?

3. **Intensity** What is her typical reaction to a situation—happy, sad, or angry? Does she react mildly or strongly to new encounters?

4. **Sensitivity** Is she physically sensitive or not to sounds, odors, tastes, lights, etc.? How does she tolerate loud noises, scratchy clothes, or spicy food, with calm or agitation?

5. **Rhythm** Is he regular and rhythmic in his body functioning, sleep, hunger, bowel movements, etc., or is he unpredictable or erratic?

(continued on next page)

*Drs. Stella Chess and Alexander Thomas, psychiatrists, did this work on temperament in the 1960s at New York University Medical Center.

6. **Approach** How would you describe her initial reaction to events or people? Is she more of a risk taker or does she cautiously hold back?

7. **Persistence** How long does he stay with a task or activity? Does he move on easily or not? Does he give up or refuse to do so? Is he focused or distractible?

8. **Mood** Is she basically an optimist or a pessimist? Is she reluctant or enthusiastic?

9. **Distractibility** Do outside things easily distract him (sounds, lights, people), and how does it affect his behavior? Does he shift attention or stay focused on a prior activity?

APPLY KIDOLOGY TO AVERT CONFLICT

Recognizing and adapting to your child's temperament rather than fighting it, is a sure path to eliminating countless battles:

- If your child's temperament makes her slow to adapt, she might need more transition time than another child. Where one preschooler might only require one or two warnings that play must come to an end, your child might need several more to make a smooth changeover.
- A temperamentally *distractible* child would do well with your direct eye contact and a touch on an arm to get his attention, while another child might only need your words, "It's time for your homework" in order to settle in to work.
- An *intense* toddler might find the circus too overstimulating, so swimming might be a happier activity.
- Springing a new last-minute baby-sitter on a child with a *slow-to-warm-up* temperament might be a bad move for you, your child, and the baby-sitter.

▶ **PYB Words of Wisdom:** *Knowing your child's behavioral style or temperament helps you adapt your parenting requests and requirements to his tempo, as well as*

*modify your expectations, eliminating a struggle before it
becomes one.*

One more word about mislabeling: Sometimes it is not misunderstanding temperament that makes us fall into the trap of mislabeling our children but our anxiety. For instance, a new parent facing the strain of getting caretaking for a new baby down pat, might react to normal and expectable glitches (i.e., a child not gaining weight or sleeping through the night) by concluding, "my child is difficult, finicky, or uncooperative" when what they might actually be feeling is insecure or quite helpless. Identifying a child as "the problem" is a way some parents unwittingly react to the strenuous demands of parenting. No one does this purposely, but it can get in the way of smooth relations with your child. If you have the urge to label, consider that you may be struggling with the daunting and sometimes scary challenges of parenting. Try to get help and support so that you don't get into this predicament. And remember, a good way to prevent this potential source of conflict is to be especially generous and good to yourself.

AVOID ACCIDENTAL MISLABELING: HE LOOKS JUST LIKE MEAN OLD UNCLE HARRY

After giving birth, one of the first reactions we and everyone else have to a newborn infant involves playing the "Who does he look like game." Sometimes this well-meaning sport can take an unfortunate turn. When a baby is identified as resembling a difficult member of the family ("Gosh, he looks just like mean old uncle Harry" or "Listen to her scream; she sounds like Grandma Tucker who always hollered at everyone.") this labeling can stick like glue. This negative labeling can also play itself out with siblings. People may make comparisons early on that "split" children in one family into "good" and "bad" categories. ("She cries so much more than her sister did: Her sister was such a good baby." or "His brother took to the breast so quickly, this one is so much harder to please.") From day one, a baby unfairly may acquire the "reputation" of being difficult, which can be a tag she has a hard time shaking. Be careful not to jump to any conclusions about your infant's personality since that can set off a potential for conflict before your child's personality is really formed. Let your baby be herself, and you will have more peaceful days ahead.

2. *Your Toddler: Thirteen Months to Three Years*

The Parade Continues: Your Toddler

Now that you're sleeping more than three hours a night, have breast-feeding down to a science, and converted your baby from nonstop crying machine to "little bundle of joy," you are thinking: "Hey, I *can* do this with a smile on my face." At this very moment, you might be feeling so relaxed about this parenting business that you're practically ready to audition for a scented-bath-oils commercial, or at the very least consider trying out for an instant mocha-cappuccino spread in *Good Housekeeping* magazine. Don't get too comfy! Before you can say, "There's a sale on infant-sized Pampers at Target," you will discover that a new creature has come to inhabit your home. The parade continues. Meet the next personality that arrives in the nursery: an inquisitive little monkey!

That little baby once content to sit, babble, and cuddle, transforms into an altogether different creature, a nonstop whirlwind of energy and curiosity ready to scoot as fast as his little legs will take him. And those little legs generally take him away from you and toward anything and everything that he can climb, pull, touch, poke, grab, and gum in his endless pursuit of exploration. *Every* toddler becomes a veritable Curious George:* inquisitive, interested, and on the go, he is endlessly and incorrigibly into everything, whether it is good for him or not. While he's high on curiosity, your toddler is still low on attention span. So, as soon as he has made one discovery, he quickly heads off in his quest to uncover other secrets of the universe, which means he is not entertained for long and is always on the go.

He may not look it, but your toddler is actually a tiny scientist at work. That's why he drops the cereal bowl on the floor: not to harass you but to discover where it goes. In his quest to see how the world works, he has yet to develop a notion of right versus wrong. Happily conducting his

---

*If you have not discovered this wonderful classic book series featuring an incorrigibly inquisitive monkey, Curious George, you should look for it.

gravitational experiment ("Where does cereal go when I dump it?"), your toddler has no idea that it is naughty, messy, or impolite to chuck what is meant to be eaten. While he is the scientist at work, it will take considerably more time before your toddler has sufficient brainpower to fully understand the complicated ways in which the world actually works. He gets into everything but he doesn't really "get it."

Essentially, you now have a dear little creature that eats, sleeps, cries, makes messes—*and* moves. On top of all this, when he's up and about, there is no reasoning with him. Your toddler is not intentionally unreasonable. He just lacks sufficient brainpower—*and* the language that accompanies it—to be rational. Toddlers are agile bodies without equally agile minds. You cannot take your eyes off your toddler for a nanosecond.

Toddlers have a wide range of moods, although they lack much in the way of language to express those feelings. Their behavior or action "speaks" of their mood. They get excited and animated, but they also can feel sad, mad, fretful, and frustrated, as they try out a world that they cannot always quite figure out or get under control—say a box that does not open or a puppy that runs from their grasp. They are long on frustration but short on words, so jumping up and down in a fit of pique may be the only way to "handle" a bad mood. Your toddler may be short on language, but "no" certainly becomes a new and ***very*** significant part of her vocabulary, and, given all the mischief she is up to, it can become a significant, if not overused, word in your parenting lexicon as well.

What to Expect of Your Toddler

Expect an Action Vocabulary

Your child has an *action vocabulary;* she expresses herself by means of her behavior. To understand the concept of an action vocabulary, imagine playing a game of charades or finding yourself in a foreign country with a language completely unknown to you. How might you express yourself? You would convey what is on your mind through gestures, motions, movements, and signals. This is an action vocabulary, and it is the only kind your toddler possesses.

A toddler is wired to move, *not* listen. Without well-developed language, what you say to a toddler just doesn't make sense. Because of this, a toddler cannot follow directions, make plans, or obey rules; therefore, do not use these strategies to get him to behave. Until he has well-developed language, you are expecting the impossible.

> ▶ **PYB Words of Wisdom:** *A child unable to talk very well is a child not yet able to listen very well. The capacity to follow directions only develops once your child can speak in sentences.*

Nonetheless, your words of warning and all your sage advice need to be spoken, early and often. Your child needs to *hear the words* long before he can fully comprehend their meaning. Even if he cannot fully understand, tell him that he must stop throwing sand at his friend's face because it can hurt, or that he has done a good job at putting on his socks even though it was very difficult to get them on. The single greatest tool for surviving battles is language. Giving your child *the words* is so central that we will come back to it repeatedly.

With a toddler, your actions must speak as loudly as your words. If you tell your curious toddler not to put a stick in the socket, you must also remove the stick from his hand without hesitation. If you don't want your child to walk into traffic, make sure to tell her so, but be just as sure to firmly hold her hand as well. *Talk while acting and act while talking.*

> ▶ **PYB Words of Wisdom:** *If your child uses an action vocabulary, use words but take action!*

Given the advent of moods at this stage, be prepared for frustration, anger, unhappiness to erupt when you take action and say "no." Realize that moods are a natural and expectable part of the toddler stage, then you will feel less crestfallen and guilty when they appear, and they will be less likely to derail your parenting. Unhappy protests when you stop her from playing in a bath because it is time for bed are par for the course and shouldn't stop you from taking good care of her. Remember: she doesn't hate you when she has a moody moment, nor is she "bad." She is just expanding her emotional range, which now includes good and bad moods, and yes, even tantrums.

Expect a Mess

With a toddler on the loose, expect your home to look as if a toddler lives there. Resign yourself to a house always in need of straightening up, with little time to make that happen. Abandon all thoughts of white wall-to-wall living-room carpeting and find a good, cheap dry cleaner that specializes in mashed-banana and finger-paint stains. Expect blocks under foot, food in the couch, and sticky fingerprints absolutely every-where.

> ▶ **PYB Words of Wisdom:** *"Living with a two-year-old is lot like living with a blender with no top. It works but it's messy," (Jerry Seinfeld). Keep this perspective and a sense of humor and you'll keep the peace with your toddler.*

Employ a sense of humor and keep a perspective: when you're ready to wring his neck for breaking your favorite lamp, remember that anything in your home *except your child* can be replaced.

> ▶ **PYB Words of Wisdom:** *The next time your toddler breaks something, be happy that he's in one piece. The only irreplaceable object in your home is your child. To calm down, try this mantra: "Don't cry over anything that can't cry over you!"*

What to Expect of Your Maturing Toddler

Expect Outbursts of Anger and Eruptions of Frustration from About Thirteen Months

Toddlers routinely erupt in frustration. They have outbursts even to the point of throwing a tantrum, and they do so for many reasons—some big, some small, some incomprehensible to even the most well-meaning parent. Toddlers melt down because they are overtired or overstimulated (be forewarned, it invariably happens at their own birthday parties). Other times they are just "out of sorts" for no discernible reason, which often happens, to your utter mortification, publicly, in front of a passel of staring strangers—say at the airport, mall, or on a bus.

All too often the world conspires against your toddler: A tall tower of blocks simply won't stand tall, clothes itch, shoes pinch, a best friend snatches their favorite toy. And, to make matters worse, you won't let him use the living-room walls as his finger-paint canvas, or baby brother as her doll. The world just does not seem to cooperate with a toddler's wishes and desires. Outbursts arise because toddlers are very easily frustrated by this "lack of cooperation," and they can't do much to cope constructively with these disappointments, because they:

- lack well-developed language, typically having about twenty words at twenty months
- have difficulty asking for things
- cannot identify and express their emotions
- have very few problem-solving skills
- have no social skills.

Fortunately, by the time your toddler is three years old, coping skills develop, and fits of frustration, as well as the more intense tantrums, become few and far between.

APPLY KIDOLOGY TO AVERT OUTBURSTS AND TANTRUMS

Outbursts and tantrums, while unpleasant, are par for the course, but many can be avoided with a little thought and advance planning.

1. **Evaluate a child's outbursts and tantrums:** Outbursts and tantrums often have a pattern that can be discovered, providing clues about how to avoid situations or circumstances that spark them. Ask these questions:

   Why do they seem to happen?
   Is there a particular event or condition that seems to trigger them?
   When and where do they seem to occur?
   Who is generally involved?
   What happens before, after, and during an episode?

Take these answers into account and you can readily avoid many a moody melt down.

2. **Set realistic and achievable goals for your toddler:** Don't unwittingly set your child up for failure. Challenges should not be too challenging, because with limited language and skills a toddler can't do things any differently than their first try. Give them a nice fat crayon to draw with, not a slim, impossible to hold and easy to break skinny crayon, and don't ask them to color in the lines, because they just aren't there yet. Asking them to "try again" won't change their behavioral readiness; it only ratchets up their frustration level.

3. **Don't offer false choices:** Don't ask, "Would you like to put on your snowsuit?" unless your intention is to accept your child's "no" for an answer. A phony question drives kids batty and sets you and her up for a fight when she gives you the "wrong" or unacceptable response. Instead, be direct and say, "It's time to put your snowsuit on, so you can play outside."

4. **Say "no" less often:** Say "no" only to things that are really important, like safety. A child who constantly faces "no" after "no" after "no" has nowhere to exercise her developing autonomy. She struggles with a high level of frustration, because there is little room for self-determination.

5. **Say "yes" more often:** There are many ways to keep your toddler in line without having to say the word "no." Try a creative compromise. Instead of saying, "No, you must brush your teeth before hearing a bedtime story," try "Yes, we can read one story before you brush your teeth and one after." This way, you maintain your toddler's hygiene but give him some say in how his life proceeds. Saying "no" by saying "yes" cuts down on fighting, but compromise only works if you stick to your guns and don't make it a series of endless negotiations that whittle away at your parenting authority.

6. **Give children a few minutes warning:** Children hate the disappointment of endings, and change can be rough. Don't blindside them; before you stop an activity, put them on notice so that they can wind down and anticipate what comes next. Say, "We are going to leave the playground and go home in a few minutes." This is especially critical for a child who has a slow-to-adapt temperament.

7. **Avoid double binds:** Try to keep from giving kids competing and/or contradictory directives, like "Stay near me in the market so you

won't get lost; stop hanging on to me, I can't get a thing done"; "Why don't you come and give me a kiss; watch it, you're messing up my clothes." Contradictory directions put kids in a bind, making them crazy with frustration.

8. **Keep life on an even keel:** Try not to overstimulate, overexcite, underfeed, or overtire your toddler. Try your best to avoid the mall before dinner; turn off the TV an hour before bedtime and encourage quiet play instead. Invite very, very few children to your toddler's birthday party; one plus your child's age is a good rule of thumb. If you feel socially obligated to invite more kids, have a few small parties instead of one overstimulating big one. A toddler who is stressed is much more prone to outbursts and tantrums. Be particularly sensitive to your child's temperament as well.

Expect Conflict with Other Children

You are admiring your sweet angel at play in the sandbox, when, without warning, his toddler buddy grabs his pail. In response to this unprovoked attack, your toddler lets out a yelp of fury, yanks his pail back, and whacks his friend over the head with his matching shovel. There is nothing like your child clashing with another toddler to make you embarrassed and annoyed. It may make you cringe, but it is to be developmentally expected. Toddlers don't ask for what they want or what they might want back, like a pail. Instead they resort to physical means to solve their personal dilemmas—they tussle—once they feel threatened. But toddlers are not bad because they "resort to physical violence"; scuffling is simply the only way they have to deal with their social problems. They don't know that social rules and practices exist, so they certainly don't follow them.

Since they are lacking the behavioral skills to be polite and civil, you can expect your toddler to:

• make "mine" and "no" her two favorite words;
• push, prod, poke, and touch as a way of exhibiting interest in another child;
• play nicely alongside another toddler in *parallel play*, but not do so well if she has to play interactively *with* another child. She will do even worse if there are more children and fewer toys;

- pinch, grab, bite, and yank to get or keep a favorite toy;
- spend as much time protectively clutching her toys as playing with them;
- think that a toy being shared is taken away and will be gone forever.

Toddlers are lousy at cooperation and sharing, so while you should certainly encourage it, don't expect that such generosity will fall into place at this behavioral stage, though it does get decidedly better as they head toward three years of age.

> ▶ **PYB Words of Wisdom:** *For toddlers, conflict comes from a deficit in skills, not morals. Just as your toddler could not be expected to do arithmetic, similarly, she can't handle her differences with other children, because she doesn't have the skills needed to solve the "social mathematics" of dividing one fun toy between two small people.*

APPLY KIDOLOGY TO AVERT TODDLER TUSSLES

Here are some ways to prevent your toddler from fighting:

- Respect your child's growing sense of ownership. If he does not want to share a favorite toy with a friend, don't force him. Put away a favorite doll, teddy bear, or truck before a play date and have your child pick out toys that he is less attached to and more able to share.
- Give small children *big* spaces to play in, so that they are less likely to get in each other's way. Toddlers have no sense of personal space and do better when they don't toddle or bump into each other.
- Give the same toys to children who are playing together—two trucks or dolls of the same size—so that it minimizes the battling.
- Stay nearby, so your toddler can come back to you for reassurance and so that you can keep an eye on things, intervening when necessary.
- When you go visiting, take a few of your toddler's own toys along. Having her own doll or truck eases the strain of sharing; knowing that she can take her toys back home helps your toddler manage the frustration of leaving fun toys behind at a friend's house.

- Keep play dates short.
- Try for playtimes with only one other child. Toddlers are not yet good at being congenial members of a group.

Expect Toilet Mastery to Be a Learning Process Throughout All of Toddlerhood (and Well into the Preschool Years)

Most parents imagine that toilet mastery comes earlier and rather quicker than it actually does. Parents frequently expect children to be able to function like adults much sooner than they actually can, *especially* when it comes to self-care, hygiene, and toileting, which sets off all sorts of unnecessary and totally avoidable hassles. Toileting is a particularly sore spot, since a toddler's lack of control makes *so* much work, like toting diaper supplies and creating messy laundry. For a good reason, parents want to hurry things up, but it is developmentally impossible to do, so don't push your toddler.

> ▶ **PYB Words of Wisdom:** *Toilet mastery can become one of the first major battlegrounds over control issues with your child. Becoming informed will increase your patience and avoid getting these power struggles started.*

To avoid conflict, be patient and know to expect:

- a span of at least two years between the ages your toddler begins to recognize when she has wet herself (about sixteen months) and when she can actually wait to urinate (about three-plus years);
- girls to learn toileting before boys (for girls, readiness may occur as early as eighteen months, and for boys, around twenty-two months);
- girls to not be likely to master staying dry—even during the day—until their third year, and boys even later;
- bowel control to precede urinary continence;
- control first to become established in the daytime and then, only months later, to progress into nighttime;
- possibility of lapses if a new sibling is born or if there is any other stress, such as moving, divorce, or illness;

- high probability of multiple accidents along the way to mastery, even as late as kindergarten.

Do not force your child to stay on a potty for more than about five minutes; it could make him dislike toileting and backfire miserably, actually delaying mastery. It can also set in motion battles over control that can trouble you for the rest of your parenting days. *Don't get angry at mishaps and never ever punish your child for an accident*. This reaction creates shame, and a child taught by shame *does not* grow into a happy and contented child. Be patient; toilet competence is a *long-term* process that begins at toddlerhood but does not fall fully into place until four years of age (and even at this age accidents are still common).

▶ **PYB Words of Wisdom:** *As you attempt to get your child to manage bathroom behavior, eliminate the word "training" from your vocabulary. Toileting is not a human trick that requires training but a gradual process of gaining bodily control as the body matures and, therefore, allows for it! Take the long view and you won't have a short fuse about toilet learning or risk setting up endless battles over control.*

APPLY KIDOLOGY TO AVOID TOILETING BATTLES

Toddlers often balk at toilet learning because they are fearful, not uncooperative. The flush of a big toilet bowl that mysteriously makes things disappear in a noisy swirl of water can alarm them. Is this a monster? Are they next to be sucked away like that? (These fears tend to be associated with learning control over bowel movements, because they can see their feces "disappear.") To avoid any battles over this source of resistance, acknowledge your toddler's fear.

- Start with a potty.
- Play at flushing the toilet before your child begins to use it. Put her in charge, or make her the "boss," of the toilet.
- Encourage your child to ask "Where do the things go?" and answer these questions simply before you ask her to use this noisy "monster."

- Be enthusiastic, clap when your child has made a bowel movement, and wave "bye, bye" when you flush the toilet. (Yes, do this; as ridiculous as it sounds, children need enthusiastic applause when they succeed in getting close to the mark!)
- If your child pulls back or fearfully withdraws from using a toilet, acknowledge his perspective, saying, "It makes a lot of scary noise, doesn't it?" or "I think it frightens you to sit high up on this big seat." Don't insist on flushing the toilet in his presence if he is frightened.
- Read books to prepare your children for toileting, such as *Once Upon a Potty*, by Alona Frankel.

Expect Your Child to Become Curious About His Body

Toilet mastery is also the first process that introduces children to their private body parts. Your toddler will probably experiment with the parts of his body that until now were mostly hidden from view and now, by contrast, are focused on intently. So expect that a toddler will:

- be very curious about his body that suddenly becomes an exciting focus of attention;
- touch and explore her genitals and rectum;
- play with his urine or feces;
- experience pleasure at urination and defecation;
- like to watch others use the bathroom or see them undress.

Many parents—especially new ones—find these behaviors startling and worrisome. *There is nothing to worry about.* This natural exploration is a first step in developing healthy attitudes about the body and sexuality. In fact, as early as at two and a half, children notice the differences between the opposite sexes. Don't display anger or disgust, or slap your child's hand away from his body; this cripples security and healthy respect for the body. A child who develops a secure respect for his body and sexuality is a lot easier in the long run because he is more likely to employ good judgment about his sexual behavior if he is comfortable with his own body.

Expect Toddlers to Be Great at Undressing and Poor at Getting Dressed

Clothing wars start early (and can be long-lasting). Getting a wriggly toddler into a dress for daycare or into pajamas at bedtime can become an ordeal. Your patience about your toddler's ability to take care of himself may help to avert this battle. Keep in mind that undressing takes far less time and effort than mastering the more complicated skills of getting all those clothes on right. Pulling off a dirty sock is far easier and is accomplished far earlier than getting a fresh shirt on and buttoned. Knowing the following developmental timeline can help.

At About Thirteen Months
Children like to take off their hat, pants, shoes, and socks (often tossing their footwear out of their stroller, like Hansel's and Gretel's crumbs in the forest), *but* they cannot put them back on. They can pull off socks in a second and lose them in an instant.

At About Twenty-four Months
Children can put most clothes back on but still stay more adept at "off" rather than "on." At this stage, they might be adept enough to pull off a sneaker and lose that, too!

At About Three Years of Age
Preschool kids are capable of both dressing and undressing, but are better at dressing their bottom than their torso: Getting pants on right comes before coats. But they are not experts, so they may get a shoe on but be unable to tie laces. *It's at this point that kids want to start making these everyday personal and independent choices.*

APPLY *KIDOLOGY* TO AVERT AGGRAVATION OVER DRESSING

- Don't spend money on expensive socks; dress your child in tights or long socks.
- Buy clips that keep gloves attached to coats.

- Buy shoes that close with Velcro.
- Buy roomy shirts, pullovers, and elasticized pull-up bottoms.
- From **about three years**, children need your help and support fashioning their independence, not supplying a fashion opinion. If you provide the latter, you are headed for a scene and possibly life-long battles over control. As long as it does not compromise safety ("Yes, you must wear shoes to go outside"), let their fashion sense direct their wardrobe. *Think of clothes as a nice, safe way for a child "to try on" their budding autonomy.*

Expect Your Toddler to Hang on to His Binky or Blanky

Toddlers are trying to make heads and tails of their world, and it makes them anxious, so expect your toddler to look for ways to comfort herself. Toddlers routinely:

- invest objects like a tattered blanket or a stuffed animal with soothing qualities;
- develop self-soothing habits, like hair twisting, thumb or pacifier sucking, sucking on a blanket, humming and/or rocking, especially around two years of age;
- invest their clothes with a reassuring feeling, endlessly wearing the same favorite shirt or cozy hat.

Toddlers do not have fully developed visual memories, so they need practice learning that if their comforting mother is not nearby, she and the comfort she brings still exist. These comfort objects and habits fulfill this need until a child learns to self-soothe without these physical reminders, which generally happens when kids have language and visual memory down pat.*

---

*This understanding of these transitional objects of comfort is based on the work of the British psychiatrist Donald W. Winnicott. (from mid 1940s to 1971)

Encourage Your Child to Soothe Himself

- If your child gets very agitated—especially at night—try giving him a silken object to rub. Blankets with satin edges are favorite comfort objects.
- If your child is very attached to an object, duplicate it before it gets lost. Some parents buy a second beloved blanket or cut the original one up in pieces for spares.
- If your child insists on wearing the same piece of clothing, let her. Say, "I know that this favorite shirt makes you feel cozy and safe." Reducing her anxiety is more important than fighting germs.

The need for physical comforters (including those attached to her own body, like her thumb or hair) is natural and does not mean that your child is insecure or babyish. Politely ignore those people who make comments suggesting otherwise. By about age four, kids give up these self-soothing objects. It isn't a good idea to try and make her relinquish these comforters before she's ready. It will make her agitated and fussy, so relax—when she's ready she will leave her Blanky and Binky behind.

Expect to Hear "No"

No Is the First Step in the Dance of Separation, Not a Declaration of War

Nothing gives rise to more battles than the arrival of the "N" word in a child's vocabulary, and arrive it does once you have a toddler. Because a toddler first has an action vocabulary, the "No" gesture—pursed lips and a vigorous headshake, often accompanied by a spray of mashed bananas—comes first, the actual word later. ("No" is often first expressed through toddler food preferences and refusal.)

For many parents, the advent of "No" sounds like the first battle cry of disobedience. It is as if on hearing "No" parents suddenly see a child's capacity for defiance born in these two letters. If you react to the appearance of "No" (and the accompanying bananas on your suit) with anger, dismay, and the assertion of your parental rule, then you are bound headlong into endless and needless power struggles with your child. Why are these battles needless? Because they do not take into account what the word "No" actually means at this stage of development. "No" does not mean defiance. "No" has absolutely nothing to do with disobedience.

The arrival of the word "No" actually signifies a glorious development taking place in the life of your child—the discovery of the self and with this the possibility of personal definition. It can and should be a cause for celebration. Get this right, and you will save yourself major aggravation. By saying "No," your toddler is *not* drawing a solid line in the sand, declaring "This is war!" He is drawing a dotted line around himself, declaring "This is me!" The child who purses her lips, shakes her head, and says "No" to mashed bananas is not being defiant—she is **defining** herself. She is saying "No" as a way of saying "**Yes**, this is who I am—and I don't feel I am a banana person at this very moment." Just consider your own behavior: At a dinner party, I am sure you have said "No" to food you do not fancy. You were not being defiant. You were simply expressing your personal preference or taste. Your "No" did not make you difficult, it just made you you. The same holds for your toddler.

> ▶ **PYB Words of Wisdom:** *"No" is the first step in the joyous "dance of separation." Do not make it the opening round in a power struggle. Take joy in this thrilling moment; your baby is becoming a person in her own right. She has discovered that she has a mind of her own. Celebrate separation, because a child with a mind of his own becomes a mindful child.*

Self-definition in a child begins—but does not end—at this stage. It is an ongoing process and continuing theme of development, as well as a potential source of conflict, as your child matures. Pay attention to this concept even if you are not currently withstanding a barrage of banana mush. It will be less of a battleground throughout your entire parenting career if you make sure to understand it now.

More to Know About "No": Keeping Peace with Your Baby

Life will be easier once you grasp another aspect of "No." "No" in a toddler's mind is a temporary state. "No bananas," means **at this very moment**. It does not mean "No bananas forever and always, until the end of time or hell freezes over, whichever comes first." "No" cannot possibly have that much force or permanence, because at this behavioral stage toddlers have no mental equipment to understand concepts such as "forever." Toddlers do not yet have a clock in their head.

So relax and don't start forcing your child to give up his decisions. "No" is not the end of the line for you or your toddler. It is a transient state. By tomorrow, it could be peaches she is spitting across the kitchen table and bananas she can't get enough of.

"No" is a rich and positive addition to your critter's vocabulary. It is the way your child playfully and repeatedly tries on the world to see how it suits her. Understand this behavioral meaning, and it won't be such a big pain to hear that little word. But do not misinterpret this information. I want you to *relax, not get lax* when you hear the "N" word. Pay attention to the difference: *Relax* means "calm down," while *lax* means "slack off." I am not urging permissiveness or a free-for-all so that every time your child says "No" you respond as if every "no" is perfectly acceptable. That would make you a doormat, not a parent.

A child needs a parent brave enough and sturdy enough to say "No" back to her when it is appropriate, when she might be at risk. "No, my little one, you can cry all you want but you can't put that stick in the socket." The challenge you face is guiding your child safely and sensibly through her "No"s and, by extension, her personal development.

Making Life Peaceful with Your Toddler

Having gained insight into this behavioral phase, what practical steps can you take to reduce aggravation? Now that your child is on his feet, you need to be on your toes. Since you can expect that your toddler will get into everything, get there first.

APPLY KIDOLOGY TO AVERT A TODDLER CANDY GRAB: GET THERE FIRST

If you are rushing through the supermarket checkout line, anticipate the inevitable toddler "candy grab" and make the first move: Unload your cart while "body blocking" the colorful lures that beckon your curious critter. To "body block," just stay at the front end of your cart with your back to the clerk while making eye contact with your little one. It also helps to have "munchies," like carrot sticks, or a toy to keep him occupied and distracted.

Stay alert. Make your child's environment as toddlerproof as possible. Cover those sockets and keep those sharp objects beyond grasp or locked up. Remove from your toddler's reach things that are not appropriate for exploration, say that heirloom crystal vase on the coffee table—which might also be a source of danger. Pad the sharp corners of your glass-topped table or just put it in the attic for the duration. Put childproof locks on cabinets storing cleaning products. Scope out your home from your child's perspective—*get down on your knees and crawl around your house to see the real hazards!* Childproof your home, thinking of it as *domestic engineering!* Make the environment suitable and safe for your toddler rather than expect your toddler to act suitably and safely. It will reduce the wear and tear of having to be the "No" machine.

APPLY KIDOLOGY TO AVERT DISASTER: AT ABOUT 24 MONTHS, RETODDLERPROOF YOUR HOME

Many parents make the mistake of doing a good job at babyproofing their home when kids first begin to be on the move (as early as five months) and stop there. Big mistake. As toddlers mature and get more competent, the dangers change. An older toddler can open gates, turn knobs, pull pots from a stove, reach a higher shelf, or climb onto the sink and get to the medicine cabinet. Periodically recheck your babyproofing. As your toddler nears two, redouble your efforts at making home a safe place to explore.

Being one step ahead of a toddler makes life calmer but it is only the beginning. Picking your battles becomes an all-consuming matter from the moment your child turns into this little roving scientist/explorer. While there are many other specific strategies to keep you from butting heads, here is what you must keep in mind: Toddlers are meant to be curious. They are inquisitive explorers discovering how their world works. Join their adventure rather than fight it.

▶ **PYB Words of Wisdom:** *Once your child is on his feet, you need to be on your toes. Winning at life with a toddler requires the strategy of a good football coach—offense as the best defense. But remember to limit the danger, not the exploration.*

3. Your Preschooler (Three to Five Years)

When you have a preschooler, a magical chatterbox has taken up residence in your home. Think of a fairytale creature, like a chatty and nimble wood sprite, to help get the picture of just who has arrived. Play, play, and play is the work of your child now. This fanciful being spends time absorbed in imaginative play, endlessly frolicking on increasingly sturdy limbs. Full of whimsy and energy, she continues to be a curious human being but one who now exults in *all* the wonders of the world, with no sense of time to get in the way of complete absorption in life. For a preschooler, time stands still, there is no clock in his head that ticks away the minutes, so he is bound to get lost in his pursuits. While walking through the front yard, a butterfly might catch your four-year-old's fancy, and she may not move toward the house for dinner until your call jolts her out of her reverie. Or, on the way to the bathroom, suddenly engrossed in a toy, your child might not make it there even if it means having an embarrassing "accident" en route. Preschoolers live in the real world but developmentally their minds don't. This is the stage of magical thinking. They do not easily distinguish between what is real and what is imagined. This can make them worried, anxious and even irritable and clingy, frightened of their very own normal and natural feelings and ideas.

This imaginative life also ushers in the age of awe and amazement. Wondering aloud with newfound words about all that she encounters— the smell of the flowers, the buzz of the bees, the splash of the rain—are a preschooler's delight. Endlessly transforming this delight into investigation, which is now *very* verbal, not just physical, she inquires nonstop. This is the age of "Why." "Why do flowers smell, why do bees buzz, why is rain wet?" When she speaks her words, they may also be silly, exaggerated, or even secret gibberish understood only by her. While life for a preschooler is filled with enchantment, it is also a place filled with threats. Dark forces seem to lurk around every turn to terrorize and terrify a preschooler, because with imagination come fears, especially when it comes to the dark or the unknown. Seized by fright, a child of this age might go from unbridled joy to inconsolable fear. Feelings are volatile and intense, and they make your preschooler imaginative but also high-strung.

Preschoolers have an explosion of imagination as well as energy, confidence, and language. More coordinated and able, your preschooler now jumps, runs, hops, and climbs with great self-assurance, agility, and enthusiasm. Sometimes this gets a preschooler into trouble, as she can scramble up the jungle gym only to find that she lacks the skill to make her way safely down to the ground and needs your help. Language mushrooms; by three years of age, sentences of three words are average; by five years of age, a preschooler can string eight words together into a sentence while making sense of about thirteen thousand words she hears. (Just think that at eighteen months your toddler could only say ten words!)

These leaps of mental advancement are the strongest determinants of this behavioral stage, so expect a delightful and challenging whirlwind. Your preschooler will keep you on your toes physically *and* mentally. Expect your job to be that of her protector while you also assist your child in getting smarter and smarter. You will need a great deal of patience and creativity to keep up with the task. Your preschooler will demand more of you as she becomes more of a person in her own right.

Nowhere will this be more apparent than in your need to listen to a preschooler and thoughtfully explain what the world is all about in terms that he or she can understand. When your daughter takes the family turtle out of its bowl for an examination, to discover where his head disappears, tell her that she must be gentle with the animal and explain that "A turtle's hard shell keeps his body safe from boo boos. It is like the plastic helmet you wear when we bike," rather than shout a reprimand or offer a lecture on the skeletal structure of invertebrates. Even if questions and thoughts seem foolish, respond seriously.

You have become your child's first and most important teacher, and the curriculum is "Life 101." I cannot emphasize enough how these verbal exchanges are crucial to peaceful family life. Study after study on child development show that children who are spoken to in this way are far more calm, competent, and better behaved than children who get terse and impatient responses from their parents.

▶ **PYB Words of Wisdom:** *Every loving and patient exchange you have with your preschooler reaps an enormous benefit, far fewer battles, because it is a proven fact that the more you converse with your child the less you will be shouting at him, now and forever. Give your child words. Words avert wars!*

What to Expect of Your Preschooler

Expect an Active and Vivid Imagination

This is what you can expect from your preschooler with her vivid imagination.

Fantasies

A "Romance" or "Adoption" Fantasy

This is common at this stage, especially when children get angry with their parents. Expect such claims as "You are not my real parents. I am a princess stolen from my real mother and father the good king and queen and put into this horrible home where no one loves me."

Tolerate your child's ambivalence. Do not feel insulted or rejected by these announcements. They have nothing to do with how good a parent you are. This is the way your child's immature mind reconciles feeling frustrated toward the same person he loves—you. It is called "splitting." Help your child see that *everyone* has mixed feelings about someone they love and that this *ambivalence* is normal and acceptable and, most important, does not threaten a relationship. Encourage your child to integrate rather than "split" his feelings. When your child tells you this, say, "I know that you get so angry that you wish we were not your parents. From time to time, everyone gets angry with people they love, but we will always love you and be your parents no matter how angry you feel."

Negative Wishes and Angry Words

When they are hurt or frustrated, preschoolers have lots of colorfully "bad" wishes, which frighten them because they don't yet understand that there is a difference between a wish and a deed. They worry that their thoughts and feelings are real and have power to make things actually happen. When they fantasize and say things like "I wish my little brother would go back to the hospital and be unborn," they believe that by thinking it they can make it come true. Only around the age of five do children start to grasp the important difference between thoughts and actions that are not one and the same.

Teach your child the difference between thoughts and deeds. Do not get angry with your child or tell him that he is "bad" if it is his feelings that are negative and not his behavior. Don't force him to feel good feelings; making a child deny or swallow his bad sentiments always backfires. It teaches a child to be phony or even sneaky. It can even encourage bad behavior. Children who are not allowed to put their anger into words are far more likely to use physical aggression. Tell your child, "Thoughts are not deeds, and I want to hear about *anything* that is on your mind." Encourage open talk about negative emotions, so that your child does not need to keep them as scary private fantasies or resort to angry behavior as his only means of expression. By *giving your child words to express negative feelings and wishes, you create the all-important separation between thoughts and actions*. Create a climate where anger is put into words.

> ▶ **PYB Words of Wisdom:** *Encouraging your child to express negative sentiments and ideas has a paradoxical effect. It makes them feel less angry, because their emotions are no longer bottled up. The more a child can say how angry he feels, the less angry he acts.*

Invisible, Imaginary Friends

Children talk about invisible, imaginary friends as if they were real. This is not abnormal or crazy and often is associated with very creative children. Expect to see it more in firstborn or only kids. (It is only a problem if it persists when a child is much older, is highly isolated, and seems out of touch with reality.) The invisible friend can serve many purposes. It can:

• make a child feel less isolated and lonely, since he always has a friend by his side whenever he wills it;
• give him someone to boss around and control, so for a change he can be the one to say, "Brush your teeth and get into bed right now;"

- provide him with someone to blame for his misdeeds or mistakes, so he can stay good. When he breaks a rule, he can claim innocence, "My friend ate the cookies before dinner, not me;"
- be a powerful ally who does everything extraordinary that a preschooler can only dream about doing. "My pal can scare bad guys away and fly just like Superman."

Respect the emotional need for an imaginary friend. Do not insist that your child give up his imaginary buddy; it actually helps soothe your child and exercises his imagination. Do not get angry with a child who uses his fantastic pal to take the blame for his misdeeds. He is being self-protective, not deceitful. A preschooler can be so harsh on himself for doing something "bad" that he uses his playmate as a stand-in to take the heat. Just gently say, "It is not possible that your invisible pal ate the cookies. But maybe you do not want me to get angry with you for doing something wrong. I may get angry if you do something that is not right, but I will still love you." While your child will treat this make-believe being as the real thing, even asking you to set an extra place at the dinner table, be patient and responsive, set a place, and add, "Please tell your friend he is most welcome to join us for dinner." As your child becomes more involved with real playmates, his need for a made-up one gradually fades.

Exaggerations, Tales, and Fibs

Expect exaggerations, fantastic explanations, and implausible stories. The child in your home is not that good at distinguishing fact from fiction. She may spin tales, like telling her teacher, "I have a real live pony at home," when it is a large stuffed one she got for her birthday. This is not a lie but a "creative" explanation when real life does not fit her wishes and desires.

Expect your preschooler to make up rules on the fly when she finds that reality doesn't work the way she needs it to. She may run a race, come in second place, and suddenly declare, "I win." When she plays a board game, she may make the rules up as she goes along, especially if it means she will triumph.

Preschool kids are incapable of deliberate deception. Do not be alarmed or angry at untruths. Don't force her to "fess up"; she is not a liar though she might sound like one. She is inventive, not cunning.

These false assertions are her wishful thinking at work. "I really do so want a pony" is what these "fibs" are actually declaring. In response to these claims let her know you understand her longings and say, "You want a pony so badly that you wish this stuffed one was a real live pony."

If your child bends the rules, she is not cheating. These flights from reality are not the beginning of a life of crime. The thrill of winning just overrides her ability to keep the rules in her head. So, do not expect her to play by them consistently and be flexible. When she has to, let her win. Say, "Winning is so fun that you make up the rules that help you to be the champion. For now we will use your rules to play. When you are ready, we will play by the rules in the instruction book." It's her reasoning that is inconsistent, not her morals. She may look like a big girl, but her logical mind is not fully matured and won't be until she is ready to start school at six.

Fears

MAGICAL FEARS

Magical fears make their appearance during the preschool years. At night, her cozy room suddenly becomes unfamiliar, and the known mysteriously transforms into the unknown. The dark shadows on the wall, clothes hanging in a closet become frightful creatures. Monsters lurk under the bed. Nightmares, which now arrive, will be about being chased and eaten by animals (people come later). They may wake your child in the middle of the night, will be remembered, and will feel "scary," because your preschooler cannot distinguish the real from the imagined. Given this imaginative surge, is it any wonder that problems around sleep emerge? Expect your child to refuse to go to bed, or to go to sleep reluctantly. Children at this age fight staying in their room alone, having the lights out, and falling asleep.

▶ **PYB Words of Wisdom:** *When your child is really scared by his imagination, it is because what scares him feels so very real.*

FEARS OF THE REAL WORLD

Preschool years are pretty anxious times for your child. Fears may be about the real as well as the unreal world. Your preschooler may develop a sudden terror of dogs or bugs, or a fear of the unexpected; loud noises like fire engines, sirens, or the roar of a vacuum cleaner might be upsetting, as well as natural events like thunder and lightning. New experiences—waves at the beach or the hot sand—might now feel scary and off-putting. Old experiences, such as going to the doctor, can crop up as a frightening outing, because, with your preschooler's maturing memory, she can now remember that the last time she saw the pediatrician she got a painful shot and so she now dreads going back. Even common everyday events can spark anxiety or panic. With eyes shut tight, a haircut or shampoo or a nap might now become a dark, scary, and unfamiliar happening accompanied by plaintive pleas or shouts of protest.

A preschooler, especially starting at about five (and still at six years of age), also has heightened anxiety over the safety of her own body, getting panicky if she bumps, cuts, or scrapes herself, because she has yet to realize that in time pain goes away and "boo boos" heal. Lacking any sense of time, or cause and effect, she fails to anticipate what might come next, like actually feeling better. All of this may make for a high-strung, weepy, and not very cooperative child.

But the greatest fear of a preschooler is losing his mother. He is on alert, anxious that mom won't pick him up from daycare or preschool, or that she won't be waiting at home when he arrives on the school bus. He may even be scared to close his eyes at bedtime, for fear of waking up in the dark and finding that mom is not around. These worries can make a preschooler clingy, or, if you are late for school or not at home as expected, very angry or even hysterical.

APPLY KIDOLOGY TO AVERT AGGRAVATION:
STAY CALM WHEN YOUR CHILD CANNOT

Shouting at your child to calm down is not the way to respond to what seems an exaggerated reaction. While no adult would dissolve into tears over a splinter, it is a catastrophe from your preschooler's vantage point. Don't overreact to your child's overreaction. Your calm, measured reassurance is the response that will avert a scene.

• Be prepared with an endless supply of kisses and Band-Aids. Give a large dose of affection while you say, "I am sorry that you are in pain. It hurts a lot now but it will go away in a few minutes. Maybe a blue

Band-Aid with stars, and a kiss, will make it feel better."

- Let your child practice closing her eyes and making the world "disappear" before she has a shampoo or goes to sleep.
- Give her a toy dog to play with to help her feel comfortable with the real thing.
- Point out pictures of the beach in magazines and on TV before you go on an outing for the first time.
- Don't insist that she confront her fears. Let her avoid dogs or not go swimming at the beach. This age of anxiety passes for most children, and she will get braver naturally and in due time.
- If she fears a destination, like the doctor or dentist, *never* lie about where you are going or what will happen once she is there in order to avoid her anxiety. Lies make her distrust you, and she will be more distraught and resistant the next time.
- Be honest about your whereabouts. Don't make false promises about showing up as a way to fend off anticipated disappointment. If you find yourself unable to be on time as planned, call. Give your cell phone number to anyone taking care of him, like his teacher, in case there is a mishap.
- You're only human. Expect to slip up and find yourself being held responsible for his frightened misery. Be affectionate, not defensive, when this happens; this can be hard since at those moments you are probably overwrought as well, feeling guilty for upsetting him. Don't try and talk him out of being distressed because you "didn't mean it," or make up excuses. Simply apologize, letting him know that you regret causing his suffering. Be gentle.

Foolish or Silly Talk

You may find your preschooler spouting what seems like nonsensical ideas or saying outlandish things. Expect to be perplexed ("where did she come up with this?") or even shocked and, if it's in public, mortified. After a talk about how babies come out of mothers, when your preschooler exclaims, giggling at her "discovery," "Babies are poop from your stomach," remember that your child has a vivid imagination but not an altogether reasoning mind. Try and redirect your preschooler's logic, and clear up the natural confusion without shaming your child, by giving correct information in accurate words, "No, babies are not poop and do not come from a mommy's stomach, they come from a special place in a mommy's body called a uterus." Don't misread these moments as provocative or rude, because they are not.

Expect Play to Be Nonstop

Play is your preschooler's work, and it is a full-time job. Understanding this may relieve you from annoyance that any of this time is frivolous or wasted. Playing with dolls or pretending to be a warrior is just what a preschooler should be doing, and you should encourage it. Studies show that children who have a rich interior life and active imagination can entertain themselves, are less demanding, more creative, calm, and well behaved.

Because your preschooler's imagination is so very absorbing, you can also expect that asking your child to give up play creates a fuss. "Come inside for dinner" or "Get dressed right now" may be the worst words to your child's ears if he is in the middle of his very important job of, say, fighting off a band of evil space aliens.

> ▶ **PYB Words of Wisdom:** *Play is a preschooler's work and it is a full-time job. Encourage it, because a child with a rich inner life will be a contented child.*

Make Gentle Transitions

Your child needs gentle help making such shifts in his attention. You will find that the battle to drag him away from his "job" will not be fierce if you:

- slowly walk toward him, bend down to eye level, touch his shoulder, and deliver a series of quiet warnings that he needs to stop playing in five minutes, then three minutes, then zero minutes. As you hold up your fingers to indicate the passing time, say, "I see you are very busy but you will need to stop playing in this many minutes;"
- communicate respect for his brand of "hard work," saying, "Come and eat dinner so that you can get stronger to fight those evil aliens," or "After you are dressed for bed you can get back to your important job of taking care of your dolls."

Expect Your Pre-Schooler to Be Finicky About His Playthings and Love Repetitive Play

Preschoolers fall in love with their toys, trucks, dolls, stuffed animals, and are very possessive and protective of them. They love to collect and arrange them, getting upset if they are out of order or, heaven forbid, get misplaced or lost. If a sibling is responsible for the misplaced plaything, it can potentially mushroom into a battle. When it comes to favorite books, videotapes, and/or music, preschoolers are similarly attached, finding it endlessly pleasurable to hear, for example, the same story endlessly retold. That means you are going to be bored to death while they are excitedly begging, "Please Mom, just one more time." And don't think you can get away with the abridged version. Expect a fit if you decide to skip a page of a favorite bedtime story or ask them to stop their beloved movie *Dumbo* before the very end even if this is the hundredth time they've seen it.

Be Patient

Make your best effort to show consideration for the things your pre-schooler loves.

- Create a special shelf for those favorite books and toys.
- Read that story for the hundredth time and try and muster up a smile on your face. It will help if you pay attention to the pleasure your pre-schooler is deriving from your efforts.
- Buy storybooks with very short stories (there are books with bedtime tales only one-page long), so that, when asked, you can read a "whole" story without feeling shanghaied by your child.
- Make sure that siblings are alerted to the fact that your preschooler's books and toys are his personal things, and that they must first ask if these things can be borrowed. Even a child as young as three has a right to privacy and personal space and respect.
- Try humor. When your preschooler begs for more play time, stories, videos, say, "This is a rule, Maggie: I will allow you one 'Puhleeze Ma' a day." Then, next time your child begins to plead for another few minutes of play or one more story, announce with mock seriousness, "Maggie, do you want to use up your one and only 'Puhleeze Ma' over this?" You will be happily surprised to find that your child will fre-

quently say "no," which will help to smooth a transition and/or end an activity.

Expect No Sense of Time as an Adult Knows It

A sense of measured time is beyond your child's present mental equipment. There is this strange phenomenon about time: To a child time seems endless, while to an adult it whisks by. You will see this difference dramatically when you have a preschooler at home. They will act as if time stands still, so they will frequently seem to dawdle or be late. Remember this difference, and it will make you less impatient when they are not measuring time by your adult clock.

Expect Curiosity About Sexual Differences

Preschoolers are particularly inquisitive about the parts of their bodies hidden under clothes, which they usually can't see. Don't be surprised if you find your child looking at or stimulating his or her genitals or playing doctor with a friend. Don't be alarmed if your boy tries to sit or your girl tries to stand while using the toilet. Little girls are intrigued by why boys stand to urinate, just as boys are fascinated about why girls sit.

The best way to react to curiosity is to take it in stride and show your child that it is normal and healthy to be interested in his own body. Validate your child's curiosity while being clear that his body is private and belongs only to him. Let him know that touching is something to be done in private, by himself, in his own room. If you see your daughter experiment with toileting, you can say, "It's very interesting to see that boys and girls are different and to see how it feels to urinate like a boy, but you will find that it is better and more comfortable for you to sit, like Mommy does, when you use the bathroom."

Expect this sexual curiosity and try to take it in stride. Sexual curiosity helps children form an accurate image of their growing bodies so that by four and five they are clear about which group they belong to. Children with a clear and respectful attitude toward their own bodies are less likely to act out sexually as they mature.

Expect Socializing to Still Have Its Rough Patches

Your preschooler will play with other children, but she will not be good at togetherness. She is just getting started at becoming a social being, and her skills are not in place. Many are quite timid or wary when first confronted with groups of playmates at a playgroup or a special event like a circus or party. Some will cry and want to leave, even though at home the thought of joining friends seemed appealing.

Don't force socializing. Forcing your child to enter a group before he is up to it will make him resistant to play dates, playgroups, preschool, and/or school. Let your child ease into those first group experiences to avoid battling. Be careful not to get angry when a child is ambivalent; let's say, wanting to go to a party and then changing his mind on arrival. Avoid taking a stand, saying, "But you wanted to come here, so now you will have to stay." Also refrain from critical comparisons, "See, all the other children are happy to be at the birthday party"; or "No one else is afraid of the clown." These responses are likely to create a meltdown, not a social butterfly.

Instead, create a bridge to help your child enter into the action. Say, "The blocks the children are playing with look like fun. Let's see if we can help them build a tower"; "The clown is making balloon animals. Let's ask him to make your favorite animal, a giraffe." It can also ease your child along if you organize small playgroups. Start by having one or two kids at your home before you go off to other places with more children. For an especially reluctant child, you might turn down invitations to large parties; ask parents how many children are expected at an event and then decline those that may overwhelm your child. See if there will be any novel events, like a clown or a magician, that may frighten your child, so that you can forewarn him. If your child is very wary, make arrangements to stay close by and say, "Mommy will stay at this party with you to help you feel comfortable." With time and experience, your preschooler will get used to being in groups, so this will not have to be a permanent arrangement. Putting in this time now will make it easier for him to separate in the long run; say, when school becomes a big part of life.

▶ **PYB Words of Wisdom:** *Your preschooler needs you to be his social lubricant, intervening to smooth the rough patches, but do not make the mistake of taking your child's* *side in preschooler disputes. This encourages antagonism, not cooperation. In a preschool fracas, help both children develop social skills.*

Expect Verbal Aggression

Do not expect social graces once your preschooler does get involved in a group; sharing is still not something at which a preschooler is an expert. Given his ideas of magic, lending a toy to a friend may still seem like a disappearing act and make a child quite reluctant to part with a favorite plaything even for a few minutes. Expect aggression to be less physical, because your preschooler will get better at saying, "I am mad," and, therefore, he will depend less on having to act it out through his behavior. His need for action will diminish. Chances are, however, that you can expect teasing, threats, and insults. "You're a big fat stinky baby" may be the way he lashes out now. Even though this is not physical, it is hurtful, and your child should be stopped from lashing out with his tongue. Tell him, "You can say that you are angry," and give him alternative words he can use. "You can tell your friend that you are very angry and that pushing and hitting are not acceptable. Big boys use their words when they are angry. Little boys who don't have their words yet hit."

> ▶ **PYB Words of Wisdom:** *Encourage your child to "use his words" early on, and you will raise a child who gets along well with others and you.*

Expect Endless Questions

Your preschooler's favorite word (which risks becoming your least favorite word) becomes "Why." Now that she has the cognitive power to observe her world, curiosity heightens. Still lacking the power to understand this world on her own, she relies on you to help her know just what is what. She has the intelligence to ask questions without the accompanying faculties to answer them. Therefore, expect to hear the query "Why?" over and over and over again. Why? Because she is built to supply the questions and you are there to provide the answers. While this "Why" attack can feel annoying, think about trading in feeling peeved for feeling pleased. At this stage of development, your child believes that you know everything there is to know. Wow! Enjoy your brief stint as the all-knowing, all-powerful parent.

Making Life Peaceful With Your Preschooler

Handling Disappearance

Children at this stage follow their fancy and are more agile and self-confident, especially as they approach five. This is the time they pull the "look how fast I can disappear from your sight" routine, so expect more than a few hair-raising moments. Preschoolers wander off in supermarkets and malls, take spontaneous and unescorted "trips" to the neighborhood playground, or make nighttime visits to friends that can leave you frantic and furious. (Though by five, and once in kindergarten, they tend to be more obedient and generally do not do things without permission.)

This is a time when knowing the facts, not just feeling the fears, can help you to keep from getting completely furious with your "happy wanderer." Despite the enormous publicity surrounding tragedies of a "lost child," most small children do not disappear permanently. *The overwhelming majority of children who wander away are, thankfully, found immediately.* Precautions are, of course, an absolute necessity. They will go a long way toward making your life with this child less stressful.

Make sure to:

- instruct her to tell you if she wants to leave your home or your side;
- lock the front gates or doors;
- fence in dangerous areas, like a pool or a well;
- show your child the manager's desk at the local supermarket, or security desk at the mall;
- have her memorize her address and phone number;
- point out which buildings or stores have a Safe Haven sticker, and let her know she can find help at these places. (Safe Haven is a community program that encourages establishments to respond to a child in distress. You can start one in your community if you do not already have this organization in your area.);
- watch your child carefully in other people's homes or places that may not be adequately childproofed for a nimble preschooler.

When disappearances do occur (and they will), do not forget an essential aspect of your preschooler's personality: *sensitivity*! Do not have a melt-down once your child is back. Do not lash out. Breathe deeply, stay calm, and count to ten. Although, understandably, you will feel overwhelmed, *never harshly criticize, yell at, scream at, or hit a child who has been lost.* Do **not** turn this hair-raising, scary experience into a battle. The minute you see her, hug her and let her know how glad you are to see her safe. Despite the fact that you might also be fuming over being made so frantic, try your level best to stay in control of any anger you feel; having her in your arms is just what both of you need.

Then, in calmer moments, you can review what went wrong and give her rules about leaving your side. "If you want to see something in the mall, you must tell me what you would like to do, not walk away by yourself. You saw how scared you felt when you did that and got separated from me."

Try to have a gentle, sensitive perspective when living with a preschooler. The more you can find the playful, whimsical child in yourself, the easier this stage will be for both of you. This is guaranteed to make life with your preschooler more fairy tale than nightmare.

BE VERY CAREFUL
OF A PRESCHOOLER'S SENSITIVE SOUL

When a small child thinks she is doing good ("Look Mommy, I cut my own hair!") and gets loudly reprimanded for being bad ("Oh my gosh, you ruined your hair!") it is often a long-remembered blow to a tiny soul. (Most adults vividly remember such incidents from their own childhood.) A preschooler is a **very** sensitive creature. When you react angrily at an apparent misdeed, remember: it is often a startling shock to her system, especially if she has no idea in the world that she has done anything wrong. Shouting, especially at these moments of vulnerability, doesn't make a preschooler better behaved, it makes her upset, confused, fearful, and teaches her nothing about getting good at being good.

▶ **PYB Words of Wisdom:** *When you have a preschooler, you realize with a mix of wistfulness and joy that your* *little one no longer looks like, or is, a baby. For some parents who want to hold on to their baby, this can be a challenging moment. Be prepared for the sadness and open to the joy, and try not to resist the change; your child will balk if you hold them back from growing up now or in the future.*

REMEMBER YOUR PRESCHOOLER'S GOOD INTENTIONS WHEN SHE APPEARS TO MISBEHAVE

One morning before I left the house for an appointment, my daughter covered her face in my best red lipstick and pressed her entire face against my pillowcase to "kiss me goodbye." I was taken aback by the sight of the ruined lipstick, a destroyed pillowcase, and a messy kid just as I was trying to run out the front door. But even though my first impulse was to yelp, "Oh no, what have you done?" I swallowed the reprimand I was about to shout and just gave her a hug and smiled at her good intentions and her love.

Corrine, mother of four

Expect Your Five-year-old to Be Ready for Kindergarten

While preschool is optional, kindergarten is the point at which most children in this country start their formal entry into a school setting. Because a preschooler has fears, has only known his family as the center of his universe, and worries about losing his mother, leaving home to attend school at age five may become a battle. Expect your child to express excitement about "big boy/girl school," but when the time comes to go through the front door and leave mommy outside, he or she may not go willingly. Anticipate protest, tears, and heartfelt pleas, "Mommy don't leave me. I beg you. Don't be mean, I wanna go home."

Don't Push

Hearing his plaintive cries makes this separation hard for both of you; you will probably feel torn and guilty while he is feeling frightened and abandoned. Parents can also feel embarrassed by their child's tearful refusal to separate easily, particularly if other kids seem more at ease. If your child has a meltdown, do not tell him that he is being a baby. Kind reassurance, not stern disapproval, is what is needed by all five-year-olds taking such a momentous step.

To avoid turmoil, develop a separation plan well in advance of the start of the term.

• visit the school during the summer before your child is to enter
• introduce him to his teacher before the year starts
• let him draw a picture of the school and classroom, and hang it up in his room
• make a fuss over buying school equipment, such as a lunch box, and let him pick out supplies
• give him a special friend, like a favorite stuffed animal, to take in his knapsack

Once school commences, establish a simple school-separation routine and discuss the sequence of these planned steps with your child.

Your ritual might be as straightforward as:

• walking your child into the classroom
• helping your child hang up his coat
• reading a picture book with him in the reading corner
• watching your child color a picture that you take with you
• waving goodbye at the door.

Your routine can become shortened over time, until you do not even need it. Chances are, if you are consistent, your child will soon tell you, "Mommy, I'm a big boy now, you don't have to stay in my classroom."

Because not all kids are ready to enter school at age five, it is important to assess your child's readiness; otherwise you may unwittingly push him to attend before he is actually up to it. The risk here is that a child develops a dislike for school, which can launch you into thirteen very miserable years of warfare. Don't get caught up in the social pressure to make your child into a five-year-old genius. Evaluate *your* child's readiness for kindergarten. Some "young fives," girls as well as boys, may not have the maturity for school, either, and might do better waiting to be the oldest rather than the youngest in their class. This is especially important for boys, who seem to do better if they start school later than girls, at six rather than five. This is not holding your child back; it is giving him a chance to become ready to succeed at learning when she is good and ready.

APPLY KIDOLOGY TO AVERT
STARTING THE THIRTEEN-YEAR WAR: ASSESS
KINDERGARTEN READINESS

School lasts thirteen years. A child who enters school when ready enters with enthusiasm, which gives you a good shot at not having these years battle-torn. It is not all that difficult to assess your child's readiness for kindergarten. Here are some, but not all, of the signs that indicate he is ready to take on life in the classroom. Your child is able to:

- skip
- hop on one foot
- catch a ball
- say his name when requested
- recognize his name when written down
- know shapes
- know colors
- cut with scissors
- follow directions in a short sequence (put your coat away, sit down, and look at the teacher)
- concentrate or focus on a task.

The above list is *not* meant to be a complete assessment. Use this readiness questionnaire *only* as an indicator for your personal use. Consult your child's school staff or a trained educational professional in order to make a complete educational assessment.

---

4. Your Grade-schooler: Six Years to Eleven Years

While your preschooler was a creature intent on making play his life's work, an altogether different person has replaced him—a serious, industrious little individual. This transformation is quite astounding. The fanciful creature makes way for the worker, the proverbial eager beaver. Your school-age child is now ready and increasingly able to study and learn.

Listening earnestly and attentively to the adult teaching him, your grade-schooler takes school and the work he finds there seriously, very seriously. His first attempt at schoolwork is OK, but the next is better. Each try is an opportunity for him to feel better about his talents and himself, but each can also be a startling moment of deflation if what happens in the classroom doesn't go right and, because he is just beginning to try out his new skills, it often does not. A grade-schooler has many rough patches: Easily disappointed at his own failings, he pouts, cries, or threatens never to try again. Getting glum and moody if things do not fall in place, he can become exasperated with himself, declaring, "I'm not good at anything." A grade-schooler is now increasingly and often painfully aware of his peers. While a preschooler caught up in his own reverie was oblivious to others, a grade-schooler, especially as he moves toward third grade, awakens to a startling and sobering discovery: Plenty of other children are also hard at work. This awareness sparks competitiveness and envy, as well as self-doubt and harsh self-criticism. Facing things that he does not like to see (like his classmate's superior skills) or that do not go his way, he will frequently bellyache: "It's not fair!"

The grade-schooler now looks to his teacher for guidance and approval. If a parent offers advice while he is practicing letters or reading, he is liable to get his nose out of joint, sputtering angrily, "The teacher knows better." If his little brother dares to touch his school things, he might become outraged, yelling, "Leave my stuff alone," even slamming the bedroom door in the toddler's face.

This child is a worker, but he is also eager in ways that parents do not always welcome. He is eager to tell mom and dad that he is no baby and that he is ready to do everything for himself, thank you very much! He is eager to be independent, but he is not quite up to the task. He is raring to fight with his siblings, especially if they are younger. He plays with friends, but only with those of his own gender.

She is also keen to compete, be bossy, tease, and to cry when her friends turn and do the same to her. She is eager to dish it out but not to take it. Given that she can be so touchy, maybe it's not so bad that she spends a good part of her time at school.

What to Expect of Your Grade-schooler

Expect School Daze

When your child has morphed into this new creature—the busy beaver— what can you anticipate? Above all, expect school to become central to his life and, to your child's astonishment, a central challenge. Expect that no matter how terrific, talented, or smart a child you have, getting competent at all the hard stuff required for school develops *slowly* and *unevenly*. A readiness and a willingness to learn come long before the ability to do it all very well. Your child's mental, emotional, and physical equipment needs *lots* of time to get fully in gear. Development will not be "finished" until he is at least a preteen. Some faculties—like good judgment—require even more time to mature and are not in place until young adulthood. This biological reality—that skills need time to fully come together—is the very reason why this stage covers so many years.

> ▶ **PYB Words of Wisdom:** *The years of middle childhood are the years when children master skills. This is a complex process that, above all, requires time. Asking a child to hurry up at mastery is about as effective as asking a fruit to hurry up and ripen.*

The single best way to promote scholarship is to encourage your child to expand or stretch his existing skills rather than demand a perfect performance in a skill set that he is not quite up to. Encourage picture-drawing before expecting your child to color inside the lines. Applaud when he first writes his name in sloppy, lopsided letters, tape the paper to the refrigerator and tell him that you would love to display more of his work. Don't insist on neatness, which will come considerably later, as he develops coordination and fine motor skills.

Forcing children to learn prematurely *always* backfires; they become resentful and resistant. What follows are ways to prevent that from happening right from the beginning of reading and writing, which are the foundation for **all** learning to come.

How to Keep Reading a Battle-free Zone

If you want to avoid fights with a reluctant reader once your child gets to school, make him into a child who loves reading before he even enters a classroom. Reading words is one tough job: it takes heroic perseverance to master those veritable hieroglyphics on the page of a first-grade reader (especially when compared to the easy and instant pleasure of TV and computer games). Knowing that reading is a source of fun and pleasure helps kids get over this hump. To have realistic expectations and avoid conflict, keep in mind these facts about reading:

- During the first years of school, there is wide variation in children's reading skills, but generally everyone catches up—no matter how slowly they first get out of the starting gate.
- Boys learn later than girls, sometimes by as much as two years.
- Reading improves notably around second grade, but it becomes truly comfortable and easy only at about fourth grade.
- Comprehension comes well after fluency, especially if a child, not a parent, is doing the reading, so expect kids to read before they understand what they are reading.

APPLY KIDOLOGY TO PREVENT READING BATTLES

- Read aloud to your children *long* after they have developed the capacity to read on their own, especially to your sons. This cozy and pleasurable experience goes a *very* long way into making a child an enthusiastic reader.
- Remind your child that, when it comes to reading, everyone catches up. When they first enter school, children are often placed in reading groups, which, they realize early on, are determined—no matter how

they are disguised by nonjudgmental names like "red," "blue," "yellow," "green"—by level of competence. That makes kids feel dejected if they are not in the "top" group. Be prepared for him to feel blue if he is not the "best reader." If your child is feeling crestfallen, say, "It's hard not to feel disappointed that you are not in the group with the most advanced readers, but, in a few months, reading will be easier for you."

- Soften your child's harsh judgment of himself: Help your child gain a perspective on the *process* of skill building. Tell him, "You are *not* a bad reader; you are a new reader. Remember when you were a new bike rider? It took practice until you got it right. It's the same with reading." Or say, "Reading is like muscles, you get stronger as you exercise, and your reading group is a place you can exercise your 'reading muscles' until they are big and strong."
- Confer with the teacher and make sure that this natural variation among beginning readers is discussed in the classroom and that the teacher makes it abundantly clear that these groupings are neither punitive nor a sign of failure. Alert the teacher immediately if there is teasing over who is a "bad" reader.
- Remind *yourself* that kids' learning differences generally even out by fourth grade. If you do not see this happening by then, consult the school, as your child may need more assistance or have a learning problem. But do not judge your child's intelligence or future school success by *when* she starts to read. It's only one factor.
- Acknowledge your own competitiveness. All parents eye with wistfulness or even envy the kindergartner who is reading before their child has even stopped sucking her thumb, but don't push your child even if you are feeling disappointed that he is not the "genius of kindergarten." Believe me, he will still make his mark.

How to Keep Writing a Battle-free Zone

Children are avid and accomplished storytellers long before they can accurately transcribe their stories or, for that matter, read them. So, do not force your child to "write" a story that in any way requires these skills. Take that existing storytelling skill, which naturally begins *orally,* and encourage it. If you do, you will not be fighting with your fourth-grader when his book report is due.

1. **Take dictation** Ask your child to tell you a story while dictating it to you, or record her story on tape and then transcribe it for her. Kids who initially "write" as they speak are less self-conscious writers and tend to develop a love of writing. Self-consciousness, not the lack of writing skills, is the single biggest obstacle to self-expression and future writing problems. *Do not edit this story, or your child will feel criticized and balk in the future.*

2. **Make up storytelling games** Children who hear creative stories become better writers, since the freedom to imagine is a positive influence on writing proficiency.

   • Before bed, make up a fairy tale where your child is the hero/heroine, Tell it in installments each night. Children love the repetitive familiarity of a good tale, and in a short while it inspires them to help you make up the tales, or take over the storytelling entirely.
   • Play this family game: Sit in a circle. Let the first person begin a story, then, as soon as that person says the word "and," let the next person take up the story. Continue around the circle, taking turns and being silly and outlandish.

3. **Play word games** Children with rich language develop better writing skills. Stretch and expand your child's vocabulary, but do not do it by rote methods, such as flash cards or vocabulary tests.

   • During a car ride, choose a word, then take turns finding synonyms, until you have exhausted all the possibilities. Keep score to see who can find the most synonyms. For example, start with "pretty," "lovely," "cute," "nice," until you have exhausted your vocabulary.
   • Find a word, post it on the refrigerator, and challenge every family member to use it at least three times with one another on the day it is posted. (Many educators find that using a new word correctly three times in one day ensures retention.)

4. **Encourage your child to write at home** Buy him a journal or diary; help her find a pen pal; and ask that they write their own thank-you notes.

5. **Hold the literary criticism** Educational research suggests that children who learn to write freely, without criticism, in the early grades,

actually become better at grammar, spelling, and self-expression as they learn the rules later on. If you demand technical competence before third grade, you will have a child whose writing is labored, slow, and not very innovative or inspired, which will make writing assignments a drag for both of you.

Expect That Others Will Become Very Important but That You Need to Stay in Charge

Your school-age child moves outside your home into the great big world, where more than half of his waking hours are spent with non–family members. Expect that with this shift you will lose status, because you will now share the limelight with others. Teachers, coaches, caregivers, mentors, and friends will become very important. Do not take it personally when you realize that you have suddenly become a person who "knows nothing," while the teacher, first and foremost, now knows best. Try and absorb the shock of being replaced as the infallible parent, because it won't be long before the soccer coach or even another eleven-year-old outranks you as the person your child seems most to admire and value. Dethroning mom and dad is an absolute necessity. It is easier for a child to leave home and enter this big, daunting world of school and friends once parents cease to seem indispensable.

Expect this "dethroning" to emerge, and expect to see it expressed as impatience, self-consciousness, and criticism.

- I don't need your help with my homework
- I'm doing it how my teacher wants it
- Do you have to kiss me when you drop me off at soccer practice?
- Don't walk me into school; I'm not a baby
- I don't need to ask you about my science project, I can find out about my topic online

These gripes are all part of his push away from you and toward independence. Rejecting attention, assistance, guidance, supervision, comfort, and even affection is a natural part of this phase of the separation process.

Expect your child to lobby hard for his "rights" and to be constantly testing the limits of what you will and won't let him do. Expect:

- **Pleas** "Can't I walk to school with my friends?" "Why can't I watch TV on a school night?"
- **Bargaining** "If I promise to do my chores later, can I go out and play?" "I'll do my homework if you let me play one more video game."
- **Comparisons** "Everyone else has a computer (phone, cellphone) of his own." "All the kids in my grade go online to IM each other."

This is the "It's not fair" stage. Expect to hear this accusation no matter how hard you try to be a good parent. ***Make room for others but do not give up your central role as a guiding force in your child's life.*** Your child will no doubt act as if she is not in need of your supervision, but she most certainly is. Actually, she will feel sad, lost, lonely, and perhaps frightened if she doesn't get a clear show of your concern. You can and must make sure that your child is safe, but leave her room to make her own decisions, and sometimes even mistakes.

> ▶ **PYB Words of Wisdom:** *Getting this balancing act right between letting go while holding on is very, very challenging as well as very, very crucial. It will make the difference not only in the battles you will wage during these grade-school years but will absolutely determine the peace you do or do not achieve throughout all of your child's adolescence.*

How to Stay in Charge While Letting Go

Here are some ways to find the balance between staying in charge and letting your children have control over their own lives. Depending on the age of your child, you might require that:

- play dates be supervised, *but* allow your child and a friend to play alone in your child's room while you occasionally check in on them;
- you first visit an after-school program with your child to ensure that you are comfortable with the level of supervision, *but* once you have attained that comfort level, allow that activity to become hers and do not constantly show up to check up on her;

- you consult with parents of peers on a regular basis, particularly if there are unusual plans in the works, *but* let your child go to a party, for example, if you establish that a trusted parent will be in charge;
- you have access to her room with permission, *but* assure her that you will never invade her personal possessions, such as her mail, diary, or drawer she designates as private;
- you allow your child to use a computer or video console *but* keep it in the family room not your child's bedroom;
- you are shown a homework assignment, *but* let your older child complete it on his own if he does not ask for help.
- you permit use of electronic equipment but employ technology to limit and control use (parental controls on computer; Time Scout, an electronic device that enables parents to program usage, www.time-scout.com.

Expect Self-Awareness, Which Ushers in Self-Consciousness

Every grade-schooler becomes *acutely* self-conscious. This emerging capacity to tune into other people is crucial, because it allows a child to move from the world of self and family into the world of society. The plight of this phase is that this awakening is often a rude one. As maturing children gain a new power—personal awareness—it creates the most challenging aspect of this push into the world of school. Your child starts to notice his peers. The result is that he makes *constant* comparisons, which invariably leave him feeling inadequate, deficient, not up to scratch.

Expect your child to be:

- a perfectionist and demanding of himself;
- his own harshest critic (lashing out when disappointed, especially at himself);
- easily frustrated (inclined to give up, leaving tasks uncompleted or done sloppily);
- seeing the world in black and white;
- a complainer (expressing emotions and opinions negatively and in extremes);
- competitive and a sore loser;
- overestimating or underestimating her abilities.

Expect your child to routinely bemoan:

- "I stink at everything"
- "I never want to go to school again"
- "Nobody ever picks me for a team (invites me to parties; saves a seat for me at lunch; likes what I wear)"
- "You're the meanest mother on earth"
- "My friends always leave me out"
- "No one likes me"
- "Everything at school is too hard for me"
- "I'm stupid"

Though self-inflicted, these wounds hurt. Grappling with self-worth, self-confidence, self-respect, your child can become moody. Expect fluctuations ranging from cocky to sad to ornery, often within minutes. In the throes of this constant self-evaluation, *everything* will feel crucial, from spelling tests to birthday parties—especially the one he isn't invited to. It tends to get harder from grade to grade, as schoolwork and social life become more complex and demanding. Eleven may be the roughest year for this misery.

> ▶ **PYB Words of Wisdom:** *If your child has reached fourth grade and you have not heard complaints or seen the moodiness, you may want to consider that he is suffering in silence. Your child may be easier to parent but he usually pays dearly. Kids who suffer in silence and bottle up feelings often explode or implode with time.*

Even when kids love school, the thrill of victory is punctuated invariably by the agony of defeat. By fourth grade, there is no child who has not felt the sting of failure, deficiency, and/or rejection. A falling-out with a best friend or being the last pick for kickball is painful but par for the course. "***Left out***" is a universal wound of this stage. He will feel the defeat more acutely and remember it far longer than the many moments of triumph. Because of this, expect him to be in a funk periodically. Also expect a negative area of school life to emerge; teasing, taunting, mocking, and, in the extreme, bullying. Starting in third grade, boys and girls can be mean to one another. Sometimes, particularly among boys, it can get quite aggressive and physical, leading to intimidation, pushing, shoving, kicking, and even eruption of major fights. Be prepared for this mean-spiritedness and be prepared to indicate to your child that this behavior is unacceptable.

You might now share the burden of raising your child with others, but the responsibility for his heart and soul are still primarily yours. Where once you needed to babyproof your home to make a toddler safe, the injuries that you now need to help your child manage are likely to be emotional. Knowing that you will need great emotional stamina and empathy for your school-age child will keep you both on course and less likely to clash.

> ▶ **PYB Words of Wisdom:** You Can't Say, You Can't Play.
> *This is the title of an indispensable book by Vivan Gussin
> Paley, which should be read by all parents and educators. It
> is about creating a school environment, beginning as early as
> nursery school, where there is no room for exclusion! I
> strongly suggest that parents of grade-schoolers read this
> book and have ongoing discussions about such problems as
> ostracism, cliques, teasing, fighting, and bullying with their
> children, other parents, teachers, and school administrators.*

Expect Differences Between Boys and Girls

This is the stage where boys and girls part company for a while and behave quite differently.* For boys, friendships are not one-on-one or intensely personal. They participate in types of play such as team sports and one-to-one contests. Who is bigger and stronger becomes very important to a grade-school boy. If he doesn't feel bigger and stronger, expect him to sulk. Also expect that your grade-school boy will be very active and not very talkative. If you ask, "How was school today?," "Fine" might be the extent of his voluntary communication. If you feel shut out from what is going on in his life, do not take it personally, but do keep talking to him in spite of his reticence. *Boys may not talk, but they need to*.

---

*Some of these differences may be the result of social attitudes. However, they still seem to exist which should not stop us from trying to change some of them, like getting boys to talk more about their feelings, something girls are more likely to do.

▶ **PYB Words of Wisdom:** *Don't fall into the trap of not talking to your son because he, like so many boys, does not talk to you. Make time to talk; before bedtime is your best shot. If at first your son does not open up, stay nearby. Once he knows you are not giving up in the face of his silence, he will probably open up. In particular, encourage your boy to talk about his feelings, something that he is probably not inclined to do.*

Unlike boys, girls have best friends and a close-knit group of peers, spending time together in a clique of friends. Girls appear caring rather than noticeably competitive: two seven-year-old friends spending time fixing each other's hair, or ten-year-olds talking intimately on the phone or via computer might not strike you as potential adversaries. Do not be fooled; girls are quite competitive but the arena for their competition may not be the ball field or a gym as it is typically for boys. Girls are socially competitive, shifting loyalties and alliances, becoming best friends one day and worst enemies the next. Girls' relationships are contradictory and ambivalent; they are love/hate friendships where betrayal and disappointment are common and recurrent. They can be cruel, especially to the outcast, but they use words, rejection, shunning, and scorn to do their work. If you have a grade-school girl, expect friendship and heartache. Being more social and nurturing does mean that girls are talkative, so expect to hear from them, especially about their social misery.

Physical maturity comes at a different rate for boys and girls; with girls maturing faster. By the time she menstruates, a girl is 90 percent of her adult height, while a boy, by age eleven, is only 80 percent of his full stature. At age eleven, a grade-school girl may seem practically a teenager, but not so for a boy. This difference means that girls seem to get interested in boys, usually older ones, before boys of their own age even notice them. It takes boys at least another year or two to get there, so expect a boy to be awkward around girls and think they are "dumb," even—or especially—his sister, which may turn into sibling teasing and tension.

The move into puberty is uneven for all children, so expect confusion and awkwardness for boys and girls, especially as their bodies change. Boys may be especially self-conscious and worried by the uneven changes; for example, pubic hair appears quite a while before chest hair sprouts. Puberty comes quite early for many girls, so expect that your daughter may be menstruating before the end of this stage. Some girls may look like well-developed teens by age eleven, and others look like little girls or even tomboys for quite a while longer. Be very sensitive to the pace of your child's physical maturation. Research has shown that girls who develop early have the roughest time; they tend to feel self-conscious, get teased, and garner sexual attention they are not yet ready for, even though they may look otherwise. Late-blooming boys, who are slight and small, tend to have the roughest time, since, among boys, size and physical stature bestows status.

APPLY KIDOLOGY: HOW TO TALK ABOUT SEXUAL DEVELOPMENT WITHOUT A STRUGGLE

Even if you are the most relaxed parent, these will be difficult discussions that kids will often vigorously resist due to their mortal embarrassment. Respect their stage-appropriate awkwardness, but, in spite of any opposition, annoyance, or anger you encounter, keep the subject open for discussion. To avert your child's opposition, try introducing books on the subject, such as *My Body Myself for Boys/Girls* by Lynda & Arey Madaras or *The Care & Keeping of You: The Body Book for Girls* by Norma Bondell.

▶ **PYB Words of Wisdom:** *Even if your daughter seems to want to look like a teenager, and may come close to pulling it off as she nears eleven, she is not one. Don't be fooled by a girl's pseudomaturity (especially if she is physically well-developed), because, despite appearances, she is not mature. Don't treat her as if she has it under control, because she doesn't. Even very precocious girls need their parents to stay in charge.*

▶ **PYB Words of Wisdom:** *When it comes to sex your child will know more than you knew at his age even if he is reluctant to talk. It will probably shock you. But get prepared for, not angry at what you encounter during your child's sexual development.*

Making Life Peaceful with Your Grade-schooler

At this stage, your child is built to overreact, so you can save yourself a good deal of grief if you do not do the same. He may think his world is ending, but you know better, so don't react as if the sky is falling just because he says it is. *Do not let your child's moodiness become a contagious disease.* If you react to her bad mood by getting into your own, tension will escalate, and you will have a fight on your hands every time this occurs, and—I am warning you—it will occur regularly!

> ▶ **PYB Words of Wisdom:** *Your child may be on an emotional roller coaster, but you don't have to buy a ticket for the ride.*

Stay calm, breathe deeply, and try your level best not to respond in kind to your child's outbursts. Practice this sort of response: "Isabella, I know that you are angry, but you must tell me about your feelings in a civil tone. I can listen to your angry words, but I will not let you scream and yell at me. If you cannot find a way to speak to me, let me walk you to your room where I can sit with you until you calm down enough to talk and not shout."

> ▶ **PYB Words of Wisdom:** *If your child succeeds in getting you to act like a kid—yelling, shouting, slamming doors, crying—the way he does, there will be endless battles to come. When your grade-schooler loses it, be firm and polite in response to his meltdown, and he will cool off. The more your kid acts childish, the more you need to act grown up. Don't act in kind; react with kindness.*

Expect your child to have feelings of rejection, self-criticism, doubt, frustration, and disappointment, but try not to overidentify, taking it as the gospel truth. For instance, if she moans, "I hate math and I'll never be able to do it,"

• take her feelings to heart but do not confuse her real feelings for real facts; remember she is rarely as bad as she thinks;

• understand that kids say "hate" when they mean that they are frustrated, anxious, or scared. Translate their language for them, so they
don't begin to believe that they actually "hate" math and then develop
a resistance to trying or throw in the towel. Say, "I think that you say
that you hate math when you find it hard. Sometimes math can be
tough, especially when you're learning something new, but I have confidence that with practice you'll learn to do your problems."

Parents who take their child's self-criticism literally frequently end
up pushing a child to "do better," "try harder." If she bad-mouths her
math performance, resist the impulse to lock her in her room until she
finishes extra arithmetic problems. Anxiously pushing makes you both
miserable and her school years a nonstop combat zone.

But do not go to the other extreme, either, making it seem as if her
concerns are nonexistent and absurd. Avoid scoffing, "Oh my gosh, she's
being ridiculous" or "Pipe down, it doesn't matter if you get picked last
for dodge ball." Do not tease, mock, or make fun of your child's pain.
"You're such a big cry-baby," "spoil sport," or any other cutting remarks
should never emerge from your lips.

These reactions—belittlement or ridicule—lead to alienation. Both
are painfully humiliating. Feeling disrespected and hurt, she will assume
that you do not take her problems seriously, that you do not care. The risk
here is that, feeling dismissed, your child will stop confiding in you. This
sets a bad precedent that will become especially troublesome during adolescence. Do not risk losing your child's trust and connection by unwittingly belittling her feelings, and you will have a friendly ally forever. The
best advice to keep the peace is that you must stay emotionally grounded.

APPLY *KIDOLOGY* TO REDUCE TENSION
OVER AN OLDER CHILD'S UPS AND DOWNS

Here are some of the most "touchy" ups and downs that an older grade-
schooler will experience, and tips on how you can smooth them out. Your
child will:

• Have a group of best friends and at least one "enemy," who can and
will change on a daily basis, making your child feel at risk for being the

next outcast. (*Take your child's worries seriously but don't get on her bandwagon and agree that her enemy deserves her ill will, since tomorrow, for sure, alliances will shift. If she is the one on the outs, sympathize and remind her that things will change.*)

- Completely define himself, by how he looks, what he owns, and what he does. Appearance, possessions, and activities become the basis on which kids judge themselves and fervently believe others are judging them on that same basis. (*Don't scoff at the need to be fashionable or "in," since your child believes entirely that this is the basis for acceptance. If you can't afford to keep up the way he would like you to—and who can these days—just say so, without putting down his desires.*)

- Feel as if everyone notices even the smallest differences in his appearance or behavior. A haircut or a hug in public will catapult him into mortal embarrassment. And when puberty sets in, and your child's body changes, this embarrassment ratchets up big-time. (*Be tolerant of the embarrassment; your child feels like he is standing in a Macy's window without his clothes on at least several times a day.*)

- Become bossy or a sore loser when she loses or discouraged when she doesn't do well in school. (*Encourage noncompetitive games, sports, and activities at home and in school, especially in the early grades. Help her set personal goals—"I will try to get seven of the spelling words right"—instead of "I will try and get the highest grade in my class on the spelling test."*)

- Be hypersensitive to criticism, incapable of accepting failure, and believe that there is no way to recover from a mistake. (*Focus on your child's successes and help her see that a mistake or failing is a way to learn to do something differently and better the next time. Instead of pointing out the spelling of a word was wrong, ask her to see if she can catch her mistake. Say, "I wonder if you can spot the word that is misspelled in the third sentence."*)

- Resist initiating things with peers that seem simple and straightforward, like calling a friend to see if he can join him to play. (*Social self-consciousness can be paralyzing. Don't push, instead be your child's social lubricant; call the other mother to help get the ball rolling. Your child may balk at your actions but in his heart of hearts he is relieved because he needs your help getting over the hump of mortal embarrassment that often gets in his way at this age/stage.*)

WORKED UP ABOUT SCHOOLWORK?

What to do if you suspect that you are too emotionally tied into your child's scholastic success

When your child falters in school, try not to get agitated, worrying, "Oh my gosh, she's going to fail" or "I have to sit on her until she does better." But if, despite your best efforts, you cannot refrain from getting worked up along with your child, there may be more going on then you first realize.

1. Parents may get excessively anxious when a child moans about a school subject that they were not good at as children themselves.
2. Parents may get anxiously disappointed when a child does not do well because they unwittingly believe that a child's success in school is a direct reflection or measure of their merits as parents, as if "A"s on a child's report card are proof of excellence in parenting and an "F" means parental failure.
3. Parents may panic because they unwittingly fear that their child has some shortcoming or limitation that will doom her to academic failure or even worse, failure throughout life.

Being overly concerned often makes parents pressure kids about school achievement. This pressure invariably backfires, setting off horrendous battles that can last for years.

- Try to separate your child's schooling from memories of your own or from your own need to feel valued.
- Rather than engage negatively, take a "parenting time out"; encourage your grade-schooler to bring her questions and difficulties to a teacher who is not so personally identified with her academic success.
- This may also be a good time for you to back off from involvement with homework and let someone who may be less invested in your child's performance to take over, like a homework helper or perhaps your spouse.

Important Advice: If There Is
Bullying, Take Action

Staying calm and not getting too caught up in the self-critical turmoil of your child is key, with one exception. If your child is the object of mean-spirited teasing or bullying, which gets started in third grade, get involved. If your child refuses to go to school or routinely comes home upset and irritable, and you discover that kids tease him mercilessly, take action. Protect your child. The effects of bullying are very damaging! Read *The Bully-free Classroom* by Allan Beane, Ph.D. It will help you formulate a plan of action.

Make certain to go to the school administration and voice your concerns. Especially if bullying seems commonplace, start to investigate the climate that exists in the school, especially in the nonacademic areas, such as the cafeteria and playground, or places where kids hang out before and after school. Chances are that your child is not the only one affected. If you discover the unfortunate news that your child is acting meanly, or is physically aggressive, and is bullying others, seek professional help *now*, before it becomes a serious problem. Children who bully are often not doing well in school or may be contending with another problem, like depression, that is getting expressed through aggression.

> ▶ **PYB Words of Wisdom:** *Many children who look angry are actually depressed! A primary symptom of childhood depression is not sadness and crying but irritability. If your child is unhappy, mean, angry, foul-tempered, isolated, and/or doing poorly in school, he may be emotionally troubled and may need help.*

Share Your Childhood Wounds and War Stories

Eventually, with your help, your children will gain a balanced perspective of who and what they are. Self-acceptance comes quite a bit later. Self-doubt and the struggle for self-acceptance can last right through young adulthood—or later! At this juncture, only you, a grownup, know that self-acceptance will be the end result of all this testing out of oneself in the big world. You can use your grownup perspective to help smooth the bumps on your child's rocky road to self-confidence and to reduce tension. One of the best ways to cut down on battles over school is to recall the ups and downs of your own childhood with your struggling youngster. This sharing sends the message "I have been through it and I can assure you it will all turn out all right."

When your son moans, "I'm no good at recess," tell him your war stories: "I was always picked last for playground kickball." When your daughter laments, "No one sits with me at lunch," describe how your own mother's peanut-butter-and-banana sandwiches made you the laughingstock of your elementary-school cafeteria.

Do not fight with your children over the bumps and bruises, real or imagined, that injure their small souls. In quiet moments together, remind yourself and your child that you made it to successful adulthood having failed far more than one geography test, and that there is, for her, as there was for you, life after not making the soccer team. Turning back the clock and sharing your moments of grade-school misery can turn a potential whining session into a parent/child bonding moment.

> ▶ **PYB Words of Wisdom:** *Kids are extremely self-critical. Revealing your school struggles makes it easier for kids to buckle down and work, because they feel less alone. They may also begin to realize that we all have our strong and weak points—even parents—and these do not have to be impediments to success. Share the wounds of childhood with your kids, and they won't see you as the enemy.*

Advice for Every Stage: Preparing for a Birth of a Sibling

While you may be delighted with the arrival of a new bundle of joy, the same may not be the case for your older child. After all, when you add another child to your family, you are asking your older child to share your parental love, to get less of your attention, and, on top of that, love an unwanted intruder when he likes things just the way they are and never asked for this change in the first place. No wonder a new baby is tough on older siblings.

At every stage, the child who comes first, whether he is a toddler or a preteen, has a lot to handle, though it often appears hardest on toddlers, who have limited language to express their feelings, and preschoolers, who feel they have lost their favored baby status to the new arrival. Bringing home another person to love, a new brother or sister, *raises intense positive and negative* feelings in your child at all developmental stages, making sibling conflict and rivalry, as well as combat, a predictable and challenging part of the parenting landscape.

APPLY KIDOLOGY TO AVERT CONFLICT WHEN A NEW BABY ARRIVES

- **Give your child plenty of advance notice about the new arrival** Let your older child know that you are pregnant before he learns it from someone else. Some parents find it helps to have a child feel the baby kick or let him "talk" to the new baby. Once you do make the announcement, include him in planning, like picking out a mobile or choosing paint for the room. Making your child feel included before the arrival, cushions the blow of exclusion that can follow.

- **Acknowledge your child's loss of attention from the beginning** From the hospital, call your older child frequently, and, if it is allowed, have her visit you there. Let her know she is missed. If you can, when you come home from the hospital, don't ignore your older child. Let someone else hold the baby, and go right to her when you arrive, even if it is only to give your daughter a kiss and say "I love you" before you get absorbed in the new baby.

- **Keep yourself accessible to your older child** Unless there are medical or safety reasons, don't close yourself in a baby's room and lock your older child out. A closed door is very painful to a child with a new sibling.

- **Give your older child a role in baby care that is appropriate for her age** Allow your older child to rock the cradle, to wind up a music box, or to push a stroller. Older children can hold the baby, with supervision. It makes them feel wanted and appreciated.

- **Don't insist that your older child make declarations of love, since he does not necessarily feel that way at the moment** He will get there, but in the meantime allow for his positive and negative feelings, his ambivalence. If you notice that your child is sullen, simply say, "It may be hard for you to be very happy or excited that we have a new baby."

- **Understand that it is normal, if your older child envies the attention, for him to revert to babyish ways of behaving** You might notice your older child talking baby talk, wanting a bottle, having accidents, wanting to be carried. Don't scold or make fun of his desire to be babied. Just tell him that you love him as he is, a big boy, and that you will try to spend special time with him even though you are busy with the baby.

- **Make good on the promise to spend some special or alone time with your older child** Kids who feel that a new baby did not ruin their life or "steal" their mother from them tend to get along better as that baby grows up.

- **Don't ask an older child to toilet-train when a new child arrives** The frustration level of your child will go to overload when the new arrival comes home, so even if she seems ready, wait until she has had time to adjust to her sibling before making more demands of her.

- **Some older siblings become physically aggressive to the new baby—stop this behavior immediately** Do not allow an older child to hit, bite, poke, or shake his sibling, but don't hit your child as a punishment, since it models and reinforces the very behavior that you do not want to see him use. If your child is unable to control his anger, do not allow him to be unsupervised with the baby for at least several weeks, until you are sure it has subsided.

Be Very Careful About Playing Favorites

Not every child of ours is the same, and it is not possible to see in one everything that you see in another. Differences exist and can be acknowledged without doing emotional damage or causing sibling antagonism. But parents who value children differently, and/or dole out emotions differently to their children, take the envy, jealousy, and rivalry that are a natural consequence of being in a family and stoke their fires, fostering sibling discord and disharmony. This is, and will always be, a very sticky problem, and here are some signs that unwittingly you might be playing favorites:

- You say, aloud or in your head, "I wish you were as nice, smart, kind, handsome, clever, and/or sweet as your sister/brother."
- You use words like "special," "extraordinary," "outstanding," "one of a kind," to describe one child and not the other; you are more likely to praise one child's accomplishments.
- You feel convinced since his birth, or early on, that one child was more attractive, brighter, sweeter, or more agreeable than the other; you may believe only one has a good character or that one is easy and the other difficult.
- You are disappointed in, and/or critical of, one child but not the other.
- You would rather be in the company of, and might actually spend significantly more time with, one of your children.
- You feel that one child loves, likes, is nicer to you, and/or admires you more than her sibling.
- You feel happy that one of your children really takes after you, and regret that the other doesn't.
- You sense that one child will carry on the family values, tradition, and/or name better than the other.
- You prefer one gender to the other; you feel more comfortable with your daughter rather than your son, or you were hoping for a boy and got a girl.
- When your children fight, you tend to see one of them at fault most of the time, or you believe that one of your children is more likely to treat the other badly and/or make the other cry.

If any of these sentiments echo your own, you may be unwittingly setting the stage for fights, arguments, and antagonism between your children that will make your days and theirs embattled. On your own, try to be aware of a possible imbalance, try your best to focus on the child who, you come to understand, feels left out, insecure, deprived, the underdog, the black sheep, not favored, the average or weak student. Sometimes these feelings are very complicated and hard to unravel, so, if you have a lot of sibling discord, consider seeing a family therapist. This can help realign the balance between siblings and restore family harmony.

> **PYB Words of Wisdom:** *There is one virus fatal to sibling peace: favoritism. Children are very sensitive to a parent's higher regard for a sibling. Be thoughtful about how you disperse and dispense your parental emotions, try to favor all your children with a fair share of love, and you will stand a very good chance of raising loving and peaceful siblings.*

The Parade Marches On

Children after age eleven through adolescence continue to morph into yet another series of interesting human beings, but, for the purposes of this book, I will end the procession here, for now. My crash course in kidology of children from birth to eleven formally concludes. Learning how to pick your battles does not. Now is the time to take what you know and discover just how to apply it to give everyday life with your children a chance for peaceful coexistence. Keep in mind that kidology is a critical tool for making much of what follows valuable and effective, so, if and when you need to, refer back to these pages and the practical knowledge you have learned here.

Chapter 2

. . . .

A Commonsense
Parenting Philosophy

You love your kids. Your heart is definitely in the right place. But, if that was all it took to raise good, easy, low-maintenance kids, this would be a very short book. To keep the peace, your head has to be working along with that big heart of yours. Having your head on straight about your role as a parent is the first and very best way to avoid unnecessary friction with your children. So, this is where we start: Take charge. Find your voice. Acquire a parenting point of view.

A parenting philosophy is vital, but at this moment, a fount of well-formed thoughts on child-rearing is probably not cascading from your own brain cells as your child is crying in his crib, refusing to bathe, or fighting with his little sister. Relax. Most of us do not have the dimmest notion of what our child-rearing beliefs might be. Especially while we are new parents, visions of an uninterrupted night's sleep are as lofty a goal as we set for ourselves. When we are sleep-deprived, the seat of our pants, not our gray matter, is all too often the location and source of our everyday working philosophy. After all, what parent of a young child has a chance to speak in complete sentences, let alone fashion those sentences into meaningful beliefs about parenthood? Understanding that it is hard enough to communicate articulately with kids in your charge, never mind spout a well-formed set of child-rearing beliefs, I have a common-sense parenting philosophy: Parenting needs to be like a good pair of shoes—***warm and sturdy, with plenty of wiggle room***.

This straightforward philosophy may instantly and instinctively make sense to you. But listen to the words of other parents who share this vision. By giving yourself a chance to hear their different interpretations, you will more fully understand this concept and ultimately find your own parenting voice. Because we are not talking about some pat formula or perfect recipe for success, I am deliberately giving you many different takes on this approach to parenting:

> *"Kids need structure. I am convinced of that. They also need what I never had, breathing room. Of course, it goes without saying that children need love and understanding."*
>
> (Yamit, age 36, ambassador, mother of twin sons and a daughter)

> *"As an architect, I do my best to build solid, beautiful buildings. Then I let people live in them the way they feel most comfortable. I see parallels in parenting: our family is the structure we as parents build, but each of our children is encouraged to 'live' in this family in their own particular way."*
>
> (Hannah, age 37, architect, mother of two girls)

> *"We stay away from extremes. A free-for-all doesn't work. I think kids are anxious and frightened if they are left to their own devices. But children can become furious or defeated if they are always under your thumb. They need to feel they can be heard and that they matter. We try to aim for the happy medium."*
>
> (Stuart, age 39, social worker, father of three daughters)

> *"It's beyond children to know how to run their own lives. I think we start out running their lives and gradually and lovingly let them grow into the task."*
>
> (Emma, age 37, full-time mother of two sons)

> *"This is my parenting motto: 'First I make it safe, then I make it fair.' "*
>
> (Mike, age 43, handyman, father of two sons)

Though these families are different, I believe you can hear a similar parental voice in all of them: warm and understanding, yet solid, sturdy, confident, assured. Self-possessed, loving parents remain in charge but attempt to maintain a balance between structure and freedom, holding and letting go, control and independence, authority and autonomy.

These parents succeed in creating family as a safe and sturdy haven. Yet while they are safely and securely holding, they are also willing and able to change and stretch, making room—wiggle room—for their maturing children. They are authoritative, sound, sensible, and seasoned. You can become one of them.

Listening to Mother Nature

It may surprise you, and even the parents I have just quoted, but this wise and balanced parenting actually starts with Mother Nature. Every human being is *raised and nurtured in a warm, sturdy yet flexible shelter!* From the very beginning, kids come packaged *double wrapped* for their own good. First, there is a pregnant mother's sturdy muscular uterus. Then, inside that first holder, for added protection and healthy development, every child bobs around in a warm watery vessel, the birth sac.

Nature's first environment is a sturdy and reliable vessel. It provides structure, protection, support, warmth, and nourishment. It acts as a sort of filtration system, letting some, but not all things in, and others out. As the child develops, grows, and matures, it adjusts and adapts to make room for the ever-changing child. You need only to compare a pregnant woman's profile at nine weeks versus nine months to see just how much stretching that container can do! Then, in the end, it delivers the baby into the great big world!

Keep in mind the contrast and, at the same time, the harmonious balance between womb and birth sac. The womb is firm and muscular yet elastic, while, inside that protective housing, the warm nurturing bath allows the child to float freely. Without the gentle balance of both elements, life as we know it could not exist.

Make your parenting an attempt to continue along the path first set out by Mother Nature. Consider your job the continual endeavor to create a safe haven in which your child can grow and develop—and eventually leave.

▶ **PYB Words of Wisdom:** *When you become a parent, take over the job Mother Nature began: build family life as a vessel, housing, holder, haven, sanctuary, a sheltering environment, in which your children can thrive and flourish.*

HOW TO CREATE A NATURAL PARENTING PHILOSOPHY

Take Over the Job Mother Nature Began

Think about integrating these qualities into your parenting *job description* and continue where Nature leaves off:

- warmth/nourishment
- shelter/protection
- filtration/screening
- limits/boundaries
- support/structure
- firmness/sturdiness
- elasticity/adaptability
- latitude/leeway
- balance/harmony
- room for growth and change
- letting go/delivery into the big world

Easy Kids: The Benefits of Balanced Parenting

Children parented in this integrated and balanced fashion—firm and free—are much less angry and less lost than those who are not. They are more content and easier to raise. Exhibiting good judgment, kids raised firmly and freely are more responsible, trustworthy, reliable, positive, productive, and resilient. With these qualities, they are far less likely to be at risk for dangerous or self-destructive behavior and much more likely to stay safe and sound. Raising a child who stays out of harm's way not only means fewer battles but also fewer headaches, heartaches, and sleepless nights.

Extreme Parenting Creates Difficult Kids:
Two Cautionary Tales

Extreme parenting—exerting too tight a grip or being too loose and lax—creates a potential for havoc. I call the first, stern style "Welcome to Boot Camp" and the second, permissive approach "Neverland" parenting. Both of these lopsided attitudes risk turning family life into a painful battleground.

"Welcome to Boot Camp" parents advocate an iron-fisted philosophy, convinced that the family container only needs to be strong and muscular, but not very elastic. Holding an icy, tight, hard-nosed grip over children, they misguidedly regard love and affection as unnecessary coddling. (Think: stiff, hard shoes without the "wiggle room.") Expecting children to listen and obey unquestioningly, they fail to listen to their children or encourage autonomy.

While some children may swallow their resentment and become compliant, this style frequently produces actively hostile and defiant children. I see the more disastrous results of this behavior in my office all too often. At almost eighteen, Tim had the dark good looks of a model.* The son of a prominent and successful orthopedic surgeon and a teacher, he was always in trouble and barely making it out of his private prep school.

Tim was constantly at war with his family. His "laziness" and "trashy friends" frightened his mother and enraged his father. His academic failure especially galled his father who had always expected his only son to also become a physician. From an early age, Tim was pushed to excel. However, following in his father's footsteps was not at all what Tim had in mind. Unbeknownst to his parents, Tim had signed on with the marines and was just waiting for his next birthday to announce that he was leaving home and school.

When I met Tim's parents, who had dragged him under duress to therapy, it became apparent to me that his father was demanding and controlling. Dad was a my-way-or-the-highway kind of guy. Tim recalled

---

*Unless noted, all people in this book are composite characters. While they are my creations, they are based on my years of professional experience and are my best effort to be psychologically authentic.

that, as early as age six or seven, he spent more than one evening in the same basement because he would not eat broccoli, and numerous other times when cold, uneaten scrambled eggs from breakfast—a food Tim detested—would be his fare for dinner at his father's insistence. His mother, more out of fear than agreement, did not object to the basement banishment and dutifully served the eggs.

Together, they exerted a tight, chilly hold with little room for their son to be his own person. The effects were disastrous for all. Constant constraints, directives, and orders left Tim harboring major resentment and believing that his only option was rebellion.

"It will kill my father to have me in the marines, of all things. I can just see him seething when I shove those papers in his face. There is nothing he can do about it. I've been waiting for this for a long time. I could never do the right thing, as far as he and my mother are concerned. So what the hell difference does it make now? At least I'll be out of their house and they'll be rid of me."

Tim and his parents are a sad example of what can happen when the grip of parenting is too cold, tight, and unresponsive. It is my observation that the tighter and colder the grip, the greater the rebellion.

Creating the "Lost" Child

Now, look at the opposite extreme—"Neverland" parenting—which often results in a "lost" child rather than a rebellious hellion. Sometimes parents adopt a stance where they take no stance at all. They permit kids to "float" completely, allowing children to do as they please, with little parental interference or guidance. Kids run the show. There are no limits, rules, or boundaries. They are *not* firmly held. In its own way, this "anything-goes parenting" is as damaging as the Boot Camp family.

I often see these lost souls in my office as well. Regrettably, and perhaps contrary to their parents' hopes, they are *not* children who grow up feeling free as a bird. They grow up *lost*, because with no structure, no embrace, kids *do not* feel liberated; they feel put out to sea, adrift, abandoned and neglected.

Unanchored and lacking direction, they invariably get into lots and lots of trouble. Lacking the benefit of parental guidance, they have poor judgment. Particularly when they reach pre-adolescence, these children run the risk of going off the deep end and becoming self-destructive.

As a therapist, I have repeatedly seen the "lost child" who acts wild and out of control, constantly "floating" on the edge of disaster.

Ally was the result of Neverland parenting. From infancy on, her parents had an "anything goes" approach. Feeling it was "wrong" to force anything on a child, they offered their child little structure, regularity, and rules. Ally's parents rarely "made her go to sleep." More often than not, she fell asleep wherever she was, and they deposited her in bed.

Her parents, exceedingly sweet and warm but also misguided, did not believe in telling kids what to do. By age nine, Ally could do a credit-card scrawl that easily passed for her mother's signature. By the time she was in sixth grade, Ally's mom and dad left her to her own devices, giving her free reign. Her dad worked nonstop, often traveling for his job, while her mother was often emotionally absent, preoccupied with her own pursuit of theater. As a result, Ally did pretty much as she pleased. Unfortunately, liquor and boys were her pleasures. She became a master at watering down her parents' booze and sneaking in and out of the house at night. She was not overtly angry or hostile, just bouncing all over the place.

Unlike Tim, she stayed on track in school. However, a pregnancy scare when Ally was seventeen was the first of a string of personal disasters that came crashing down on Ally and her parents. The sparks flew, and the family desperately sought a therapist.

Ironically and sadly, in Ally's situation, as with others like her, she and her parents were relatively conflict-free in her younger years. She was left to her own devices until the mud hit the fan and she was reeling out of control. Crashing is the sound heard most often by Neverland parents. Unfortunately, when parents take what appears as the easy way out, allowing a child to run the show, they invariably end up as Ally's parents did, paying for it later.

Lopsided Parenting Creates Difficult Kids

The parents of Tim and Ally were on opposite ends of the caretaking spectrum, but both led to the same end: Ally and Tim were difficult to parent.*

---

*Each of these children—Tim and Ally—presented me, as a therapist, with a different corrective task. Tim needed empathy; room to feel listened to and understood. He needed a warm, safe space, the very thing he did not get enough of in his family. Ally needed anything but room. She needed a very firm and sturdy container.

Arguments, antagonism, animosity, and rebellion ruled the day. Frequently and frighteningly, the battles they chose made them unsafe and put them at risk.

I do not want to go overboard on the cautionary tales, especially because wise parents can avoid these heartbreaking situations. It is important to focus on the positive message. Create a warm, sturdy, flexible home. Strike a balance—firm *and* free. It works. Employ this common-sense child-rearing approach, and—you know those kids you see at the mall, the really sweet and well-behaved ones, the ones that make you want to go up to the parents and ask, "Gosh, those kids are so delightful, what did you sprinkle on their Cheerios this morning?"—they will be yours!

(To see where you may fall on this parenting spectrum, try the quiz "What Is Your Parenting Style" at the end of this chapter.)

Good Is Good Enough

Fortunately, while raising delightful kids requires this firm/free balancing act, it *does not* require a philosophy that assumes parental flawlessness. Nature may require balance, but she does *not* ever demand perfection. You can raise perfectly agreeable children without having to be a perfect parent spouting a model philosophy.

Let's return to the womb for a moment, to understand why this is so. Nature's first container is *not* a perfect environment. It doesn't have to be. While developing human beings do require a safe and sturdy vessel, it does not have to be a flawless habitat. It only has to be *good*. What does this mean? No developing infant needs precise, exact, or ideal conditions in order to grow. The human race would become extinct if our perpetuation depended on flawless precision during every step of conception and pregnancy.

Babies in the making just need everything to fall within a manageable or tolerable range, to be adequate, sufficient, OK, quite all right, or, in other words, *good enough.** Keep this good news in mind when constructing your parenting philosophy: Mother Nature cuts herself some slack. You should, too. So, from this moment on, stop thinking that you need to be the model

*Good-enough mothering is a concept developed by Donald Winnicott.

parent charged with producing blue-ribbon offspring. Thank goodness, there is no exact mark you must hit in order to turn out cooperative kids.

> ▶ **PYB Words of Wisdom:** *When aiming to parent, think*
> *target, not bull's-eye. Thankfully, it does not take perfection*
> *to have perfectly wonderful kids. Just get it about right.*

The immediate effect of incorporating good rather than perfect into your parenting philosophy is evident. You will have less tension on the home front. Perfectionism is so taxing. Flawlessness is such a strain on everyone. A parent who demands perfection is creating an unnecessary minefield of frustration and exasperation. Frustrated, exasperated parents have more conflict, because they and their offspring are frequently in a bad mood.

So, it is simple: *Do not strive to be perfect.* It makes you and the kids grouchy, grumpy, crabby, and cross. Eradicate a whole realm of conflict just by taking your cue from Nature—good is certainly good enough!

The Screening Room:
Getting Good at Setting Limits

While Mother Nature may not require saintly perfection, she is still pretty darn careful with her developing babies. Even in the security of the womb, she *limits* a developing child's exposure. In fact, the womb comes with its own filtration system. As a growing fetus bobs around in a mom's "belly," nature has worked it out so that only some things get through from mother to the developing fetus.

As a parent, you need to provide a screening system, a selective barrier between your child and the world. Permitting exposure to things only as long as your growing child can safely assimilate them is part of your job. Indeed, "too much too soon" can have adverse consequences. This philosophy means that *a parent sets limits and boundaries.* To help your children grow sturdier, you must act as a thoughtful, watchful guardian of their environment and decide what gets through to them.

Adopting the idea that screening is well within your parental duties will help you calmly reframe your role. You will become more comfortable, self-assured, and authoritative about staying in charge. You won't be afraid to be firm or to acknowledge that you *are* wiser than your child. You will understand when and how to say protective words like:

No
That's not allowed
You may not
Don't
This isn't appropriate
Stop
I don't think you are ready for this

> ▶ **PYB Words of Wisdom:** *Be selective to be protective . . . and effective. Parents need to set boundaries and limits. Remember, "No" is a safe, wise, and loving word.*

Perhaps in your wisdom you will decide to "filter" the amount of violence to which your children are exposed by taking action, such as turning off the TV news when your preschooler is in the room, or firmly saying to your older child, "This video games is not appropriate for your age." Ultimately each decision that you make in this area will be your own and suitable for your family. But no matter what you eventually select to filter, if you want to be a self-assured, authoritative parent with less rambunctious kids, do what Nature does—mind the gate!

> ▶ **PYB Words of Wisdom:** *Knowing how to "mind the gate" is very much the heart of becoming a take charge parent adept at raising well-behaved kids. Therefore, a good deal of what follows in Part II will help you become skillful at carrying out this all-important aspect of your parenting job-setting limits and boundaries.*

Remember to Change the Filter

Your offspring do not need the same degree of parental "filtration" throughout life. Earlier on, when kids are tiny, helpless, and most vulnerable, the screening system needs to be *highly* regulated. As a child grows, the monitoring can and must ease up. As you raise your children, recognize that regulations need to evolve in ways that reflect their maturity level. Your preteens need to have more of a say in their choices than your preschoolers. You need to let kids grow up and take on more of their world!

When you permit and support this transformation, you can stay in charge without becoming rigid and controlling, making life with a child much more tranquil. Parents who do not readjust their limits as a child grows more capable and competent are asking for trouble. Stay controlling when your children need autonomy to govern themselves, and you set the stage for all-out warfare. Arguments, quarrels, and even angry estrangement are a much less likely scenario when parents allow children to develop jurisdiction over themselves.

> ▶ **PYB Words of Wisdom:** *Change the filter and you will keep the peace. Children need less control as they become more able.*

Some parents fail to change the filter not because they are controlling but rather because they are frightened. Anxiously overprotective, they try and keep everything out, depriving their child of the opportunity to take on the world and interfering with the development of life skills. They risk creating a less than competent kid with an unhealthy dependency. This can make for a whiny, clingy, needy, or demanding kid who whittles and wears away at the patience of the most concerned and well-meaning parent. If anxiety keeps you from changing the filter, it isn't fights you will encounter. Instead, your overreliant kid will drive you to distraction!

> ▶ **PYB Words of Wisdom:** *If anxiety keeps you from changing the filter, you risk raising a child who grows big without necessarily growing up.*

Delivery: Letting Children Grow Up and Letting Them Go

Mia Farrow's mother, actress Maureen O'Sullivan, was a grand matriarch, the mother of eight children, thirty-two grandchildren, and thirteen great-grandchildren. Asked about her off-screen motherhood, she commented, "The real way to bind children to you is to let them go. Clutching is no good; it simply makes them determined to get rid of you. But once they're free, they surprisingly want to come back to you as friends." She understood the wisdom of letting go.*

Mother Nature's vessel serves a purpose, but she tells us loudly and clearly that there comes a time when a child is ready to leave it behind. A child needs room to grow and a womb to grow in, but, ultimately, the goal of any parent is *to make a delivery*, to set our children free to make their way in the world. We need to let our children grow, but we also need to allow them to grow up and let go.

Ponder the paradox we face. Children bring us into the parenting business, and then, all along the way, proceed to put us out of it. As we go on, children need us less rather than more. They begin as helpless and vulnerable, then, with our help, they become independent and sturdy. Isn't it ironic? As parents, we give our all so that our children will need us less and less.

How does this knowledge reduce conflict? Keeping this "delivery" goal in mind will make you less prone to feeling rejected, cast aside, or hurt as your children move away from you into the larger world. Incorporating the goal of "letting go" into your philosophy forestalls feeling personally injured, as if your child is leaving you in the dust as she fashions her own life. Do not fight the inevitable—kids are meant to separate from us and go their own way—and you will have far fewer battles at home.

"Making the delivery" *can* hurt. Any woman who has gone through labor will attest to that, but it is also a miraculous part of life. When children make their exit, it may well feel sad and painful. However, when you have raised a child who can make a break and separate, it is a glorious sign. You have done a good job. Your philosophy has worked! When you do a good job as a parent, you are on the road to becoming less central to your child's life. *Not less loved;* just less needed. Don't fight it, and kids won't fight with you.

> ▶ **PYB Words of Wisdom:** *Kids bring us into the parenting business, then proceed to put us out of it. Don't take it personally.*

*Quote from her obituary, *New York Times,* June 24, 1998.

A Nice Warm Bath: A Key Ingredient to Our Parenting Philosophy

I have saved what I regard as the most important element of a sound parenting philosophy for last. The parenting embrace you create must always continue to be warm and responsive: nourishing; a soothing, comforting space. Most people find this part of the parenting job a matter of doing what comes naturally. Tender affection is what most parents have in abundance for children from the very first day. In those early days, creating serenity with our baby is straightforward. Chiefly, it's a matter of the basics, i.e., love as expressed through physical care and attention. We hug, kiss, pat, rock, and sing to our little one. While these basic ministrations *always* remain essential and are effective ways to soothe and calm, later on we need more than "tender loving care" to make this happen. As children grow more complicated, and as they acquire mobility, language, a social life, and minds of their own, it is far more challenging to calm them down and keep things peaceful. Our instinctive capacity to pacify and create tranquility by tending to our child's physical needs will not work solely on its own.

As your child grows and ventures out into the world, acquiring speech and reason, he needs your empathy and thoughtful words of understanding to find calm. Nonverbal gestures always retain a power to defuse tension. A loving look, a hug, a kiss, all work wonders to engender calm. But in the course of parenting, emotional understanding conveyed through words becomes an essential ingredient in creating a warm, soothing space.

In response to a frightened preschooler battling bedtime, such empathetic words as "It's scary to go to sleep if there are monsters under your bed" will go a long way toward making a bedroom into a comfort rather that a war zone. Commiserating with your child who has not made the team will make him less irritable and sullen at the dinner table. A parent's capacity for empathy is a critical tool in eliminating and surviving battles. Emotional recognition reduces battles dramatically. All people—kids included—calm down when they feel understood. Understanding washes over them, soothes their souls, and makes them a lot easier to handle. This is why we will pay a good deal of attention to helping you develop empathy skills.

▶ **PYB Words of Wisdom:** *At some point in the life of many families, parents need to share the tasks of raising a child with adults outside the immediate family. When you make decisions about choosing such adults, consider whether they, too, can follow Mother Nature's lead. If they can offer your child responsiveness, warmth, and sturdiness, your child will be in good hands and will get even more help in becoming a well-behaved kid.*

PARENTING QUIZ
WHAT STYLE OF PARENTING DO YOU HAVE?

Is your parenting style Boot Camp, Neverland, or Mother Nature? In this quiz, it is not all that hard to guess which answer reflects the balanced parenting style. But don't choose that one because it's "right." Be honest and select an answer that actually comes closest to your spontaneous reaction. Use these scenarios as a way to gauge where you are now, so that you better understand the work that you have yet to do. (Make sure each person in your house responsible for raising your child takes this quiz. It is very important to discover if you have opposite, unbalanced styles.)

1. You are at your favorite diner. Your eight-year-old son has a milk mustache, chews with his mouth open wide, gobbles everything in site, and just spilled his soup on his pants. You:
   a) Tell him he's unbearable to look at across the table and order him to leave the restaurant.
   b) Explain that his table manners need to improve or you can't take him out to a restaurant again. You show him how to chew with his mouth closed and help him clean up his mess.
   c) Think everyone makes too much of a fuss over manners, and as long as he's enjoying his food, that's all that counts.

2. Your child comes home an hour later from after-school sports than he said he would. You:
   a) Give him a piece of your mind and ground him for a week.
   b) Continue watching TV. Kids will be late, and at least he's in one piece.
   c) Explain that if he must be late, please call, since it worries you if he breaks an agreement.

3. While playing around in the family room, your toddler picks up a vase and drops it. You:
   a) Angrily tell him he's clumsy.
   b) Are secretly pleased, because you didn't like the vase, which was a gift from your mother-in-law, and you're not going to take him to task because you like to see your child feel comfortable in his own house.
   c) Check to see that your child is not hurt, tell him that he must touch some things gently, because they will break, and plan to review childproofing the family room tomorrow.

4. Your child loves math, but he struggles with his math homework, because he cannot read the problems. You:
   a) Tell him to relax and go to sleep. Now that there are calculators, who really needs math?
   b) Tell him that he cannot come out of his room until every problem is done.
   c) Tell him that his math skills are ahead of his reading, and that soon he will be able to read the way he needs to for school. You suggest he try as best he can, and you plan to schedule a conference with his math teacher to explain his problem and help figure out a way to handle this.

5. Your six-year-old tells you he "hates you" after you tell him he cannot have the new bike he wants now. You:
   a) Tell him parenting is a thankless job and that he's ungrateful.
   b) Tell him that you know that he's very disappointed and that he hates the fact that you are making him wait for something he really wants, but that he can get it for his next birthday.
   c) Like his spunk and wish you had had the guts, as a kid, to let your parents have it when they weren't nice to you.

Chapter 3

....

Creating Family Policy

Putting Philosophy to Work:
Turning Ideals into Guidance

Now that you've acquired a parenting philosophy, you need to put it to work, and family policy is the very best way to translate your child-rearing beliefs into action. A family policy is the customs and practices that you establish to guide your children, actively conveying on a day-to-day basis what is truly meaningful to your family life. Family policy transforms admirable parenting ideals and values into actual guidance. And kids need—no, make that *crave*—guidance. Without it, they risk feeling lost (and getting lost), while with it, they feel well-grounded and secure.

The Four Rs of Family Policy

To make your parenting ideals tangible, integrate the Four Rs of Family Policy into your home life: Each one is essential for creating a warm and sturdy family.

- Routines
- Rules
- Responsibilities
- Rituals

Routines

Routines give children an idea of what they can generally anticipate and expect. Kids need and want parents to supply this blueprint for their own lives. It makes them feel safe and protected. Don't wing it, or make child rearing up as you go along. That uncertainty makes kids confused, insecure, and unruly. Let your child know that home life is predictable and will unfold in an orderly way—especially on a day-to-day basis. This is enormously reassuring and soothing to say nothing of the fact that it reduces tension and makes daily family life run a lot more smoothly.

- **Institute schedules** Write down a schedule with a timetable for the usual features of your child's day: waking up, meals, hygiene, playtime, and bedtime (i.e., wake your child up every morning and put her to bed each night *around* the same time). Make predictability, not punctuality, your goal.
- **Lay out the steps** Make arrangements about not only *when* but *how* various routines will unfold—even the most ordinary ones of daily life. Be specific and clear:
  - First you get into pj's and put your clothes in the hamper;
  - Then we will read a good-night story;
  - Then the lights go out, and you get a big kiss and a hug and go to dreamland.

  Break routines down into small pieces: it's easier for kids to manage and carry them out.
- **Create a system** Particularly when school becomes a part of your child's life, create a system to handle routines that occur outside the home. Keep it simple. When it comes to school days,
  - Decide who will take your children to the school-bus stop;
  - Have someone escort them to their after-school program;
  - Ascertain who picks them up at the bus stop when the day is done.

A "system" requires advance planning, but, once it's in place, you will have less to be aggravated about. Be sure to make the system clear to your kids.

- **Develop fallback strategies** Have backup plans. When you can't be where your child expects you to be, say at school for a pickup, you might set up a buddy system with another adult who can pick up the slack for you. Let your child know in advance that this other person will pinch-hit for you from time to time. There is nothing that reassures a child more than the knowledge that you have all the bases covered for their care.

- **Develop well thought-out transitions** Give kids a heads up about what will happen to them. A warning that it is a few minutes to dinner or lights out, being reminded that there will be homework to do when snack time is over, posting a calendar in the kitchen that marks the day that school starts, all reinforce a child's sense that life is predictable and doesn't come with a lot of unsettling surprises. When kids know what's coming, it makes them more inclined to go along.

- **Foster good habits** Establish good habits about hygiene, the care of personal space, and possessions. Encourage hygiene regimens. Insist that your children respect their clothes, room, toys, and books, as well as themselves. Good habits are a tangible demonstration of loving respect that you display toward your child, which you ask him to show himself, others, and his belongings.

> ▶ **PYB Words of Wisdom:** *You will have calmer kids and a more peaceful home if you don't ad lib parenting.*

Rules

Families need bylaws that govern the conduct of parents and children. Kids need "do"s and "don't"s. They need limits and boundaries. This includes establishing general rules of morality ("We will be truthful") as well as those that govern everyday existence ("We will not leave you unsupervised"; "We will check your homework.")

Children need to and want to know what is required of them and what is not permitted, what is acceptable and what is not. Especially as kids get older, guidelines governing their activities are of *enormous* importance to guarantee their safety and well-being. As they get older, don't be misled by your children's growing independence; they still need you to run the show—just be careful not to go overboard.

(Guidelines that come to define limits and boundaries are so essential to good discipline that much of what follows in Part II focuses on this critical area.)

> ▶ **PYB Words of Wisdom:** *Once you are clear about the conduct you expect from your child, indicating actions that are acceptable or not permissible, good behavior follows. Kids make fewer mistakes and missteps if standards of conduct are unmistakable.*

Responsibilities

Make accountability a key element of family life. Let children:

- Assume responsibilities, duties, and jobs at home and, as they get older, outside the family A child may be given the job of setting the table, caring for the family pet, or helping with the laundry. A fifth-grader might walk a neighbor's dog, while a sixth-grader might prove to be an able homework-helper for a younger child on the block.
- Learn that family life comes with mutual obligations and that they must help other members of the family, parents, or siblings do their assigned jobs An older child can see to it that dinner is ready when mom or dad is working late, or help a sibling clean his room on a day that that sibling has a lot of homework.
- See that expectations include emotional mutuality and show kindness, affection, and understanding to others in the family A mother can kiss a little one's "boo boos," but it is also fair that she gets a special hug and kiss when she is feeling sad, or that a brother offers TLC when his sister is disappointed that she didn't make the soccer team.

Encourage Service to Others When they are small, start children on projects focused on helping others. An effective first step is to encourage community service with a local organization, church, school, firehouse, or family shelter familiar to your kids. Start by collecting pennies for a new fire engine at Halloween, wrapping holiday presents for disadvantaged kids residing at the local shelter, or contributing cans to a food drive at school. As children mature, encourage them to undertake more hands-on community service such as visiting a nursing home or working at a soup kitchen along with you. Learning early that there are others who need your help and assuming that it is your job to do something to make the world a better place makes for pleasant kids. Yes, studies actually show that throughout life people who "do good for others" are calmer and happier. Be thoughtful about your choices especially for young children, as some charities, for example those visit very sick children at a hospice, that would be too emotionally overwhelming for a small child. Let kids grow into that level of service, in time they will be up to it.

▶ **PYB Words of Wisdom:** *Kids who "do good" are more likely to be good kids.*

Rituals

Rituals, traditions, customs, and ceremonies weave family life into a warm and joyful tapestry. They make a family recognizable to itself, creating a family personality and identity. Celebrating milestones—birthdays, anniversaries, christenings, bat/bar mitzvahs, baptism, sweet-sixteens, and/or graduation—pulls families together, making kids feel grounded. Whether it is the tradition of holiday dinners, celebrations, religious observance, communing with nature, vacations, or something dreamed up by and for your family alone, like an annual family slumber-party in a backyard tent, every custom you create defines your family. A well-defined family where children can declare "Yes, that's us," is one where parents have successfully breathed life into their parenting philosophy.

▶ **PYB Words of Wisdom:** *Rituals provide meaning. They are memorable events, anticipated when they will come and missed when they are over. They are the emotional punctuation marks of family life, which make children feel they belong to a caring family.*

FAMILY MEMORABILIA

Kids *love* it when parents save things that document their personal history; it makes them feel valued. Try making:

1. a memory box, into which you occasionally put childhood memorabilia: baby clothes (first shoes); favorite "retired" toys and or books; drawings; first schoolwork; birthday decorations;
2. keep a baby book, which chronicles milestones, i.e. first step, first word;
3. keep a family scrapbook;
4. encourage children to keep a personal journal.

Every once in a while, pull these collections out of the closet and take a walk down memory lane together with your child; it's very calming, because your kids will think: *"These customs are anchors that connect me to myself and to my family."*

CREATING FAMILY TRADITIONS

"We specialize in inventing our own family traditions. We have Lazy Day, when we all stay in pjs and just hang out and relax and Family Sundays where each of us has a turn at choosing an activity in which we will all participate. Then we always try to do things that are special for each season: We go pumpkin- or apple-picking in the fall. We take a trip to see the leaves turn in New England. In the summer, we have an annual bonfire at the beach, and in the winter, each child gets a special sleepover party with their friends. Nothing we do is a big deal, but each special event seems like a way to mark our sense of togetherness as a family."

(Amy, mother of Rochelle, age 13, and Audrey, age 11)

▶ **PYB Words of Wisdom:** *Routines, responsibilities, rules, and rituals convey a reassuring message to children—my parents take their job of raising kids seriously so they must truly care about me. Cared-for kids, act with care. Kids raised without this structure invariably feel neglected and abandoned, which regrettably puts them at risk for bad behavior.*

Practices That Fit Your Family Are Practices That Work

While these practices—routines, rules, responsibilities, and rituals—are a must, there is no uniform code that dictates your decisions; practices only need to have a good fit with the character of your family. Daily routines, especially around morning and evening, are indispensable practices for *all* families, but they do not have to be identical to be wonderful. Some parents feel comfortable with exact bedtimes and storybook readings, while others prefer tuck-ins with a degree of flexibility and the spinning of imaginary bedtime tales. Families with school-age children may create homework routines that are altogether different but equally effective: One child may be permitted to play before work and another required to work before play.

The religiously observant family may establish customs about religious rituals, while the secular family may find their spiritual rites in the joy of nature. The former might find peace in prayer, the latter in retreats to the woods. Both will be providing their children with steady grounding.

By the way, there is no rule that says that you can't have fun while being a responsible parent. Being funny and silly and whimsical can often be delightful ingredients for effective family practices. The ritual of snuggling in bed on a weekend morning, or making homemade cards and presents for birthdays or holidays with your kids can also bring family cohesion. Families that work *and* play together have children who develop good character.

Why Practices Make Cooperative Kids

There are six very good reasons why policies help families run smoothly. Routines, rules, responsibilities, and rituals are essential because they:

1. establish quality time
2. create rhythm
3. lay out clear expectations
4. eliminate uncertainty
5. keep children from wielding too much power
6. develop character and good citizenship.

Establish Quality Time

Practices create a serene family space. They are not strict requirements as much as they are gifts, a parental offer to spend important, meaningful and tranquil time together, made good on a daily basis. This is the essence of quality time. *However—there is no getting around it—quality time takes time.* Put the time into quality time. Meaningful "heart to heart" exchanges don't take place when you're taking out the garbage, watching the news, or nagging kids to clean their room. Without a serene space and a peaceful interlude, communication is next to impossible. With it, families do more than just talk—they actually converse, developing intimacy and trust.

> ▶ **PYB Words of Wisdom:** *If you take away no other wisdom from these pages, be certain to absorb this: Creating the opportunity to communicate—to listen and to be heard—is without doubt the single best way to reduce discord with children.*

A DUAL BENEFIT OF QUALITY TIME: KEEPING AND RESTORING THE PEACE

Kids who have a calm space tend to bring to parents problems with which they are grappling **before** they turn into trouble.

A Saturday morning nature walk, where a child unloads the burden of a classmate asking him to cheat on a homework assignment, may avert an error in judgment as well as uproar when a phone call comes from a dismayed teacher.

After the peace has been broken, a serene space becomes a route to restoring it.

Many a grade-schooler who has shouted. "I hate you Mommy!" during a stressful day finds the placid bedtime ritual of a tuck-in and bedtime story a place to say "I am sorry" and make amends.

Create Rhythm

Customs, conventions, routines, and rituals establish order and regularity in a child's world. Life develops rhythm, and kids do very much better with it. It makes them feel secure; they know what to expect from life, but it doesn't magically eradicate conflict. Nevertheless, the battles you have with a child who feels secure are of a different magnitude than the ones you face when a child does not stand on such a sturdy foundation. Risk-taking is not so risky (read: self-destructive) in kids who feel safe and secure.

▶ **PYB Words of Wisdom:** *Give kids rhythm, and they happily fall into step.*

Lay Out Clear Expectations

Set an expectation in place for a child, and it becomes a given. Then whatever you ask of your child feels downright ordinary. Any request simply feels comfortable, like the natural order of things, as if there is just no other way to do it. Once a ritual becomes a comfortable habit, you have absolutely nothing to nag about!

Eliminate Uncertainty

Family policy clears the air of indecision and uncertainty. It declares, in effect:

• This is the way we do it in our home
• There are no options
• We don't waffle, waver, or shilly-shally
• There is nothing to debate, discuss, or question.

Above all, we are not open to on-the-spot revision or seat-of-the-pants decisions. Children accept that dinnertime is dinnertime, no TV is no TV, church is church, getting up and out is getting up and out, bedtime is bedtime, so they don't trouble you by moaning their protest.

▶ **PYB Words of Wisdom:** *Thou Shalt Not Waffle. They Shalt Not Whine. Kids get crabby if they sense a lack of clarity or indecisiveness.*

Keep Children from Wielding Too Much Power

One of the big problems these days is that many kids have far too much power over parents. Sometimes, in our kid-centered world, it can feel that children rule. What a child wants—often above and beyond what a parent can manage—seems to dictate family life. Some parents run themselves ragged in pursuit of happiness for their kids: "You're bored? Well, what would make you happy now? Stop crying, I'll get you a different toy." Some seem intimidated by their children, even when they are very young: "You don't want to go to Grandma's house for Sunday dinner? OK, we won't go."

This turns family life upside down. It gives children far too much power and, though they may seem desperate to have it, *it scares them—a lot!* No child wants to be wielding the power; that feels too unsafe. Kids recognize that they do not as yet have what it takes to be in command. If they do succeed in getting control, it often makes them go haywire and out of control.

The message conveyed by rituals, customs, rules, routines, and traditions is "Your parents lead this family, and you need to follow." *All children desperately want and need a parent out in front of them, responsibly leading the way.* Family policy puts you firmly and lovingly in that critical position.

> ▶ **PYB Words of Wisdom:** *You are wiser than your child. Don't be afraid to let them have the benefit of the fact that you've been around longer than they have and that you intend to stay in charge for as long as you are needed.*

Develop Character and Good Citizenship

Family policy endorses a spirit of cooperation, thereby sending a magnificent message—life works best if we work together as allies.

Expecting your child to join agreeably with the family definitely lays the groundwork for achievement in *all* aspects of life and community. Succeeding and flourishing, whether in relationships or a career, calls for teamwork, collaboration, reciprocity, and mutuality. To get on in life, we need to get along with others. Learning this cooperative spirit at home, from the beginning, is essential.

▶ **PYB Words of Wisdom:** *Family and all of life is a team sport. Policies are a way to train children to be good team members.*

People who cannot learn this, who are selfish, uncooperative, at odds with or warring with others, do not do well in love or work. As a therapist, I constantly see people deeply compromised or even jeopardized because they do not possess these social-emotional skills. Jobs are lost, friendships sacrificed, and marriages ended because people never learned the basics—relating to other folk. Success in life requires being able to join others, not to fight them. Policy is also a daily wake-up call, a reminder that the world does not revolve entirely around your child. Life is not a one-way street. This can be a bit of a jolt to your child, to discover that he has to fall in step with the family and, by extension, with the world. However, it is a necessary and civilizing jolt into becoming a solid citizen inside and outside of your home.

When It Comes to Family Policy, Conviction Counts

Conviction is your key to success. Policies only work if your commitment is genuine; you cannot fake it and then count on obedience. Expect cooperative kids only if your beliefs are sincere. Try banning TV if you are a tube-lover, or sending kids off to Sunday school when you don't care to go to church, and see how lame that policy is. Kids take to heart policies that come from the heart. But they also know when words are only words and not more. Then they act or act up accordingly.

▶ **PYB Words of Wisdom:** *Kids are human lie detectors, so don't try faking conviction.*

All of this is not to say that your children will fall into lockstep obedience. Life is far too complicated for that to happen, and anyway, it would be a deadly bore to have perfect Goody Two-shoes for kids. Of course you will have family friction. Wherever there is contact, there is friction; that is inevitable, because not every objection is laid to rest by establishing family policy. You can, however, anticipate that protest will be relatively mild, reasonably good-natured, and not shrill.

In a solid, well-grounded family, friction will not cause dangerous sparks to fly. Conflict arising in families with sound policy is manageable and not toxic to the family unit. This is key. Set family policy in place, and you may have good kids acting badly but you won't have bad kids acting awfully.

Five Key Ingredients That Make Family Policy Succeed

- **Start Early** Begin setting out these family bylaws when kids are small, and it becomes second nature to them; if they grow up *with* them, they grow *into* them. Through active participation, children learn what counts, especially if you start early.
  - Your toddler who joins you for dinner while still in bib and high chair will not need a lecture about your commitment to sharing meals.
  - Your son who has visited Grandma with you weekly since "before he can remember" will not require a sermon from the mount about the value of family.
  - The kindergartner with a piggybank earmarked for giving will know the meaning of charity before he knows what the word actually means.
- **Be Consistent** If you make a plan, keep to it. If you can't, it is fine to revise it. Perhaps you were overly ambitious. But once you have established a tradition that suits you, keep it up regularly. Erratic or haphazard observance backfires—kids balk even more.
- **Make the Practice Kid-friendly** Practices best remembered and followed are those kids actually enjoy. Not everything must be fun and games for children, but even responsibilities can be carried out with good cheer. Don't unwittingly become a taskmaster. Making traditions, rules, or responsibilities too demanding takes the joy out of them and does not make for family teamwork.
- **Discuss the Meaning and Purpose** Explain why a particular practice is important. Children who "get" why they are doing things and feel that their efforts make a difference are more responsive and involved.

When you explain the value of a practice, it creates a pride of purpose in a child, and that makes for a good kid and a better world.

- Even quite a young child can place food donations in a community food box while you explain that she is doing a good deed and helping take care of other children who may not have all the things she has.

• **Inform Other Parents** As your children become more social, let other parents know about your family practices. Communication makes other parents your allies, able to intentionally reinforce, rather than unwittingly undermine, your child-rearing. Kids don't get in as much trouble if other parents are your eyes and ears. Stay connected to other parents, and you will have better connections with your children.

Creating Your Own Family Policy

No family has cornered the market on thoughtful choices. It will be up to you to decide what feels most meaningful and how you can actively weave that meaning into everyday life. To begin, ask yourself these questions: What do you *feel* you most want to impart to your children? Which values or characteristics strike at your parenting core? Are honesty, reliability, generosity, responsibility, and/or competence most meaningful to you? Or perhaps spirituality, thoughtfulness, concern, social consciousness, family closeness are the characteristics you hope your child develops.

Considering your core values, in what realm of family life can these find expression? Might your religion be the centerpiece of your practices? Maybe your daily home life together—bedtime, mealtime, and playtime—will be the area where you set these practices in place. Charitable endeavors or social activism may be another area of possibility. The decision is all yours; just make sure it is well thought out.

Learning from Others

While assessing your own family priorities and values is essential, you do not have to reinvent parenting. Let me pass on eight wonderful practices that make for cooperative kids:

1. Sharing Meals
2. Family Time-out
3. Family Forum
4. Imaginative Play
5. Financial Planning
7. Reading
8. TV watching

Sharing Meals

"Happy eating makes for happy family life."

(Japanese proverb)

Regular dinners with time for talking *and* listening are a calming custom for families (which means that the TV **must** be turned off, and you **must** converse). This time gives parents an opportunity to learn what is going on in the lives of their children. It brings families closer, which goes a long way to helping you and your children get along amiably.

Not every family can make dinners together an unbreakable ritual. A mother juggling two jobs, a dad on shift work, and a child in extended day care make it tough to get mealtime togetherness going. I know this. But even if it means starting to eat together on a limited basis, perhaps just one Sunday night a month, try to make this happen.

> ▶ **PYB Words of Wisdom:** *Food nourishes the body, and intimacy nourishes the soul; a family dinner is the time for both. Make sitting down together a part of your family policy, and your child will not starve for attention and then be at risk for behavior problems.*

FOOD FOR THOUGHT

Here are eight recipes to make meals that truly nourish your family life:

1. **Have uninterrupted dinners** Make dinner a "techno-free zone": TV, computers, beepers, phones, cell phones, video games, and all other gadgets are not allowed to interfere. Use your answering machine to protect you from interruptions. Agree that *no one* leaves the table just to grab "this call" or check e-mail.

2. **Encourage uninterrupted talk** Go around the table and allow each child a few minutes of time to talk without anyone else making a comment. Don't permit interruptions or comments.

3. **Declare "family only" suppers** Try your level best to have at least one meal a week where everyone is expected to show up and where you don't have guests.

4. **Find a favorite family restaurant** If eating around the dinner table at home doesn't work, find a favorite restaurant and go there regularly. Ask for the same table and waiter. It may not be home, but it can become a cozy and familiar gathering place, and it relieves the pressure of having to prepare a meal and clean up.

5. **Treat "take out" seriously** If work eliminates home cooking as an option, do "takeout," but treat the meal with the same respect you would home cooking. Just because you can't cook doesn't mean a meal can't be a nice family occasion. Set the table and put the food out on "good" china. Think of it as "taking the 'take' out of takeout."

6. **Treat meals as a spiritual event** Encourage reflection. Ask your children what they are thankful for this week.

7. **Have traditional family dinners** Once a month, have a meal with relatives or close friends and serve your family's traditional or favorite food.

8. **Cook together** During the weekend, prepare a meal together and then share it. Cooking is something kids enjoy, and you would be surprised at the things kids say when they are peeling carrots!

Family Time-out: Stay Connected

While we may *live* with our children, parents—especially once kids attend school—spend relatively few hours a week *interacting* with them. If we are not careful, we can end up *rooming* with our children, not *living* with them. As an antidote to this, I strongly advocate a ritual—a family Time-out—where parents set aside regular blocks of time with children and fix these times into their schedules.

HERE ARE SOME WAYS TO CREATE A FAMILY TIME-OUT

- Try your best to stay home on school nights. Alternate staying home if both parents can't be home.
- Make an effort to tuck in your child at night.
- Devote a specific part of a weekend to your child.
- Make special dates with your child.
- Mark your "Family Time-out" on a calendar (i.e., Family Sundays).

▶ **PYB Words of Wisdom:** *The easiest and most natural family "Time-out" is bedtime. Let children talk, and even if they don't, just be there and available. Sit on the edge of your child's bed, and it forever takes the edge off your relationship.*

Family Forum

Hold regular family meetings where you can discuss your family affairs. If you have been able to establish the custom of family dinnertimes, this may be your natural forum for such discussions. If not, carve out a time, perhaps weekly, for this round-table to take place. During these meetings, observe the tradition of permitting children to speak without interruption. Your children will feel acknowledged and attended to, which will lead to less arguing in the long run. You can use these meetings as a forum to update, modify, and alter family policy. This is especially important since family policies need to change as children develop and mature.

▶ **PYB Words of Wisdom:** *Parents and children who make conversation a natural part of family of life tend to* *get along. Carry on a meaningful conversation with your kids, and your kids won't be mean or carry on.*

Imaginative Play

Imaginative play is activity that encourages children to rely on their own imagination to furnish their play and become the *active inventors* of their own amusement, in contrast to such entertainment as TV and video games, where they are the passive recipients of stimulation. When children engage in imaginative play, like singing and dancing just for fun, being silly, making up plays and puppet shows, playing house, throwing tea parties, and, when they are older, writing stories and poems, they are generally in a better mood than children who are only passively entertained or amused. They are not prone to boredom, restlessness, or short attention spans, and, most significantly, they are generally better at self-soothing, which helps them to manage frustration. Parents who not only encourage but join their children in playing house or school, participate in tea parties and space-alien roundups, or watch performances, have children who feel close to them, and *closeness is a very good insurance policy against discord.*

JOIN WITH YOUR CHILD THROUGH IMAGINATIVE PLAY DON'T BE AFRAID TO LET DOWN YOUR HAIR WITH YOUR KIDS

"My parents always encouraged whimsy. My father who was a pro-fessor and older, who looked so serious to the outside world, would let me dress him up in outlandish costumes, usually during our summer vacation. Then we would do silly dances. To this day there is a sign in our house that reads, 'Dance Like No One Is Looking!'"

(Bev, age 27)

"On long car rides my mother and I would make up 'operas.' One of us would sing a few lines and then give the other person a chance to continue. My mother, who could hardly carry a tune, would encourage funny verses. It could really get goofy. One long trip flew by as we "sang" an entire opera about a whale in love with a min-now: our aquatic version of Romeo and Juliet. My parents were busy professionals but they let their hair down when they played with me. I think it helped me become and stay close to my parents."

(Cindy, age 19)

These activities may sound silly but there is nothing foolish about creating close and joyful connections between you and your child. And if you balk at the idea of "finding the time" bear in mind that it takes less effort to share joy with your children then it does to disci-pline them.

MAKING YOUR BABY INTO A GENIUS VS. IMAGINATIVE PLAY

The baby toy market is now inundated with DVDs, videotapes, and CDs, designed to instruct even the tiniest infant. (Actually, some suggest exposing children to learning while they're in the uterus). Even before they can sit up, babies, propped up in front of screens,

(continued on next page)

work at becoming baby Einstein. Overused, these products are counterproductive to the all-important development of your child's interior life. They are bombarding your child with stimulation, at the possible expense of having her develop her own imaginative and creative capacities (to say nothing of the pressure they put on a child to achieve).

If you do use these products—and of course you will—do not let them replace the role of imaginative play in the life of your child, which affords opportunities for wonder, self-discovery, and interaction with the world and others. A sock doll, pots and pans, blocks, finger paints, clay, and other unstructured toys are a must. Encourage children to dance, sing, act, write poems, pretend so that they develop the all-important faculty—to *actively create their own amusement*. Set aside special moments—perhaps before bed—to playfully babble, coo, and sing with your infant, to make up stories with your preschooler, or to paint with your older child. These shared rituals, and the delight lighting up your eyes as you play with her, not images flickering across a screen, will actually advance speech and language development, create emotional attachment, and make for a calm contented child who doesn't constantly whine—"Dad, get me another video game" or "Mom, I'm bored, there's nothing to do."

Family Contact

Regular contact with extended family or a close circle of friends is a practice that is very centering for children, reassuring them, making them feel that life comes with a safety net. It can also make life less tense for parents. Parents who are isolated can be burdened by feeling that the family responsibilities fall on their shoulders alone. With a close-knit extended family or circle of friends, there is often someone to turn to for help. Parents do better with a safety net, too.

SPECIAL RELATIONS

"My parents encouraged me to call their best friend, Cecile, Auntie CC. She was my godmother and, above all, she was my confidant. I could go to her with problems that I wouldn't dare tell my parents. I wonder if my mom realized the aggravation she avoided because I had my aunt's ear. My relationship with Aunt CC is still a rock to me."

(Annie, age 34)

Family contact may be as informal as dropping in over the weekend for lunch or sleepovers. Or it may be more formal, as in establishing a family circle, cousins' club, or periodic organized reunions. When extended family is not available, close friends can certainly take on this role, becoming what I dub "Family by Choice."

> ▶ **PYB Words of Wisdom:** *Some people are born into loving families, for others loving families are born in their heart and imagination—a* **"family by choice."** *Keep stability in your children's lives by anchoring them to a group of people—relatives and/or friends—who deeply love them. It creates another envelope of security, an atmosphere in which children do well and stay calm.* **The greatest family value is the ability to value family.**

Financial Planning

We are often trying so hard to earn money to give our kids everything that we neglect developing their sense of financial responsibility, which is a source of **many** parenting battles, especially as kids get older. Avoid money wars by helping your kids become financially savvy. Start early with a piggy bank; later, help your kids open their own savings accounts. Providing an allowance can give them a chance to handle decisions about money early on; help them become financial planners early. Encourage discussions about spending, so that they see that their choices have consequences. ("Do you have enough money for that video game? Think ahead: is there any other way you might want to spend your money?"

**MAKE KIDS SMART CONSUMERS
TO AVERT TOY WARS**

There is no better way to cut down on buying battles than by making your child a savvy consumer.

- Teach kids about marketing and product hype that are directed at children. (Let them compare the advertised product to the real one before they take it home.)
- Take kids to stores for "looking trips" before "buying trips," to discourage impulsive spending.
- To build up their critical thinking about fads and trends, save old toys/clothes that your child loses interest in. Six months later, ask them which they would recommend (or not) to another child and why.
- Encourage children to consult Web sites that evaluate products for kids.

Reading

Reading is a mindful, *not* mindless activity that encourages thinking. A child who is mindful is more likely to make good and safe decisions, so encourage reading.

- Read to kids at bedtime and continue to do this even after they have learned to read.
- Let children read out loud to you if they choose to. Don't force them.
- Let little ones pretend to read. They usually love to do this if they have a favorite book that they know by heart.
- Listen to an audio book of a favorite author while you are in the car.
- Write a family storybook. Let every member of the family contribute a story, whether oral or written.
- Go to the library as a regular family outing. Attend library activities, such as storytelling hours and summer book-reading contests. Get children their own cards. Let them choose their own books.
- Make a family library, a collection of favorite storybooks that your children can choose from. *Goodnight Moon, Curious George,* Dr. Seuss books, *The Very Hungry Caterpillar, Eloise, Babar, Chicken Soup and Rice,* are wonderful for starters.

- Create a family book club. As a family, select a book and read it aloud together in installments instead of retreating to your own separate activities or watching TV.

> ▶ **PYB Words of Wisdom:** *Reading expands your child's mind, giving her language and ideas. Kids who think are kids with whom you can reason!*

TV Watching

Have a policy about TV: use it to enhance family life. Just about every family in America has one or more TVs and spends numerous hours a day watching it. It is preposterous not to harness the power of this activity in the service of making family life more cohesive. How can you transform *viewing* time into *together* time?

- Make TV part of the family rather than have it part your family. Is your family room a room for family? TV viewing tends to be a passive and rather solitary venture. Families watch a lot of the tube yet spend little time having any exchange over what they have seen. Avoid TV in your child's bedroom. It is very isolating and disconnects your child from the family.
- Turn television into a group activity. Regularly watch a favorite family program together. A tradition of sharing laughs or tears about favorite moments in your favorite show can bring you closer.
- Transform television into *tell-a-vision*. Make it a custom to choose an educational program (news, nature, history, science), watch it with the kids, and then chat about it. TV as a shared experience can be as useful as any other family activity.
- Monitor what your children watch and cut down TV viewing by 25 percent. Give kids a choice of picking one hour's worth of TV-watching an evening. Recent studies suggest that just cutting down on television-viewing reduces aggressive behavior in kids.
- Make certain times TV-free. You can try making school nights TV-free, or evenings after dinner.
- Turn off the television during meals.

AVOID RAISING A CRIB POTATO: SET LIMITS ON THE ELECTRONIC ENTERTAINMENT

Increasingly the crib, not just the couch, is where kids are exposed to electronic entertainment.* A recent survey shows that more than 25% of children under 2 have a TV in their room, and that on an average day, 59% of kids 6 months to 2 years watch TV, while 42% watch a video or DVD. Word is not in yet—nor will it be for quite a while—on the impact of all this early exposure to electronic media on children in these very formative years, but here is my best advice: Moderation! My concerns, echoed by others in the field, are that too much of the moving image may contribute to:

- passivity
- lack of imagination, creativity, and ingenuity
- need for instant gratification and difficulty managing frustration
- shortening of attention span
- desensitivity to violence
- reduction of reading and writing skills
- obesity
- social isolation, withdrawl from outside world

All of these are not ingredients for creating happy and resilient kids who are fun to parent. Remember to be a good filter: avoid over-exposure, especially until there is more known about the long-term impact on kids. When you grab that next video to get a few minutes of peace, consider the battles you might end up waging in the future if you have created a crib potato hooked from infancy on visual entertainment.

"Too Busy" Is a Bad Excuse

Some parents may be ready to throw up their hands and sputter: "My life is so hectic and full of demands; I'm *extremely* busy, and so are my kids. This policy stuff is not doable." Well, yes, this may be true, but all the more reason to get this policy "stuff" in place and in gear. Despite all

---

*"Growing Number of Video Viewers Watch from the Crib," *New York Times*, October 29, 2003, pg. A1.

your efforts, getting excessively caught up in your own activities leaves a child feeling neglected. Ask any child who has been neglected; there is no substitute for showing up. If you don't act as if your children are a priority, they will act up.

It is easy, all too easy, for a child to become a stranger to us, even if he lives under our own roof. As your child gets older, he becomes more active, comes to spend almost half of his waking hours at school, eight hours watching TV each week, to say nothing of countless hours on the Internet and phone. If he feels unanchored to his home, it can pose risks. A child who floats in and out of your house is one who is more likely to act up, and you may not know it until it gets very bad. If you lose track of your child, he risks going off track or, even worse, getting derailed. Spend time with your child, and it won't happen.

> ▶ **PYB Words of Wisdom:** *Kids never read "extremely busy" as a mark of parental devotion, but interpret it as "My parents don't care about me." Try hard not to become a parent who visits your home rather than lives in it, and you will live peacefully in your home.*

Chapter 4

How to Eliminate No-Win Discipline: Conquering Bad Habits to Stay in Charge

How Can I Scold You? Let Me Count the Ways

One more sound out of you and you are in *really big trouble*." As soon as these words leave your lips, you know that they are a useless attempt at discipline. No matter how red-faced with outrage or tearful with frustration we get, our children do not become better behaved because we bellow at them. No battle with kids, large or small, has ever been won by warnings, threats, scoldings, reprimands, tirades, lectures, or sermons. Never! Most disputes get worse, or, at the very least, go on a good deal longer than they need to when we resort to such tactics. We know all this, yet, like a bad habit, when we reach a certain breaking point with our children, these no-win discipline reactions kick in.

When our child acts inappropriately, or just plain misbehaves, we invariably and automatically spout one or more of these oh-so-familiar rants:

"Enough!"
"Did you hear what I said?"
"My head is pounding."

"Right now—or else!"
"OK, just stop whining."
"Next time you really will be punished."
"See if I care."
"This is the last time."

If you listen to yourself, you will discover that, like most parents, you have a tendency to fall back on a fixed number of these responses. Each of us tends to have a no-win discipline style that we unfortunately and unsuccessfully overuse. Trapped in the grip of bad discipline habits, our angry automatic responses rob us of parental authority *and*, most important, do little to meaningfully improve the behavior of our kids. After years of observing parents and children, I have identified eight of the most common self-sabotaging discipline patterns where well-meaning parents unwittingly mishandle anger. These no-win discipline styles include:

- **Threat Makers** Parents who, in the face of misbehavior, angrily level empty threats with promises of punishment that are never carried out.
- **Shifters** Parents who respond to misbehavior by hastily passing off, or shifting, their anger and all responsibility for discipline onto another person, frequently a spouse.
- **Cavers** Parents who, while initially angry over misbehavior, eventually *cave in* under pressure from their children; their angry resolve fades away and the kids have their way.
- **Camels** Parents who tolerate misbehavior until they reach the *last-straw* point and only then finally erupt in excessive anger.
- **Short Fuses** Parents who continually feel edgy, irritable, impatient, and, as a result, have a *short fuse*, which means they rapidly fire off bursts of anger at every and any infraction, scolding, reprimanding, and battling with kids nonstop.
- **Erratic Erupters** Parents whose angry outbursts and punishment for misdeeds are unpredictable, inconsistent, and random; they *do* lose their temper over misbehavior but *erupt erratically*.
- **Fault Finders** Parents who are controlling, critical, hypervigilant, and/or suspicious, constantly and angrily *finding fault* or detecting that their children are up to no good; they are always fuming at and squabbling with their kids.

- **Deniers** Parents who *never* get angry at their children's misbehavior because they disconnect from these feelings by *denying,* burying, displacing, suppressing, or swallowing their frustration. The net effect is that anger disappears and, along with it, appropriate discipline.

Springing from the No-Win Discipline Trap: Four Simple Steps

Escaping from these no-win discipline traps and establishing a positive pattern of discipline takes just four steps:

1. *Identify* your own pattern and see how it goes wrong in spite of your best intentions.
2. Gain *key insights* into the hidden reasons why you are in the grip of this self-sabotaging style.
3. *Reflect on your own childhood in your family of origin* in order to uncover how your own personal struggles gave rise to your present no-win discipline tactics. Even if we try hard to shed the past, it can have a powerful grip on our efforts to raise cooperative kids, often in ways we do not recognize. Like an unwelcome ghost, your own, original family problems may haunt your present parenting, interfering with effective methods of discipline. These hidden forces can be banished once identified and understood.
4. *Break no-win discipline habits: turn personal insight into action.* Adopt new, constructive discipline strategies so you can eliminate unnecessary fights for good, to become an effective, take-charge parent.

> ▶ **PYB Words of Wisdom:** *Every parent caught in a no-win-discipline pattern unwittingly mishandles anger and loses the crucial opportunity to teach a child to become a better, more cooperative kid. Eliminate no-win-discipline and gain great kids.*

MIXED MARRIAGES

Often parents have two very different no-win discipline styles. An Erratic Erupter may be married to a Caver or a Fault-Finder may co-parent with a Camel. Once you have identified your own pattern, it can be enormously useful for each of you to get a handle on your co-parent's style which can help both of you get on the road to good, consistent discipline.

Are You a Threat Maker?

Step 1: Identification: How Does Anger Go Wrong for a Threat Maker?

Do you regrettably fall victim to the self-defeating habit of making empty threats in the face of misbehavior?

> *"You have one more chance and that's it."*
> *"This time I really mean it."*
> *"Try that one more time and you'll be in really big trouble."*

Children are exquisitely sensitive to parents who do not make good on their promises to take disciplinary action. It is the parenting version of "crying wolf," and, just as in the fairy tale, children come to disregard the warnings. Then, at the very moments when you need your child to listen, he ignores you. At its worst, overusing this pattern emboldens a child and can foster a growing disrespect for his parents. For example, kids tend to get "fresh" with parents who regularly tender empty threats, sometimes even calling their bluff and becoming more defiant ("Yeah, let's see you do it!"). Sadly, the great learning device—cause and effect—is lost on your child.

Children often regard the Threat Maker parent as foolish, weak, and not to be taken seriously. "Full of hot air" is not a flattering figure to cut for your children, and that disrespectful attitude does not encourage cooperation. What's more, kids may well act worse, in the hope that you will stop threatening and start enforcing a code of conduct. They know they *need* parameters.

Step 2. Key Insights: Why Does It Go Wrong for a Threat Maker?

Consider that these hidden factors might make you vulnerable to being caught in the Threat Maker style:

- Perhaps you are a parent who mistakenly sees following through as hurting, not helping, your child, as if consequences were delivering a harmful or painful blow. Unwittingly, your unreliable anger might come from not having "the heart" to make your child unhappy. Ironically, you may end up being too nice for your child's own good.
- Insecurity, lack of self-confidence, or timidity may make you pull back from being firm, committed, or consistent.

Step 3. Reflections: How Did I Come to Adopt the Threat Maker Style?

Ask yourself: "Where in my own childhood are the clues as to why I have acquired this style?"

- Did anyone in your childhood family use threats, bullying, or intimidation? The unfortunate fact is that even if it caused pain, we often adopt the destructive anger strategies of our own family of origin. This pain of childhood may make it impossible for you to follow through with your own children. You may want to "protect" them from feeling anything close to the intense suffering or fear you endured.
- Did you have a mother or father who was weak, tentative, shy, or frightened? The absence of an effective parent in your family of origin may make it hard for you to carry out your intentions.
- Did you have a parent who was excessively punitive, cruel, harsh, or physically abusive? With a parent who misused discipline in this way, you may be loath to carry out *any* consequences. You may unconsciously fear losing control as they did, and stop yourself from taking any action at all as a way to prevent that hated outcome from ever coming true.

REFLECTIONS

As a child, Shelly came home from school to find that her beloved dog had been given away; according to her father, it was the way Shelly would learn her lesson for not taking care of her pet properly. When Mark's mother felt angry, she threatened to "send him to the orphanage" and periodically locked him out of the house when he was "bad." With childhood pain like this, is it any wonder people become parents who resort to threats without consequences?

Step 4. Break No-Win Discipline Habits: Put a Halt to Threat Maker Tactics

Here is what you can do to turn these insights into change for the better:

- Stop the empty threats. Stay focused on the actual misbehavior and make your consequences measured and specific to the misconduct ("Clean up the milk that you spilled." "Give the toy back to your friend and apologize.") so that you don't feel harsh or out of control, like your own parents.
- Flag words that are the hallmark of this style ("wait," "next time," "soon"). Try to eliminate them from your discipline vocabulary.
- Be brave enough to express your anger, but only in words. Verbally expressing your distress sets you far apart from the destructive ways of your parents. (Make sure to read chapter 9.)
- Stay in charge. It is good for children to know when they have done something bad and to experience the consequences of their misbehavior; children actually feel comforted, *not injured*, by a parent who follows through.
- Work on building parenting self-confidence. Practice sounding assured and *consistent*. Develop a *firm voice*, not a threatening one. A firm voice is one that is quiet, measured, strong, no-nonsense, and conveys the feeling that anything that you say must be taken seriously. Use your "firm voice" sparingly, only when you are ready to be taken seriously.

▶ **PYB Words of Wisdom:** *When your child acts up, warn her by saying,* "This is my firm voice," *which gives her a signal that the next words you speak are the real thing.*

Are You a Shifter?

Step 1. Identification: How Does Anger Go Wrong for a Shifter?

Do you get upset at your child's misbehavior but then *shift* the anger and the responsibility for discipline to another person? Do you say, for example:

> "Your teacher will be very angry that you did not finish your spelling pretest. I bet she lowers your grade."
> "If you don't write that thank-you, Grandma will be so upset that she might stop sending you birthday presents."
> "We will see what your mother has to say when she gets home and hears about your lost bike!"

With this no-win discipline tactic, a Shifter is often perceived as weak and ineffective by children who lose respect for this parent because they can walk all over him. But, with this style, there is an added problem. A child can become worked up or pitted against a third person; often it is the other parent, but it can easily be a teacher, friend, relative, coach, or neighbor. This *triangulation* ratchets up fury, because it draws in the third person negatively rather than constructively. Mom becomes the "bad cop," and dad the good one, which is not good for parenting, as conflict escalates, often becoming a three-way melee.

Step 2. Key Insights: Why Does It Go Wrong for a Shifter?

Perhaps one of these insights will unlock the real but not altogether apparent reasons why you must shift your anger.

- A shifter is frequently a parent who is actually fearful of intense anger. It is as if anger is such a hot potato that it must be shifted to another, a way to offload an overwhelming emotion.
- Parents who are afraid of being authority figures can develop this pattern. Reluctant to take charge, they give their own parenting control over to someone they believe is more commanding, effective, respected, or powerful, i.e., the other, "stronger" parent.

Step 3. Reflections: How Did I Come to Adopt the Shifter Style?

- Did people take sides or gang up in your family? A Shifter has often seen a lot of *triangulation* during conflict, so she may become a parent who is not good at fighting her own battles, and instead reflexively draws another person into the fray.
- Did you doubt that you yourself deserved respect? Did you learn helplessness and/or subtly get rewarded for staying dependent? Any one of these can lead to your believing that anger and power need to be in the hands of someone who, you assume, is more capable of handling them.

Step 4. Break No-Win Discipline Habits: Put a Halt to Shifter Tactics

- Try to maintain privacy and boundaries: don't bring others into your conflicts. Be sure not to invoke names of people outside the immediate family. Keep in mind that the more *positively* connected your child feels to people he admires and loves, the better he will behave.
- When conflict arises, find the courage to take on battles with your child. She will feel you care if you do. If you are not up to handling a fight on your own, do not feel pressured to do so. Tell your child that you need time to think, and that you will get back to him about your reaction to his misbehavior. Once you have collected your thoughts and have a chance to formulate a plan, you will feel sturdier about disciplining your child and won't need to drag someone else into the fray. (See chapter 6).

Are You a Caver?

Step 1. Identification: How Does Anger Go Wrong for a Caver?

Do you begin with resolve about your child's conduct, then start to waffle, and finally capitulate in the face of your child's resistance? Do you *cave in* when your child whines long enough and loud enough, until you finally shout:

"OK, OK, you can go out before you do your homework."

"Go ahead. Just put on the TV and pipe down."

"Alright, you can have a new toy if you'll just quit crying."

"OK. Whatever you want."

The well-meaning Caver hands power to children, and a child who knows he rules the roost causes long-term conflict and misery. With a parent who caves, a child quickly catches on that he can get his way as long as he puts in the time, effort, and, if need be, "creativity." Children of Cavers are superb at making up "but I have to"s as a way to coerce a parent or get their own way. "But Dad, I have to go to practice even though I'll miss my test, or else the whole team is out of the playoffs." This style encourages "negative creativity": white lies, manipulation, and even deception, which, of course, are not qualities of character that will make your child grow more cooperative with you or the world at large. Cavers' children are also consummate whiners!

Cavers are inclined to use bribery to gain cooperation and peace. This parent offers anything from toys to privileges if the child will "just stop acting up."

Though a Caver has very different intentions, being nice or indulgent sends a message that a parent is a patsy, a pushover, or, at worst, a fool. What's more, a child gets things he ought not to have, or does not deserve, simply by insisting. A Caver's child may not develop the all-important capacity to tolerate frustration and disappointment and will have the unreasonable expectation that the world will always meet his demands. This makes a child you will one day want to call a "spoiled brat."

> ▶ **PYB Words of Wisdom:** *Caving to the demands of your child collapses your foundation for good discipline. Keep your parenting resolve and you will not only win many a battle, you might just win the whole war!*

Step 2. Key Insights: Why Does It Go Wrong for a Caver?

Here are some of the not-so-obvious forces that compel a person to use this anger style:

- A Caver may feel emotional insecurity and believe that love can evaporate because a child feels frustrated or angry. Behind a parent who capitulates may be a parent unsure about how much he is truly loved.
- Uncertainty about your parenting skills and authority may be the hidden reason for giving a child's insistence undue clout. A child can easily influence you if you doubt that you are parenting correctly.

Step 3. Reflections: How Did I Come to Adopt the Caver Style?

- Did your parents withdraw when they were angry? You may believe that anger destroys love. Then, as an adult, you may still feel emotionally insecure and unable to risk antagonizing your children.
- Were your parents poor role models; did they not make parenting a priority? Were they self-involved or even absentee? If you did not have parents to show you how to do it, you might understandably lack security about your own parenting, feeling like a phony when you are in charge of your children. Therefore, when your children become insistent or adamant, you cave, because you are not sure you really know any better than they do.

Step 4. Break No-Win Discipline Habits: Put a Halt to Caver Tactics

- Watch your language! The telltale sign of this style is that your sentences get longer and more qualified. You engage in far too much back and forth with your child. Stop talking so much! (Learn talking techniques in chapter 7.)
- Join a parenting group. You will benefit from the support and guidance of others to help you feel more secure with your parenting decisions.
- Stay at the helm of your family. Kids may insist on power, but remember, it really scares them to know that they can take over.
- Respect your own feelings not just those of your child.

> ▶ **PYB Words of Wisdom:** *A parent is a person. She has the right to pay attention to her own feelings, needs, and desires not exclusively those of her child. Don't let your*

*child use guilt or any form of emotional blackmail to
manipulate you into caving into his demands and giving
up your rights and your anger.*

• Write down the last five times you caved in. You probably will find that
your reaction clusters in certain areas (school, bedtime, hygiene, etc.).
Choose *only one* of these issues that come up regularly and practice
being resolute in this one area only.

> ▶ **PYB Words of Wisdom:** *Make this your new parenting
> mantra: There is love after anger. Love does not do a disap-
> pearing act, and anger will not make it go away.*

Are You a Camel?

Step 1. Identification: How Does Anger Go Wrong for a Camel?

Do you have a "slow burn" style, tolerating your child's undesirable
behavior far too long before you finally reach the last straw and then go
ballistic? Do you take it and take it until you can't take it "one more
minute" and then finally lash out, which makes you go from quietly
appeasing to loudly frantic, and sounds like this:

> "I'll be off the phone in a second, Jack. Just a moment. I'll be right
> there. Jack, just give Mommy another minute to finish. I'll be
> right there. Get away, you're driving me nuts!"
> "No sweetie. Don't, darling. Can you please stop, honey. Please
> stop, now. That does it!"
> "I've asked you nicely ten times, this is the last straw. Stop it this
> instant!"

One of the predicaments with this reaction—especially if you tolerate undesirable behavior in silence or by muttering under your breath, or
attempt to appease or humor your child—is that a child may not get any
anger cues that tell them they are misbehaving until it is too late. Frustrated mutterings are not a clear "stop sign" for a child. Saying "yes"

when you want to say "no" is not, either. Raising a child who is not clued in to behavioral expectations can make your kid into a big pain. He does not know when to stop because he has not learned clear warning signs cautioning him that he is going over the limit. As a result, a Camel's kids can become agitated, jumpy, and end up getting into everything.

By tolerating your child's behavior, you unwittingly provide opportunity for him to practice the very conduct you want to see controlled. Ironically, every phone call gives Jack a "practice session" at "How to bug my mom on the telephone." The inevitable Camel blow up also makes things worse. The aftermath of the "I am fed up with this" tirade is battles and tears, which is not at all what you are trying to accomplish.

Step 2. Key Insights: Why Does It Go Wrong for a Camel?

- A parent resorts to this style because she feels a pressure to please or do everything "right." Wanting to make everybody happy, she tolerates misbehavior far too long even if it drives her to distraction. An angry outburst may actually be the desperate cry of an overwhelmed parent forcing herself to try too hard to be good.
- A Camel parent does not feel she deserves her own space. For example, a mother may not believe she is entitled to say "No" to a child unless she is feeling extremely put upon or put out. Setting boundaries early is not comfortable, so a parent's initial protests are weak and thus not taken seriously by a child. This all adds up to a "No" that doesn't really mean "No" until things get explosive and maybe out of control.

Step 3. Reflections: How Did I Come to Adopt the Camel Style?

- Did you have volatile parents with a short fuse? Frightened by angry outbursts as a child, you may hold back on getting angry as an adult. However, trying to dam up anger cannot work. You can only do that so long, and then you erupt. Ironically, your effort to prevent being like your own volatile parent might unwittingly trap you into your own form of delayed eruption.
- Did your family expect children to be there to make your parents happy, and did they get harsh, angry, or disappointed if you did not?

Were you in the middle of an angry marriage or a divorce where you ended up trying to be the peacemaker? A Camel has often been a child who, for any number of reasons, feels she must please and be accepting, and does so with her own children until she "bursts."

• Were your parents intrusive and controlling, did they refuse to respect your privacy and boundaries? Did they deny you the right to determine your own life or to say "No" to them? If you have parents who never respected your personal space, it may be difficult to establish this with your own child. You may have learned that it was unacceptable to say "No," and this may be why you accept the unacceptable for longer than you should.

Step 4. Break No-Win Discipline Habits: Put a Halt to Camel Tactics

• Write down the sort of behaviors that eventually send you over the top. When one of them *begins* to occur, immediately stop everything else, make direct eye contact with your child, and say in a firm voice, "This is unacceptable."

• Practice saying "No" with determination. When you believe in your right to say it, so will your child, and it will dramatically cut down on eruptions (review chapter 1 on the importance of "No"). Make yourself a sign "PARENTS HAVE RIGHTS, TOO." When he is *not* misbehaving, discuss this idea with your child. (Review ideas about family meetings in chapter 3).

• Try to take better care of yourself. This style often rears its head when you are feeling pulled in too many different directions or when you feel depleted. Try to do less for others and more for yourself.

> ▶ **PYB Words of Wisdom:** *Losing control is bad for a parent but it is always worse for a child; it is very damaging to a child's soul and models poor impulse control, which does not make for a well-behaved child.*

Are You a Short Fuse?

Step 1. Identification: How Does Anger Go Wrong for a Short Fuse?

Are you so wrung out and strung out that you cannot help but fire a volley of quick, stern reprimands that do not make your child more cooperative? In spite of yourself, are you frequently impatient, short fused, edgy, and/or irritated when your child acts up, which makes you fly off the handle issuing a constant barrage of directions, corrections, and orders until you feel all you ever do is scold your kid so you sound like this? (Hint: Short-fuse parents shout their child's name in exasperation so often that a child's very name sounds like a reprimand.)

"Sit still. Don't move. Stay put. Get down. Sit."
"Don't touch. Leave it alone. Keep your hands off. Watch it."
"Adam, no. Stop, Adam. Adam, cut it out. Adam, enough ADAM!!"

A parent with this style often sounds like a worn-out trainer in an animal obedience program with an unruly critter who does not "get" the commands. (Think: Heel! Sit! Down!) This response-set is often associated with parents of very active or restless children and is more likely to be operating with "on the go" boys rather than more subdued girls.

Unfortunately, this volley of reprimands has a boomerang effect: An active child is *not* calmed or soothed by a constant string of rebukes. A barrage of directives makes a restless child more fidgety and more agitated, then kids listen less, which keeps them *very high maintenance.*

The child of a Short Fuse parent hates the sound of his own name and, as a result, often ignores it altogether, because his name spells trouble. He may grow to hate the sound of his own parent's voice as well, run from it or defy it. "Don't wear out my name" was one child's memorable and cheeky response. The Short Fuse's child resorts to tuning out, becoming virtually deaf to parental reprimands no matter how loud they get.

Regrettably, these tactics do not convey much other than "You are making me crazy." A child is not given information about what line they are crossing or what behavioral crime they are committing. And while he gets the message that he is doing wrong, he never receives directions or demonstrations on how to do things right. Reprimanding rather than soothing a fidgety child, giving him no instructions on how to behave, is a recipe for nonstop battles.

▶ **PYB Words of Wisdom:** *Shining a spotlight on your child's misbehavior but keeping him in the dark about how to do things right won't give you or him a sunny disposition.*

Step 2. Key Insights: Why Does It Go Wrong for a Short Fuse?

- Short Fuse parents may struggle with impulse control and not be able to hold on to anger, because it feels too uncomfortable, so they discharge their fury.
- These parents can feel overwhelmed by their family responsibilities, feel helpless, and try to offset that by barking orders; out of desperation, they try anything to gain control, but shouting doesn't do it.
- A parent with an active boy may unwittingly equate activity with trouble, not just temperament. Every time he acts up, this parent issues a reprimand and an unfortunate message "you are bad," until it becomes a self-fulfilling prophecy, which, of course, makes things worse!

Step 3. Reflections: How Did I Come to Adopt the Short Fuse Style?

- Was there a lot of shouting, screaming, and verbal disrespect in your family of origin? If all you knew was bitterness and acrimony in your childhood home, it is understandable that you might evolve into a parent who has a negative volley of responses to your child's misbehavior.
- Was your family chaotic? You may have lived in a home without guidance or instruction. It is difficult to become a good discipline coach if you lacked such basic guidelines.
- Were your parents poor in communication skills? Was there little or no conversation and an abundance of reprimands? Short Fuse parents often have not developed verbal skills because no one communicated with them. Unwittingly, this makes a one-word reprimand seem as if that should be enough when it isn't.

- In your childhood home, were there negative views of boys as "bad" or "trouble"? Was there any boy in your family who was difficult or even delinquent? A Short Fuse parent may have been raised with a sort of emotional prejudice that makes her see a boy's active behavior not as a reflection of temperament but as a warning sign of trouble to come. This may have set up a cycle of overreacting to boys and coming down angry and hard rather than offering them a much needed gentle touch.
- Do you recall being difficult, unruly, hard to manage, doing poorly in school, and/or having trouble paying attention and focusing? You might have had undiagnosed Attention Deficit Disorder (ADD). This can lead to a lifelong problem with impatience and irritability that may now be interfering with your capacity to be patient with your own child. There is also growing evidence that this problem runs in families, and your child may be struggling with it as well.

Step 4. Break No-Win Discipline Habits:
Put a Halt to Short Fuse Tactics

- Count to ten. Slow down your reaction time. Try to give yourself a space between seeing what you want to correct in your child and reacting to the misbehavior. For more help in lessening your reactivity, learn relaxation techniques: breathing, meditation, yoga, deep-muscle relaxation. Teach these techniques to active children. It can give them the tools to become self-soothing, too. (See chapter 11.)
- Give up the one-word reprimands. Talk to your child in *complete sentences* even as you correct him. Learn the art of firm *and* kind: If your child is in jeopardy, react swiftly but not harshly. Use a full sentence and guidance as you intervene decisively yet gently: "I want you to be safe, so come down immediately. Let me show you how to climb down safely." (Make sure to pay special attention to chapter 8 on helping your child to develop self-discipline.)
- Join a parenting group or get "one on one" assistance from a counselor who specializes in family guidance. You need a good coach to help you become a better parent.
- If you think that your child may be suffering from ADD, ask the school how your child can be evaluated, since there is much that can be done to help. Bear in mind that while ADD is more common in boys, girls can be affected as well.

• Your impatience, if it is a result of undiagnosed ADD or any other underlying problem, like the very common problem of depressive irritability, can be treated by many different approaches: go to a mental health professional who specializes in this area. Medication and cognitive therapy are both useful in gaining more peace of mind, which will help get your child to mind you!

▶ **PYB Words of Wisdom:** *Raising your voice is not an effective tool for raising well-behaved kids; a quiet firm voice is. Lower your voice if you want to be heard.*

Are You an Erratic Erupter?

Step 1. Identification: How Does Anger Go Wrong for an Erratic Erupter?

Does your child get to you but not all the time? Do you react intensely but unpredictably to misbehavior? Are there times when misbehavior goes unnoticed and other times when a similar misdeed puts you into frenzy? Do you lose your temper erratically? When your alarms do go off, perhaps you sound like this:

> "You will be the death of me."
> "No, this can't be happening."
> "I'm losing my mind."

An unlucky parent caught in this pattern hardly knows what is happening to her. She can feel calm in the face of a child's behavior one day and the next go-round find herself flying off the handle for nearly identical conduct. With this style, it is a parent's frame of mind or mood that determines her discipline; if she is relaxed and/or happy, there will be infinite understanding and little punishment, but if she is tense and/or depressed, there will be abundant fury and penalties for misdeeds.

When feeling cheerful, this parent may see a failed spelling quiz as inconsequential, yet, when feeling less buoyant, a below-par grade may seem like an academic disaster. It may prompt distress calls to teachers, tutors, and even the principal. It may also prompt a screaming match with a child who, this mood-driven parent now suddenly insists, must shut himself in his room all night and study, study, study! This mercurial parent may be a child's best friend and coconspirator one moment ("Oh, don't worry about your homework, I'll write you a note") and the enforcer the next ("You didn't finish your homework, so I'm taking away your computer for a week").

This inconsistent discipline style backfires badly, making children unruly and, in time, rebellious. A random discipline pattern confuses kids. They never know what to expect, and they do *not* get needed parental feedback or consistent follow-through that can help them gauge their behavior. Our poor speller, for example, is not continually encouraged to study, only sporadically forced to work when there is a perceived crisis. When the crisis ends, so does the studying. This adds to a child's confusion: Just how am I supposed to behave? Which face of my parent—the smile or scowl—is the real thing?

With older children, the volatility of this Erratic Erupter style makes them feel treated unfairly, and they rebel against it. With time, children also tend to discount this parent, reacting with a here-we-go-again indifference, turning a deaf ear to rants and raves. Worst of all, this style fosters avoidance. Kids want to stay away from home, because they never know when they will "get it." They are children who don't confide in a parent, keep secrets, and hide information, especially when things go wrong, because they cannot take the chance of revealing themselves for fear of setting off an Erratic Erupter. An erratic erupter may be an understanding confidant when in a good mood only to throw it back in a child's face when his mood changes. This isolation and estrangement sets the stage for battles galore, which get worse as a child gets older.

Step 2. Key Insights: Why Does It Go Wrong for an Erratic Erupter?

- Erratic Erupters look very angry, but, it may surprise you to know, they are actually very frightened. The way they try to manage the panic and anxiety they feel is to keep from noticing what is going on. Finally, when they do see something wrong, panic takes over. They are then flooded with fear, which spills out as angry agitation.
- Parents like this are often struggling with mood problems, even depression. On a good day, they have a "good child," while on a down

day everything their child does seems as dark and ominous as they feel. It is their mood fluctuations that make them appear "two-faced" and confusing. These shifting moods are responsible for preventing consistency, reliability, and follow-through.

- Frequently Erratic Erupters carry on their shoulders a load of responsibility that feels overwhelming: They may be single or divorced, the only breadwinner or able-bodied parent. They may be the nonaddicted or nonabusive parent. If they are preoccupied with carrying great burdens, it may be difficult for them to tune into their children. Then, when they do so intermittently, and see something awry, it pushes them over the edge and they erupt. They always feel on the edge of losing control over their life and their children.

Step 3. Reflections: How Did I Come to Adopt the Erratic Erupter Style?

- Did you have a home with a great deal of uncertainty, or beset by catastrophes and calamities, which made you feel fearful, unsafe, and unprotected? There are reasons why a child can grow into a frightened adult. Perhaps these created an underlying anxiety, or even terror, that now interferes with your parenting and causes your eruptions.
- Is there a history of mood instability or depression, perhaps postpartum depression in your family? Were you unhappy, sad, moody, or melancholy, even as a child? If you struggle with an unstable mood while parenting, it is quite likely you've grappled with this problem in your past. Without your realizing it, this dark cloud may have followed you into your own current family, accounting for your unpredictable discipline style. If you had a postpartum depression, this is an indicator that your mood tends toward instability.
- Was there a lot of drama in your home? Did people react intensely? Was your mother the hysterical type or your father given to black moods or rages, perhaps fueled by alcohol or drugs? If you grew up in a home where feelings were frequently running high and wild, this emotional roller coaster unintentionally becomes the model for your discipline approach.

Step 4. Break No-Win Discipline Habits: Putting a Halt to Erratic Erupter Tactics

- Find a support group to help you with whatever is creating undue stress. Groups exist for everything that burdens you (e.g., Al-Anon for family members of alcoholics; Parents Without Partners for single parents). Nothing takes the weight off parenting shoulders more effectively than a group of fellow travelers, especially if you are pulling the parenting load on your own.
- In a calm moment, look at the things in the life of your child that you reacted to strongly over the past week. Rate each event from one to ten, with ten indicating "life-threatening" crisis. Did anything actually rate a top score? It is unlikely. Try to use this perspective next time you have the urge to erupt.
- Find a quiet time with your child, during which both of you have the opportunity to get to know each other without stress. Reading together at bedtime creates this very good space for the two of you. Even a small increase in this calm quality time can eliminate loads of parent/child tension. (Reread chapter 3 for more details on establishing these routines and rituals.)
- You do not have to be a victim of your mood, dragging yourself and your kids along for the bumpy ride. Talk to a professional about how to get greater mood stability. Medication, exercise, and talk therapy can help. Cognitive therapy and a new form of treatment, Interpersonal Psychotherapy (ITP), are short-term talking treatments proven highly effective in regulating mood. The same is true for the panic that besets you. Help is nearby. Go for it!

> ▶ **PYB Words of Wisdom:** *Problems with mood regulation in parents and/or children can play a huge role in no-win discipline patterns. Fight the real enemy—depressive irritability—and you will have far fewer discipline battles on the home front.*

Are You a Fault Finder?

Step 1. Identification: How Does Anger Go Wrong for a Fault Finder?

Are you exasperated by your child who doesn't listen when all you tell him is just for his own good? Do you keep an eye out for his bad behavior and spot naughtiness, mischief, and sometimes, sadly, wickedness in him? When things go wrong, do you suspect that your child is often to blame or the culprit? Do you worry that your child is bad, a troublemaker, devilish?

> "I tell you this for your own good, but you don't listen to a thing I say."
> "What have you done now?"
> "It's just as I suspected."
> "Everything I say goes in one ear and out the other."
> "I can't let you out of my sight for a minute before you get into trouble."

A parent in the grip of this cycle has the best of intentions, but *execution* is the problem. She is deeply concerned about the welfare of her child and wants to make sure nothing goes awry. However, with this style, control *and* vigilance are excessive. A Fault Finder is always telling her child how to do things right, while having her antennae up at all times looking for the possibility that her child is doing wrong. With such hypervigilance, a parent *is* bound to see something wrong (look hard enough and long enough at anyone, and you are sure to find fault), which, of course, stirs up conflict.

Suspecting the worst about a child's behavior, this parent doubts a child's moves, motives, or explanations and finds it hard to take a child at his word. Always needing to know what is going on, this parent peppers a child with questions and, in her zeal, may even breach privacy in the interests of keeping her child out of harm's way. Earnestly protective, she often asks questions for which she already knows the answers or might even try to trip up a child's explanations for his misbehavior in order to get to the "truth"—for his own good.

Single-minded determination to raise a good, obedient child backfires entirely in this pattern. It creates a cycle of distrust. Always feeling under a microscope, the child of a Fault Finder does not feel relaxed in the presence of his parents; his guard goes up. Guardedness arouses parental suspicion, mom and dad assume it is a sign that their child must be doing something wrong, and they go after him. Unable to recognize that their suspiciousness, not their child, is the problem, parents react: "I can tell just by looking at you that something is going on." Feeling angry at unfounded accusation, a child lashes out, tempers flare, and battles ensue.

A Fault Finder's child may also stop trying to be good, concluding, "I get into trouble no matter what I do, so what's the use of being a good kid?" Seeing his overprotective parents as hypercritical, this child may become a self-protective liar. Because a Fault Finder parent gets so angry so often at a misdeed, real or suspected, a child may think there is no way to recover from a mistake. As a result, he may learn to lie and claim he didn't do it. Once detected, the lies ironically become further proof that a child is losing his way, which scares these parents, raising their blood pressure and family tensions.

Parents trapped in this style convey the message that they are always right while their child is always falling short of the mark. One of the most serious outcomes of this is that a child may not only grow up to resent his parents' "always knowing better" but also come to believe that he is bad. This negative self-image can start early (even a toddler can begin to feel like a bad little boy or girl) and last a lifetime, causing more battles than you would ever want to imagine.

> ▶ **PYB Words of Wisdom:** *Believing the worst about your child sadly makes them believe the worst about themselves, and they act accordingly, fulfilling your own worst fears.*

Step 2. Key Insights: Why Does It Go Wrong for a Fault Finder?

• A Fault Finder is an emotional pessimist who sees the world through dark glasses. Though loving the child very much, someone with this burden cannot have a sunny parental disposition toward his child. Hidden in her heart are darker feelings of tension, suspicion, and distrust, which cloud family life.

- Parents with this style may suffer from an imagination that runs wild; it is as if they see their worst nightmares about kids going wrong run through their heads nonstop. Uncontrolled bad thoughts are the hidden reason why a Fault Finder parent thinks the worst of his child, must always know what is going on, and then gets agitated and angry if he detects that something is amiss.

- These parents may believe the world to be an unsafe place full of bad influences. Certain that danger lurks, they live on high alert, which makes them vigilant and hyper about their kids. They are in a fearful, tense panic, but, to the child, they seem to be always worriedly scrutinizing. He sees them as punitive and always on his case!

- A Fault Finder parent may not know it, but she is hyperresponsible and overprotective. She unconsciously believes that a child's survival, emotional and physical, is entirely up to her. If she lets down her parenting guard, even for a moment, all is lost. This is her hidden burden. She appears cross when actually she strains under the weight of responsibility overload.

Step 3. Reflections: How Did I Come to Adopt the Fault Finder Style?

- Were you overexposed to or flooded by traumatic, frightening experiences, information and/or images during your childhood? Flooding a child too early with fearful experiences, images, ideas, and information can have damaging and lasting impact. Too much horror too early can traumatize a child, leaving an indelible impression that the world is a scary place, which may be a way the Fault Finder style gained power over your parenting life.

- Were you raised to believe that the world was a scary, devilish, sinful, or immoral place? If you grew up to believe the world was bad and wicked, it may still be your worldview and, unwittingly, your view of your own child.

- Were you very sheltered or overprotected and/or isolated from outsiders? Did your parents urge you to be very careful and cautious? These actions can send a subtle but powerful message: Inside our home, it is safe; outside, it is not. Perhaps this is the origin of your supercautious parenting approach.

- Were there any very bad, shameful, or secret things that went on in your childhood? Did anything happen in your childhood for which you felt great guilt, such as sexual abuse? Fault Finders often have heavy hearts and *guilty consciences*. They may even hate themselves for some past and early shame. These terrible memories are hard to forget. A Fault Finder may unwittingly worry that her own child might fall prey to the same evil she experienced. As a parent, she keeps a vigilant watch to prevent that.

Step 4. Break No-Win Discipline Habits: Put a Halt to Fault Finder Tactics

- Catch your child at being good. Make a vow to react to one success a day with as much energy as you do to your child's shortcomings.
- Protect yourself. You may have an overactive frightening imagination. Do not stimulate it. Cut down on scary information overload. Do not watch the late news, skip horror movies, and ditch the tabloids. Less is more: Less negative input means more inner peace with your child.
- Work on having good thoughts. Yes, you can actually train your mind to think more positively. Cognitive therapists are specialists at this. Tapes training you to develop positive imaging can help, too.
- When you think a negative thought about your child, reframe it. For example, if your toddler pulls at your hair, and you suddenly think, "He is showing a mean streak," stop that negative thought. Replace it with a reframed positive thought: "My curious toddler is trying to discover if my hair really belongs on my head." (Review chapter 1 for help.)
- Trust your child. Know that *all* children want to be good and do good, and, with your positive support and encouragement, your child will find the right path.
- If there is some painful, secret shame or torturous guilt that you carry, get help taking that dark burden off your conscience. Talk to a religious or spiritual advisor or a mental health professional. Let the truth come out. Sunlight is best disinfectant. If you feel cleansed of the bad feelings you harbor about yourself you will *detect* more good in your child.

Are You a Denier?

Step 1. Identification: How Does Anger Go Wrong for a Denier?

The Denier, the last of the no-win discipline styles, is in a class by himself. In this pattern of responding to misbehavior, anger is not mismanaged, it is more apt to say that it does a disappearing act. While in the first seven styles anger rears its not so attractive head and is handled less than effectively, the heart of this final pattern is that anger is denied, suppressed, buried, swallowed—in short, eliminated—which makes it impossible for any parent to be effective at handling misbehavior. Many parents unwittingly employ this self-defeating pattern and do so in a remarkably *wide* variety of ways.

> ▶ **PYB Word of Wisdom:** *Deniers rarely feel or display anger toward a child when he misbehaves. Beware of hidden or invisible anger. When anger goes missing from your parenting, appropriate discipline vanishes as well.*

Instead of blowing a fuse when your children misbehave, do you unwittingly eliminate anger? Do you avoid confrontation and conflict, and feel relieved? There are nine different ways that Deniers can unintentionally make anger disappear: Deniers banish anger and, therefore, inadvertently sabotage meaningful discipline by *excusing, rescuing, giving up, complying, forgiving, bribing, negotiating, displacing, blaming,* and *ignoring.* Bear in mind that a denier may use one or many of these conflict-avoiders.

Excusing
Do you make it a habit of *making excuses,* explaining away, justifying, and/or defending your child's mistakes so that she doesn't run into trouble or make a fuss? Do you avert discord by automatically validating your child's misbehavior to reduce friction, sometimes bending the truth or even sounding ludicrous so there won't be a to-do?

"You're just tired, that's why you are acting so rudely."
"You weren't being a bad boy, you just pushed that girl because she wasn't being nice to you."

"I'm not angry, because you couldn't have realized that the new
   video game you bought was so expensive when you ordered it
   online."
"It's OK that you took the money for yourself; it was just lying
   around on the table."

EXCUSE ABUSE

Here are some excuse notes reportedly received by school secretaries from parents:

"Please excuse Laura from being absent yesterday. She was sick
   and I had her shot."
"Please excuse Lynn for being absent Jan. 28, 29, 30, 31, 32, and 33."
"My son is under the doctors care and should not take P.E. Please
   execute him."
"Irving was absent this morning because he missed his bust."
"Please excuse Rochelle for being. It was her father's fault."

These are laughable, but when it comes to raising cooperative children, endlessly excusing behavior may end up being no laughing matter.

Rescuing

Do you get *actively* involved and intervene when your child misbehaves? Do you come to your children's *rescue* by fixing things up, patching things over, or bailing them out, covering for them? Are you adept at making trouble go away by cleaning up after your child's misdeeds? (Rescuing is a close cousin to excusing, and, if you are a denier, you probably do both.)

"Don't cry over the broken crayons. Daddy will go right out and
   buy you a new big box for yourself."
"You don't have to share your toy. I'll get another for your
   brother."
"I know you didn't have a chance to study, so you don't have to go
   to school and take the test today."

"I'll pay for those jeans you bought on eBay, so you won't get a
    bad feedback rating."

Giving up

Perhaps you sound like the harassed Denier who defuses conflict by *giving up*. If your kids act up, do you throw in the towel and implode rather than ever explode? Perhaps making yourself sick or sad rather than angry or mad?

"I have a headache from all of this, just leave me in peace."
"Your behavior upsets me too much; I'm going to lie down."

Complying

Are you too nice and *complaint,* a pushover, or a softy who never gets mad? Do you automatically say "Yes" and rarely stand your ground by saying "No"?

"You're the boss."
"Sure sweetie, it's up to you."
"I don't care, whatever makes you happy."

Forgiving

Are your battles rare because you all too rapidly *forgive,* and forget even more quickly, perhaps too quickly? Do you bend over backwards to take an apology without expecting any remedy from your child? Do you offer the apology before it is even extended by your child and, through this, avoid conflict and confrontation?

"I know you didn't mean to do it."
"Don't worry, I accept your apology."
"It's not so bad that you broke my computer. I really needed a
    new laptop anyway."

Bribing

Is *bribery* the tactic you routinely employ to steer clear of hostilities and keep the peace? Do you regularly offer your child inducements, to buy your way out of battling? Do you exchange goods for good behavior and family peace?

"Stay with the baby-sitter tonight, and I'll bring you a present."
"You can have a dollar for every chapter you read."
"Eat your broccoli and you can have ice cream for dessert."

Negotiating

Do you use *negotiation* to appease your child and prevent warfare, bargaining your way out of anger and conflict? Are your expectations of your child always ready for revision? Do battles evaporate because you always do the compromising?

"All right, just one more story before bed."
"Five more minutes on the (phone, computer), and then you
    come to the table."
"I'll let you buy sneakers if you promise to study for the test."

Displacing Blame

Might you unwittingly fall into the habit of *displacing blame* for misbehavior from your child onto someone or something else? Do you often fault others in order to deflect anger and avoid a melee with your own child?

"I'm not angry that you can't finish your homework. It's your
    coach's fault for making practice so long."
"If Charlotte didn't grab your toy, I know you wouldn't have hit
    her. That Charlotte is a bad influence."
"That teacher of yours has some nerve giving you such a bad
    grade."

Ignoring

Sometimes a stressed out Denier can fall into the trap of habitually *ignoring* misbehavior as a way to unwittingly avoid conflict. Loving parents who somehow miss the cues, clues, or hints that something is going awry, do not spot the skirmish in the sandbox over sharing a toy, for example. Theirs is the parenting error of omission. They do not witness the fight between two brothers over who is watching what TV program. They aren't aware of the homework that is not completed or the teeth that are not brushed before bedtime. Are you a parent who puts on blinders or even shuts down in order to get a reprieve from arguing, fighting, or quarreling with your child? How do you sound if you are a Denier who makes anger vanish? *Silent!*

All deniers are conflict avoiders. Discipline can feel too much for some beleaguered parents to handle, so they back away from battling kids. While I am very keen on helping you pick your battles with kids in order to reduce conflict, this is *not* the wise way to do it. Choosing your battles is *not* the same as running away from them, any more than surrender is the same as victory. Yes, of course, steering clear of confrontation makes life with a child more peaceful in the short run. (After all, surrender *does* end the war.) It can be a quick fix for battle weary moms and dads.

When we are trying to keep our heads above water as parents, this conflict-dodging style does the trick. It gets us off the hook and kids off our backs. It offers relief. Buying time without a hassle or headache from our children is very tempting, especially these days, when hardworking parents feel frazzled—and that's on a good day. The only problem is that the price you pay, especially if it is overused, is always high. Remember, *peace at any cost is costly!* Kids become more difficult, not less so. The more you shy away from taking on the management of discipline in your offspring, the higher maintenance they become. Try to keep this in mind, because it is hard to give up a bad habit when it offers relief, and this style of short-circuiting anger certainly does just that. Pay close attention, because *many* well-meaning parents fall into this last, all too common discipline trap. Why wouldn't we?

The need to bypass conflict is one all parents routinely have. There are times when these tactics are useful and necessary. A new toy "if you're good" for your squirmy preschooler makes the Christmas-card photo shoot memorable rather than ghastly. "Five more minutes until bedtime" when you are on an important long distance call gives you the breathing room you need without doing discipline damage. An occasional ice cream bribe or a personal day off from grade school is not going to be anyone's undoing. The latter might even become a day for special bonding with your soon-to-be teen.

If you periodically *decide* to use these tactics, that is fine. Becoming a slave to these responses and carrying them out automatically is what creates trouble, not your occasional choosing to use them. Making these avoidance reactions habitual deprives your child of the basic building blocks of good behavior, because your well-meaning but misguided tactics send a child the following destructive messages:

Excusing: My behavior is always justified, reasonable, and/or acceptable, and, therefore, I do not have to change or suffer consequences. I owe no one an apology. It is all right to bend the truth or even lie to get what I want.

Rescuing: I can get away with anything. I bear no responsibility for my misdeeds. My misbehavior *never* affects me adversely. I do not have what it takes to make things right on my own.

Giving up: I don't have to worry about my actions, because I can make people back down. I have the power to dispose of authority.

Complying: No one else's feelings count but mine. I am in charge.

Forgiving: I can do wrong without having to right my wrongs.

Bribing: I only have to do good if I get something out of it. I can be bought. I can manipulate people to get what I want.

Negotiating: I never have to be frustrated or disappointed. I never have to tolerate hearing the word "No." I can make people do what I want.

Displacing blame: I can do no wrong. Everyone else and/or everything else are the problem, not my behavior and not me. I am helpless to do right, because my mistakes are not my own.

Ignoring: I can do just as I please. No one cares how I behave. I am unwatched, neglected, and abandoned.

These nine outcomes are strong indications that habitually avoiding battles for all the wrong reasons is a recipe for discipline disaster.

Step 2. Key Insights: Why Does It Go Wrong for a Denier?

- Unbeknownst to them, Deniers are often disturbed and even frightened by anger and frustration. They avoid angering their children, fearing they will stop liking or loving them, perhaps cut off communication, all of which feels too risky, so they dare not discipline their kids.
- Deniers often have the misguided idea that they are protecting their children. They can't stand to see their kids unhappy or suffer, and mistakenly see bearing consequences as suffering. Deniers don't see anger and conflict as a way to inform their children of wrongdoing and guide them to better behavior; they see it as hurtful and/or destructive.

- Some deniers have a longing to be admired nonstop by their kids, making it impossible for them ever to be the "bad guy."
- Deniers may have a hidden terror of their own anger, imagining that if they got angry with a child, they could lose control and perhaps even be violent. To avoid that possibility, they do not let themselves get anywhere near such feelings.

Step 3. Reflections: How Did I Come to Adopt the Denier Style?

- Did you hate your parents? Were they demanding, tyrannical, rigid parents, icy, mean, and/or ungenerous? Did you suffer because of burdensome chores, strict rules, harsh discipline, punishment, and/or abuse? If you were subject to a very controlling upbringing, you may be more inclined to back away from conflict; it brings back too many unbearable memories. A childhood under the thumb of strict parents may make you too gun-shy to battle with your own children. Enforcing discipline might feel as if you are becoming like your mean and hated parents, so you react by going in the opposite direction—leniency or even permissiveness. Because of your painful past, you overidentify with your child and must be a beloved parent no matter what.
- Was your first family full of rage, wrath, and retaliation? Was there arguing and even physical fighting? If you lived in a first family overstressed by anger, you may have grown into an adult ill equipped to handle turmoil in your life, and may do anything not to "go back" to those days even now. With this as a model, you may believe all anger is out-of-control anger, and avoid going close to the "edge" at all times, even when your child misbehaves.
- Were you the "black sheep" in the family, the one singled out for angry negative attention? Did parents or siblings pick on you? Were you ostracized, teased, or left out as a child? Did you feel ugly, stupid, or feel painfully different? Did you cry over these childhood pains? Families often handle anger by splitting it off and directing it at one child in particular. If you felt singled out in this way, always the brunt of family frustration and disappointment, you may be loath to have your child experience anything that reminds you of those bad times. Perhaps, as an adult, you are unwittingly trying to "protect" your child in ways that no one ever protected you in your first family. "I do not want my child

to suffer the way I suffered" may be the hidden motivation behind eliminating confrontation. Deniers who recall a childhood of sadness, suffering, and hardship can't bear to make their children feel any unhappiness.

Step 4. Break No-Win Discipline Habits: Put a Halt to Denier Tactics

• Confrontation, when handled well, is a moment of growth for your child. Give your child the benefit of learning to tolerate disappointment and frustration, discovering that actions have consequences, that others have feelings, too, and that mistakes need to be redressed. The importance of being a loving source of frustration to your child starts when she is an infant, and if you yourself have had harsh parenting, it is not something with which you may have much experience. (Go back and review the importance of frustration in chapter 1.)

REFLECTIONS: DID YOU SUFFER FROM PARENTAL RAGE? THE DAMAGE OF TOXIC ANGER

A Denier frequently has had a harsh upbringing. Marly recalls her mother's wicked temper: "She expected perfection. I can remember the dinner table, when she saw my brother's elbows on the table, without warning, she slammed his arms out from under him and, in her fury, sent a milk container hurtling across the kitchen. I lived in perpetual terror and spent my childhood trying to go unnoticed." Charlene has vivid and unpleasant memories, as well. "My mother was a slave driver. I think that she resented being a mother so much that she made my sisters and me into scullery maids, like Cinderella—except she wasn't the wicked stepmother, she was our mother! I remember my father constantly saying, 'But they're only *children*.' The only problem was that he never did anything to stop her."

If your own childhood was contaminated by toxic anger—rage—it can be very difficult for you to normalize your anger and use it appropriately in your own parenting.

• Anger, when put into measured words, is a gift in that it can be a source of information to allow your child to discover when he has bumped up against someone else in the world. Knowing how to use anger appropriately and how to properly respond to it are essential. Unfortunately, conflict avoidance does not advance this cause. Anger is a tool for navigating the world and finding a peaceful place in it. Managing anger productively is what your child and the whole world needs. Who better to present it to them than a loving parent? Learning how to make this possible is the heart of much of what follows. Pay close attention, since you may believe that all anger is the toxic anger of uncontrolled rage. (You will find out otherwise chapter 9.)

• Practice being constructively angry in small steps. Make a point of saying "No" to one of your child's demanding moments today. Do *not* bail him out of the next misbehavior. Watch what happens over the long run. Initially, he will get angry about being frustrated, but you will discover that your child will still love you, even if he hates what you are asking of him.

> ▶ **PYB Words of Wisdom:** *If, when you are fairly disciplining your child, he says he hates you, it's the frustration he can't stand, not you. Take heart: There is love after anger. In fact, children love you more, not less, when you respond with concern and attention to misbehavior. It is a sign that you love them.*

MIXED MARRIAGE

If you are fuming "My spouse lets the kids get away with murder," you are probably married to a Denier. If you are muttering "My spouse is so darn hard on the kids," you may well be the Denier. Couples in a mixed marriage like this often fight furiously about child rearing issues. Eliminate this no-win discipline style, and you will have better behaved kids *and* a more peaceful marriage.

Part II

*Surviving Hassles
and Headaches: Strategies
and Tactics*

Chapter 5

Rules of Engagement:
Setting Limits

Where Do You Draw the Lines?

Here is a multiple-choice quiz that no parent in his right mind could possibly fail. The scene is a suburban kitchen. A mother comes upon a four-year-old playing with a ten-inch kitchen knife. Which is the appropriate response?

1. Not wanting to upset her little dumpling, she says, "Sure sweetheart, just keep playing Kung Fu Fighter with my brand-new set of all-purpose Ginsu carving knives while I stand by the phone in the event that you need somebody with all their fingers to dial 911."
2. Seeing a disaster in the making, mother confidently strides toward her preschooler, firmly wrests the knife from his grip, and calmly says—even in the face of a full-throttle Kung Fu Warrior protest, "These knives are dangerous. You may not play with them under any circumstances; knives are not toys."

No parent in her sound mind would do anything other than take the knife away from her child—fast. This absurd example overstates the obvious: Kids need limits, and responsible parents set *and* enforce them. For your child's well-being, you must draw a line and take action if and when it has been crossed, even if it means clashing with him. Yes, there are battles worth waging, and the safety of a young Kung Fu Warrior is one of them.

While it is evident that playing with carving knives is one of those nonnegotiable moments, many times setting limits and taking a stand is just as necessary if not nearly as obvious. How do you know when you must pick a battle? Establishing boundaries by setting behavioral expectations for children is always a challenge. Seeing how several experienced parents have arrived at their various "rules of thumb" for setting limits can be a helpful start.

Practical Pointers on How and Where to Draw the Line

After four kids, Molly knows where her lines are drawn.

"When it comes to picking battles, my shorthand is: the good, the bad, and the ugly. In my mind, I think of my children's behaviors falling into those three possible categories:

- the good = cooperative behavior
- the bad = uncooperative behavior
- the ugly = risky or harmful behavior

"I try my best not to let everything turn into a showdown. However, I do not let anything that falls into the 'ugly' category get past me if I can help it. Just the other morning, my nine-year-old daughter Nancy was haranguing me about letting her walk to school alone. I told her that it is too dangerous for an adult, let alone a kid, and I wouldn't give her the nod.

"If Nancy were to turn verbally abusive, I wouldn't let it slide any more than I would her physical safety. Nasty words are hurtful and ugly in my book, so I take a stand against them."

Joanne, mother of seven-year-old Eden, has her method for sorting out the "Big Deals," as she calls them.

"To decide what is over the top, I ask myself one simple question: *What will this mean for her at thirty?* It helps me to put things in perspective and decide if it really is a 'Big Deal.'

"When Eden started first grade, she got into a 'favorite shirt thing.' Hard as I tried, I could not peel this red turtleneck off her back. I stopped fighting. I took the long view and told myself: 'It's no *big deal*—I am sure at thirty she will not be wearing the same shirt!'

"On the other hand, I absolutely insist, even under protest, that Eden sits in the back seat of the car and stays buckled in—no exceptions. As far as I'm concerned, buckling up means she will be alive. If the answer to my question ever includes dead, maimed, or jailed, I will battle to the finish. This is what I think of as the *good fight*, because it is for my child's own good. I want my daughter in one piece when she is thirty."

Marian, an easygoing, self-described pushover of a mom, uses her well-developed sense of humor to help her make discipline decisions. Like Joanne, she applies the long-range view.

"In my head, I'm always having conversations with myself about my kids' behavior, to try and keep a perspective. When I get annoyed at my son's thumb-sucking, I say, 'No one walks down the wedding aisle with his thumb in his mouth.' When my daughter went through a cheese-only phase, I reminded myself that my kid won't starve to death. I try to consider *the real consequences* of my kids actions, not just squabble over the things that annoy me."

Mike, a direct, no-nonsense father of two college-age boys, has a simple rule of thumb for selecting the worthy fight. "When the boys were growing up, we gave them plenty of rope, but if it looked like they were going to hang themselves, we put our foot down. There are certain lines we didn't let them cross, and if they did, they heard from us loud and clear."

PRACTICAL TIPS FOR SETTING LIMITS ON BEHAVIOR

- Is it good, bad, or ugly?
- What will it mean when she is thirty?
- If it's a *big deal*, fight the *good fight*.
- Is it just annoying, or does it have *real* consequences?

The Right Reasons and the Wrong Reasons
for Setting Limits

When instituted for the right reasons, limits and discipline are the ways parents protect and guide children so that they stay safe and acquire the fundamentals of how to get on and get along in this world. However, sometimes limit-setting has little or nothing to do with child guidance and much more to do with control, compliance, or even manipulation; limits can become a way of getting a child to do what you want just because you want it. When they serve this ill-advised purpose, they are of little value, or, in the extreme, create a good deal of strife.

> ▶ **PYB Words of Wisdom:** *Limits are behavioral expec-*
> *tations or standards of conduct that you require of your*
> *children to ensure their safety and well-being. Discipline*
> *is your response, to correct and guide your child's behav-*
> *ior when these limits have been breached. Even as kids*
> *chafe at limits and discipline, they crave both. Your atten-*
> *tion to their welfare is extremely reassuring; a child feels*
> *loved, protected, embraced, and cared for.*

Four Good Parenting Reasons
for Setting Limits

To help you get a better grasp on precisely how to set limits that work, let me give you my idea of the four good reasons for setting them in the first place. While there is some overlap, having these categories in your head will make it far easier for you to set appropriate limits and decide how vigorously you must enforce them. Here are the four good parenting reasons for setting limits:

1. Safety
2. Values
3. Civility
4. Routines and Responsibility

Safety: Limits to Assure Well-Being

Limits are a way of keeping children safe by making sure that they do not hurt themselves, others, or property. Just think about these safety-limit statements.

  You must:

- not play with matches
- hold my hand when you cross the street
- pet your dog gently
- sit in the car seat
- not hit

Safety-based limits keep your child secure in this world and make your child a person who, in turn, will take care to keep his world a safe place. *Ignoring or condoning the breaching of safety limits may give rise to destructive or even dangerous behavior.*

Values: Limits to Assure Good Character

Setting boundaries is a way to see that your child develops moral values and personal integrity, so that he grows up as a person of a sound character. Consider these values-based limits:

- Tell the truth.
- You must pay for what you take.
- Copying your friend's math problems on the test, or homework, is cheating, and that is unacceptable because it is dishonest.
- Do not call your brother or anyone else nasty names; that is hurtful.
- Take whatever you found of value to the lost-and-found; you cannot keep anything that is not yours.

Limit-setting grounded in the transmission of values is essential for guiding your child so that he develops into a moral, ethical, and responsible person. *Ignoring or condoning the breaching of values-based limits may give rise to deficiencies in character, immoral, or indecent behavior.*

Civility: Limits to Assure Interpersonal Skills

Instituting civility limits—expecting your child to respect the feelings, rights, needs, property, and/or personal space of others—are ways to set in place your child's capacity to get along with other people, to become adept at interpersonal relations, and, therefore, to grow as a well-adjusted member of society. Here are examples of boundaries that endorse civility:

- You must share the candy with your brother.
- Wait and take your turn.
- Grabbing is not acceptable; ask to borrow the toy.
- Say "Excuse me," if you are trying to get my attention.
- Thank Grandma for the gift.

Limits in this category are the building blocks of *all* personal and social relations. They help them develop such skills as cooperation, patience, and collaboration, essential for getting along in groups. *Everything* in life, from love to work, requires these essential interpersonal skills. *Permissiveness in breaching of civility limits may give rise to disrespect or disregard for others.*

PLEASE, MAY I, THANK YOU
TEACHING KIDS TO CONSIDER OTHERS

Asking kids to practice politeness, courtesy, and good manners are effective ways to teach them to acknowledge others. They can be good daily reminders that life is a two-way street and that everyone deserves respect. Don't underestimate the value of teaching a child consideration, which is a basic for getting along with others. Just be certain that this is your motive, so you don't mistakenly demand good manners as a way to control your child's behavior.

▶ **PYB Words of Wisdom:** *Civility lays the cornerstone for the recognition that others matter, that others assist us in our lives, and that we are all inter-dependent. From this recognition grows a human being's capacity for apprecia-*

tion and gratitude, which makes for a child that you will appreciate and be grateful to call your own. Kids capable of gratitude are by definition, good kids.

Routines and Responsibility: Limits to Assure Life Skills

Life needs to move along in a reasonably orderly fashion, otherwise nothing much would get accomplished in a family, or the world at large, for that matter. Also children must learn to take charge of their lives, to pull their own weight. In other words, children need routines and responsibility to grow into productive human beings. Here are limit-setting statements that can serve to promote orderliness, regularity, and responsibility in your offspring:

- You must wash up, brush your teeth, and go to bed by nine o'clock.
- Do your homework before you watch TV.
- You can have a play date for an hour on school nights but not on a night before you have a test or a book report.
- Set the table before dinner, then help clear the table.
- The dog is your responsibility; you must feed and walk her.

Limits that fall into the arena of enforcing routines and responsibilities are a way to ensure that your child learns to be accountable, productive, and in charge, as well as to make life move along. These are critical life skills.

Requiring kids to fulfill these obligations is also vital for your well-being, because you, the parent, are entitled to expect that the group you are in charge of, your family, will run with some degree of regularity and orderliness. It is fair to expect that school buses are boarded and meals eaten in a timely way, and that you get assistance from your children in taking care of family needs, as soon as they are able to give it. These limits make the life of your family more manageable, and that is another very good reason for setting them in place!

Permitting children to breach routine and responsibility limits can make life disorderly and even chaotic, or give rise to disruptive, undependable, or irresponsible behavior.

▶ **PYB Words of Wisdom:** *The clearer you are with your children about what it is they are required to do in order to be members in good standing of your family, the less you will battle over these issues.*

TESTING YOUR LIMITS

Four Key Questions to Determine If You Are Setting Good Limits

To assess whether or not you are setting limits for *all the right reasons*, ask yourself these four questions
Does a limit that I establish:

1. Keep my child safe and teach her to safeguard herself and others as well as property?
2. Promote my child's character and develop her value system?
3. Encourage my child's interpersonal skills, her civility, respect, and consideration toward others?
4. Advance my child's development of life skills, her orderliness, and sense of personal responsibility, and/or make family life more manageable?

Limits You May Need to Limit

Personal Taste: Limits to Make Parents Feel Comfortable

Parents frequently set limits that have little to do with providing protection or guidance; rather they institute behavioral standards for kids, which suit their parental personality, temperament, and/or style. And families can have very different styles:

- private versus open
- religious versus secular
- serious versus playful
- conventional versus unconventional
- adventurous versus cautious
- formal versus informal

Because there are no two families that are alike, limits that reflect personal taste and style vary widely from family to family; anything from cleanliness to privacy may feel important, depending entirely on a family's personality. For example, parents who value neatness might establish behavioral expectations like these:

- Your toys are to go back in the colored bins on the shelf when you are through playing.
- Always take your shoes off before you come into the house.
- Don't eat food anywhere but the kitchen.

Parents who want formality might institute these rules:

- Take your elbows off the table.
- Don't start eating until everyone is served at the table.
- Don't call a grown up by his first name

Parents who feel comfortable with a particular style of dress may issue these directives:

- Put on a suit, not jeans, for Thanksgiving dinner.
- You can't wear that same shirt to school three days in a row.
- Get your hair cut short; you look sloppy.
- You can't wear that party dress to school.

Distinctive ideas about home, personal space, privacy, and/or family life may be reflected in these standards of conduct:

- Your friends need to play in the family room.
- You may not use the guest bathroom.
- Do not discuss family matters with anyone who is not your immediate family.

Remember that these behavioral expectations are really a matter of taste and style and what parents may have grown accustomed to and, therefore, prefer. They have less to do with child guidance and more to do with pleasing or displeasing you and making you comfortable in your own home-life. These are certainly things that you *can* ask of your children and hope they comply with, but they are *not* generally good reasons to pick a major battle or fight to the finish. Don't call them on the carpet if they:

- use the guest bathroom.
- put toys in the wrong colored bins
- play rock-and-roll music
- wear to school clothes that look unattractive or ridiculous to you

You can certainly encourage your child to emulate your preferences, but **never** insist that your children entirely conform to your personal expectations. Take the long view: After all, what will it mean when your child is thirty if she used the guest bathroom, put her toys in the wrong bin, or wore the same shirt repeatedly? If you are adamant that your child mirrors your taste and style, it will become an unending source of conflict.

> ▶ **PYB Words of Wisdom:** *Insisting on taste- or style-based limits is the single biggest area of unnecessary parental aggravation. If you are holding your own on the first four good parenting limits—safety, values, civility, routines, and responsibility—your child will not go haywire if you allow him room to make his own decisions about matters that are essentially decisions about personal preferences.*

Children need some room to be different from parents; give it to them. They need to be themselves. And here is the paradox and your payoff: If you give them that room—to be different from you in matters of personal preference—as they mature, your kids will come to feel that they *do* want to be quite a lot like you. Children emulate parents only if they have not had to constantly fight for room to be themselves.

> ▶ **PYB Words of Wisdom:** *If you allow a child room to be different, to express her own taste, you will probably be surprised to see that she will find her way back to many— not all, but many—of the things you would like her to appreciate. Lead by example, not by insistence.*

Control: Limits to Guarantee the Outcomes in a Child's Life

Sometimes parents feel that they are not just in charge of their child's welfare but always know exactly what is best and right. They want to control, not guide their child, so they may insist on all sorts of rules that they staunchly believe must be followed, leaving little room for a child's personality to take shape. Diet, friendship, clothing, school work, even extracurricular activities may all be areas in which parents feel obliged to dictate their precise expectations:

- You can only play with children who I think are suitable for you.
- I don't care about what's in style; I'll decide what's proper for my child to wear to school.
- You will take piano lessons, because it's better than dance class.
- Broccoli is good for you, so eat it *all* up before you leave the table.
- You can't go out looking like that, I won't have it; it's embarrassing to be seen with you.

Often parents who want control are not ill-willed or mean-spirited but have a misguided notion that they can guarantee the outcomes of their children's lives. They want the best for their children and believe that insistence is the way to make it happen. **This never works. Never!** Pushing piano lessons on a child who wants to be a ballerina rarely makes a happy virtuoso. Forcing children to eat their vegetables makes them have bad feelings toward broccoli *and* you. *Be careful not to exert control when what children need is guidance.*

> ▶ **PYB Words of Wisdom:** *Ask yourself, "Am I unwittingly imposing my taste or trying to control my child's life when I set down expectations or rules for my kids? If the answer is "yes," try to relax your grip. Regulate rather than police your child's conduct.*

Parental Comfort Zones:
Comfortable/Uncomfortable/Intolerable

I've given you four broad categories, safety, values, civility, routines and responsibilities to guide reasonable limit-setting. Within these, parents can make a wide variety of possible boundary decisions. Where does that bring you? Limits that you set are ultimately *your* decision. This is not one-size-fits-all discipline; there are no uniform rules of engagement. As this is not the case, picking your battles, especially the big ones, depends on determining which behaviors fall within *your* acceptable range and which go beyond *your own* limits of tolerance. For your own family, *you* will need to draw the lines and to decide which behaviors fall inside the *"comfortable"* range; which behaviors push the envelope to create a zone of *discomfort*; and which behaviors careen into the "red-hot" zone of *intolerable*. Using these categories as guidelines, parents pick battles according to what I call *parental comfort zones*. Since there is *no* exact or uniform parenting code for rules of engagement, every parent will make different choices. Not better, just different.

THAT DOESN'T MAKE ME COMFORTABLE

Your friend may be ready to send her fifth-grader off biking to the park for a summer afternoon with friends, while you are not quite there yet. All you need to remember when you make a decision about limits for *your* child is the phrase "That doesn't make me comfortable." Feel free to say this to other parents when you encounter differences, and elect to act within *your* comfort zone. Respect your right to make your own boundaries, and other parents will respect you for doing so, as will your kids.

If a situation arises where you feel extremely uncomfortable, say you have reason to believe a parent is routinely careless or thoughtless, reserve the right to limit your child's contact with that family or make a decision to have play dates only if you are there to supervise them. Let your child know that this is not just about "family differences" but about your commitment to keeping her safe, a concern that extends to every and anyplace she goes.

Establishing Your Own Parental Comfort Zones

Because limits and boundaries are crucial for discipline, I would like to give you additional advice on how to establish your own by using a rating scale that I have devised. I call my rating system **the *D* scale,** because you use it to evaluate your child's behavior as having a potential range from **Delightful** to **Dangerous.** You will see that this rating scale incorporates the limit categories and the risks of not enforcing these limits that I have described earlier.

On this ***D* scale** below, you can divide the entire range of behaviors into three comfort zones. Actions that feel acceptable fall into **Zone I.** Everyday lapses and behavioral mishaps that annoy you and make life difficult and generally come from a child's failures to carry on routines and responsibilities fall into **Zone II.** The most serious infractions—the conduct of your children that angers and alarms you and represents serious and intolerable limit violations, such as destructive and harmful actions—fall into **Zone III.**

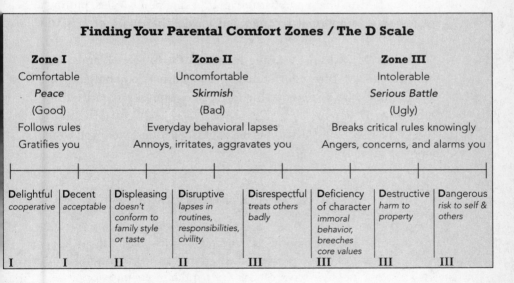

Finding Your Parental Comfort Zones / The D Scale

Zone I	Zone II	Zone III
Comfortable	Uncomfortable	Intolerable
Peace	*Skirmish*	*Serious Battle*
(Good)	(Bad)	(Ugly)
Follows rules	Everyday behavioral lapses	Breaks critical rules knowingly
Gratifies you	Annoys, irritates, aggravates you	Angers, concerns, and alarms you

Delightful	Decent	Displeasing	Disruptive	Disrespectful	Deficiency	Destructive	Dangerous
cooperative	*acceptable*	*doesn't conform to family style or taste*	*lapses in routines, responsibilities, civility*	*treats others badly*	*of character immoral behavior, breeches core values*	*harm to property*	*risk to self & others*
I	I	II	II	III	III	III	III

Practice Getting in the Zone

To see where you stand on setting boundaries, consider into which of the three zones (Comfortable, Uncomfortable, Intolerable) you might place the following behaviors, and, more specifically, where on the ***D* scale** these fall:

- will not wear a helmet when he rides a bike
- eats hamburgers, well-done, with peanut butter
- teases a child during a play date
- refuses to bathe and go to bed on time
- saves her allowance for the church offering
- doesn't clean his room
- hits other kids
- hurts the cat
- wants to wear her party dress to school.

Here is a rating of these behavioral breeches:

1. Not wearing helmets and hitting are *d*angerous and *d*estructive and fall into the *Intolerable, Zone III*, because they are unsafe and do harm. Hurting the cat seems to fall in this area as well.
2. Teasing is unkind and *d*isrespectful of others, so it is also a serious limit violation; *Zone III.*
3. Resisting bed and bath are *d*isruptive, breaking family rules, putting a wrench in an important routine, and making life more of a hassle; *Zone II.*
4. Not being "Mr. Clean," wearing a party dress to school, and eating food that might turn your stomach, like burned hamburgers with peanut butter, are *d*ispleasing but not serious offenses to go after full-force; *Zone II.*
5. And, of course, being charitable is *d*elightful and just what you would hope for; *Zone I.*

KEEP AN AGGRAVATION DIARY

During the next week, make a list of those things that provoke annoyance or anger or perhaps even alarm with your child. Then see where each of these gripes falls on the D scale. Doing this will give you a perspective on whether or not you are reacting appropriately to your child's misbehavior and how seriously you are or are not taking limit-setting and discipline. Evaluate your reactions: Are you under- or overreacting? For example, are you angry over matters of taste when you should really reserve that reaction for more serious and dangerous misconduct?

**BECOME SKILFUL AT MINDING THE GATE:
BUILD A BOUNDARY VOCABULARY**

As you work on learning to set limits, here are the words through which you can clearly express boundaries to your children.

Zone III

When you want to convey your most deeply felt limits, use only a few select, strong words, making it clear that this behavior is

>   completely unacceptable
>   intolerable
>   wrong
>   violates (abuses) our family rules
>   absolutely not an option
>   under no circumstances
>   is a "Big No No"

Zone II

When the stakes are heartfelt but not extreme, you might try stating that this behavior is

>   not allowed
>   not the way we do it in our family
>   unsuitable
>   makes us uncomfortable
>   displeases, frustrates, annoys, irritates, aggravates us

Kidology Should Have an Impact on Limit-Setting and Discipline

At different ages stages, kids require different responses to broken limits, and you need to be more or less tolerant, depending on your child's developmental phase. The most effective rules of engagement take into consideration what kids are like at different maturity levels. After all, the boundaries you set for a toddler will not be the same as those for a school-age child.

Consider a child who hurts his cat, to make this clear. A toddler is developmentally curious. As a result, he might grab at anything that passes his way, including the tail of your beloved cat, even causing it some harm. But he is acting on a *developmentally appropriate impulse*— to touch and clutch. On the other hand, that seven-year-old who injures your family pet, pulling her tail until she screeches in pain, is *not* responding to some developmental urge. He is acting on his *own nega- tive impulse*—to harass or even torment the cat! Strictly speaking, both children "do harm," but, developmentally, they are *not* the same infrac- tion. Your toddler did *inadvertent harm*, indulging curiosity that is entirely appropriate to his stage. Your seven-year-old did *deliberate harm* that may well reflect cruelty, a potential problem of character. Only the grade-schooler is violating a serious Zone III boundary.

As a parent witnessing tail-pulling, you would certainly stop both children from hurting their pet and potentially themselves (cats do not take kindly to harassment). But the reaction that you have to your curi- ous toddler needs calibration different from your reaction to your not-so- nice seven-year-old. Your toddler needs *gentle correction and guidance*, while your grade-schooler needs to hear in no uncertain terms that you are angry, that his behavior is intolerable, and that there will be *serious consequences* for his actions. When you are making judgments about dis- obedience, and decisions about discipline, include your child's age/stage in your evaluation.

LIMITS INFORMED BY KIDOLOGY TO STOP EVEN THE RUDEST BEHAVIOR

Once your child reaches school age, you will see and hear things that might well stop you in your tracks and be a challenging disci- pline moment. Laurie recounted one that she had with her five-year- old daughter:

"At the mall, Lana, my kindergartner, asked me for a doll, and I told her 'No.' To my utter astonishment, to say nothing of embarrass- ment, Lana raised her hand in an obscene gesture that completely floored me.

"Even though I was mortified, I was sure that at five Lana couldn't fully understand what she had done, and that she had probably seen this on the school playground. So I swallowed hard and asked, 'Lana, do you know what that means?'

(continued on next page)

"Not surprisingly, my daughter answered, 'No.'

"I said, 'Lana, I think you want it to mean that you are very angry with me for not getting you a doll, but this is not what it means.'

" 'What does it mean, Mommy?' she asked.

" 'It is very bad and rude, worse than calling someone stupid or saying 'shut up.' This hand gesture is very, very mean. And, Lana, if you use it when you are angry, people will misunderstand what you are feeling. They will become very, very upset. You must *never* use that gesture, and, if you are angry, you must put your anger in words, not actions. You must never be mean to Mommy or any other person. In our family, we treat people with respect even when we are angry with them.' "

Especially at the most shocking moments of misbehavior, know your child's age/stage, swallow hard, set limits, and offer guidance. This can nip objectionable behavior in the bud.

Boundaries Become "Family Commandments"

Do not keep your behavioral expectations to yourself. Let your children clearly know the most sacred, never-to-be-broken family rules, which will help you avoid serious battles. The easiest way to do this is to transform your boundaries into a written set of "Family Commandments" that you can post on your refrigerator, tack up on your bulletin board, and/or hang on your child's bedroom wall. Think of these as commandments, because you want to transmit a message to your kids—*Consider these rules written in stone!*

Make them brief, definite, and few. Remember, the rule of law generally works best when there is a limit on regulations. (After all, there are only *Ten* Commandments). We only regulate what truly matters. (Maybe this is why "Thou shalt floss after every meal" never made the list.) Perhaps yours might look something like this:

FAMILY COMMANDMENTS

Family is a place where we will show love, respect, care, and concern for one another:

- We will be kind, decent, and moral.
- We will keep each other and ourselves safe.
- We will be constructive, *not* destructive, in words and deeds.
- We will put our angry feelings into words, *not* actions.
- We will respect property, our own and others.
- We will join in taking care of our family.

These rules create your safe family-container. They are your family filtration-system, keeping harm from invading your home life and permitting your children to grow and flourish. They are instrumental in making sure you raise your child to be one of the "good kids." Children need Family Commandments to develop the all-important moral compass—a conscience—as you will see later in these pages.

▶ **PYB Words of Wisdom:** *Children emulate what parent's value, so make your values very clear to your kids and live by them yourself if you want them to follow your lead.*

TO GAIN SUPPORT FOR YOUR LIMIT-SETTING, KEEP IN TOUCH WITH OTHER PARENTS

Spread the word to fellow parents about your family standards and find out about theirs. All parents welcome knowing what is going on in their community, because it is far easier to enforce limits if you have the support of others. By making your expectations clear, you prevent another adult from unwittingly creating a limit violation with your child. It reinforces your boundaries with the message, "These are so important that we want them in place at all times, even when you are in the care of another adult." Children also get a boost from seeing that people outside their families respect the family limits— even if they are very different from their own.

(continued on next page)

"When our daughter bellyached that she was the only fifth-grader not allowed at this older kids' dance party, we made a few calls to the parents with whom we usually network and found out that no one liked the idea. We all agreed to a joint veto, which helped weather the whining."

(Shapiro family)

"Our faith is very dear to our family. Our children attend Sunday school each week. We make it a point to the parents of their friends know about this, so that if, for example, our eight-year-old has a sleepover, they "get him to the church on time." Our kids are very social and more than occasionally resistant to the idea of going to religious school. It would be very easy to lose track of this if we did not enlist the help of others."

(Hackele family)

"After the first time our daughter came home and announced she had a hot dog at the park with her friend, we realized that we had assumed her friends' parents knew we did not eat such meat, because we observe halal laws as part of our Muslim faith. Since then, we have talked about this with any parent who takes our daughter home. We have only encountered respect for our practices."

(Ozery family)

"We ask that when our daughter has an after-school date, that the kids do homework before they play together. We just let other parents know that this priority, schoolwork first, feels right for us. Now that our daughter is in fourth grade, she has a lot of homework, and it gets to be a nightmare if she comes home from an afternoon at a friend's house and hasn't done it."

(Hordy family)

When Parents Openly Fight About Limits: How to Avoid This Discipline Disaster

One of the biggest problems in families occurs when parents have vastly divergent views of where the lines should be drawn and then openly argue over these differences. Typically, one parent is the "harsher," or stricter, disciplinarian than the other. For example:

- Mom insists that TV on school nights is out of the question, while dad, who enjoys sitting down to Monday night football with the boys, feels that this bonding time is important.
- Every morning before school, dad is aghast at the "sloppy clothes" his daughter wears and forbids her to walk out the door looking like that, while mom thinks that being comfortable and fashionable in sweats is just fine.
- Dad believes an eleven-year-old should feel free to spend birthday money that he's saved as he pleases. Mom is adamant that her son request permission before he makes purchases with money from his savings account.
- Dad insists that homework must be started immediately after school, while mom firmly believes that kids need time to unwind before settling in to do their schoolwork.

When parents have this split and argue, they can sound like this:

- Are you kidding? You must be nuts to think that a ten-year-old should be allowed to do that.
- You're always undermining me in front of the children.
- You want to be their friend, not their parent.
- Why do you have to be so hard on the children?
- You always make me the bad guy.
- For a change, can't you try and listen to what the kids want?

Parents who disagree on where lines should be drawn make a **serious** mistake if they do not try to resolve differences, because continually fighting over limits destroys their very value: You are neither protecting nor guiding kids if you spend all your time battling over rules and regulations rather than firmly establishing them.

Disagreements that turn into parenting disputes are very destructive and, in my experience, actually create disobedient, unruly, and even wild kids, because children:

- Get confusing, contradictory, and inconsistent messages about behavioral expectations.
- Witness disrespect or disregard that parents have for one another's point of view and values.
- Risk growing to dislike one parent while favoring the other. For example, they may see the stricter parent as unreasonable or unfair, and the more lenient parent as the "nice guy."
- Come to disrespect the parent who "loses" the limit-setting dispute. For example, an exasperated dad who finally just gives up on "fighting" his wife over Monday night football may seem weak and spineless to his boys, while mom may seem harsh.
- Feel a split in loyalty, as though following one parent's limits is disloyal to the other, so they feel anxious and/or end up ignoring both parents.
- Learn to be manipulative, pitting one parent against the other. For example, going to the one parent they realize will endorse their behavior or "protect" them if they break the stricter parent's rule.

FIGHT OVER LIMITS AND KIDS LOSE OUT

Kids who can get between their parents fall between the cracks. Regina recalls, "My parents were so busy disagreeing about how to raise me that all I had to do was go to one of them, usually my dad because he was more lenient, and I could get whatever I wanted, because he would take it as point of pride not to give in to my mom's way. It was a case of 'divide and conquer,' and I exploited it big-time. Unfortunately, I got away with much too much as a result."

Achieving Harmony in Your Limit-Setting: Six Steps to Reducing Family Conflict

1. Don't angrily disagree or argue in front of kids

It's damaging to you and your kids and undoes the very thing that you are trying to achieve. Discuss your differences and resolve them in private.

THE RIGHT TO RESPECTFULLY DISAGREE

Parents do not have to walk in lock step agreement on limit setting. What is critical, however, is that differences don't turn into arguments and power struggles, which can make parents lose sight of the task at hand; making good child rearing decisions. If you find that you are not aligned on a parenting issue, let the kids know that you need time to work out a shared point of view. You can say, "It looks like Mom and I don't see eye to eye on this matter right now. We need some time to decide how we are going to handle this together. We will discuss things and get back to you." This attitude conveys your mutual respect as well as the clear notion that you are a parenting team even when you have your differences about limit setting and discipline.

2. Set limits before they are needed

Parental discord can be greatly reduced by advanced planning. Discuss limits *before* you need to set them. For example, before your child starts to get homework, agree on the routines you want to establish before they become an issue.

3. Don't let your kids ambush you; before setting limits, consult with your coparent

Kids like to get their way. Sometimes, to accomplish this, they ask only one parent to respond to important limit issues at a moment's notice or an inopportune time; they make a request of "lenient" dad when "strict" mom is not at home. This leaves you open to setting a limit that your coparent might not agree to. Unless you know that you are reading from the same parenting page, delay responding. Say, "Mom is not home, so this is not a time when *we* can give you a decision."

4. Don't put down your coparent

Be very careful to avoid belittling, criticizing, or attacking your coparent if you are having a disagreement. Watch your language and especially your body language: Don't roll your eyes, crinkle your face, or moan at a moment when you are far apart in your parenting approach. This conveys contempt, undermines both of you, and breeds disrespect in your child.

5. Become a parenting team

Make joint decisions about behavioral expectations and inform your children that this is the way the two of you operate, as a parenting team. At a family dinner table or family meeting, clarify your approach: You act as one when it comes to protecting and guiding them.

6. Give a little to gain a lot

If your coparent has a limit that feels so important to him, as long as it is not damaging, respect his wishes and ask that next time you need it he reciprocate. This give-and-take works wonders on defusing tension, making for more relaxed parenting.

A HIDDEN REASON FOR DISCIPLINE DISCORD

If there is fierce fighting over your limit-setting, it may actually not be discord over discipline but a sign of tension in your marital relationship. If you have tried to negotiate your differences peacefully, and, after due time, not been able to accomplish that goal, your marriage is probably the issue, not your boundary-setting. If marital strife is spilling over into your parenting, get assistance in straightening out your relationship, because you are unwittingly using your child as a pawn in your marital skirmishes. Your responsibility to protect and guide gets lost in the fray, and so does your child!

What's Next: Discipline Strategies Based on Boundaries

Boundaries and limits are essential for raising cooperative children, but so is discipline, once kids cross the lines that parents have drawn for their protection and welfare. What follows in these pages are boundary-based discipline techniques and tactics to help you take charge when kids break the rules. And, by the way, if you are a parent who has ever wondered why ear plugs are not standard-issue equipment for moms and dads, you will be overjoyed to learn that you can use this boundary knowledge to develop strategies that put a halt to that obnoxious, insufferable, and altogether maddening scourge—*the whining wars*.

Chapter 6

Put an End to Whining:
Developing Your Child's
Self-Discipline

Standing Firm in the Face of "It's Not Fair"

Here is what you now know about boundaries:

1. Good limits have to do with safety, values, civility, and routines and responsibilities.
2. Each parent creates his or her own limits.
3. No two parents will have the same "zones of comfort."
4. Limits are different, *not* better.

Here is the scene, the one that makes you wish for wax in your ears: You set an important safety rule that your nine-year-old daughter may not have play dates at a friend's house where no adult is present. One afternoon, itching to visit a friend at an unsupervised home, she whines, "It's no fair, Julie's mother lets her have play dates even if no one is home the whole night. Julie's mother, Pauline, lets her do anything."

This, of course, can be the beginning of the longest afternoon of your life. It does not have to be this way. You can win the whining war soon after your child takes the opening shot. You stay in charge, because you understand and apply all there is to know about boundaries and limits by remembering or referring to the four points on the checklist above. How does this happen? First, you do not buy the notion that Julie's mom has thrown caution to the wind and given her daughter free rein. Pauline giving the OK to nine-year-olds, alone, "the whole night," is a *highly unlikely* scenario, no matter what your child tries to tell you.

So, while your little one is earnestly trying to test the limits, you realize that her information is *not* accurate. You take her feelings seriously, but *not* her *facts*. As a result, your child's perspective does not cloud or alter yours. What's more, if there were a slim chance that a mother did *not* set a safety rule, you would certainly not go along with it, given that safety is a critical, nonnegotiable boundary.

But your little angel has also thrown at you that Julie's mother *"lets her do anything,"* and perhaps you are aware that Pauline has looser parenting rules than you do. Julie's bedtime might be later than your daughter's, and she may have her own twenty-seven-inch digital TV in her bedroom, while you have your seventeen-inch with the missing remote under lock and key.

Do these boundary differences intimidate you? Do you begin to tremble and cower at the thought that you are not nearly as "nice" as Julie's mom? No. Instead, you realize that parents are certain to have *different standards*. Comparisons neither unsettle nor disarm you. You do not worry that other parents' standards are superior. *Different is not better.* You do not get self-conscious, apologetic, or defensive.

With an unswerving, unwavering, committed mindset, you will stay calm and composed. You will *not* resort to any of the following:

Six Most Common and Guaranteed to Backfire Responses to Your Whining Child:

- *Get defensive* and snap, "I don't give a fig what any other mother does."
- *Throw your weight around* and demand, "I'm your mother and you are going to do what I tell you."
- *Beg for reason and cooperation*, and implore, "But honey, try and understand; I am only doing this for your own good."
- *Negotiate* and sheepishly bargain, "Well, don't go today and I'll talk it over with Daddy."

- *Capitulate* and surrender, "OK, if Julie's mom lets her, I guess I will, too."
- *Turn over power to your child* and completely abandon anything that remotely resembles boundaries and limits and declare, "All right, you can do anything you want as long as you stop whining."

Demonstrating an attitude of resolve as your child snivels and complains, you stay *firm, undeterred, clear, unflappable,* and *unstoppable,* and you say with full force of *all* this conviction behind your every word:

"I am sorry that you are disappointed about the play date, but being unsupervised in anyone's house is ***absolutely unacceptable.***"

Then what? Then you say nothing else. Period! That is all. This is your boundary-based strategy to eliminate whining. Let your words reflect your sure, secure, and definite commitment to your important limits and your child's welfare. Do not fall into the abyss of indecision and doubt. For those of you who are habitual conflict-avoiders, this will take practice, so take these warnings seriously:

- Do not give your child one morsel of information other than your conviction.
- Do not feed your child one crumb of doubt or ambivalence.
- Do not nourish a child's hope that you will change your mind.

Your tactic is to deprive your child of any scrap of uncertainty, because uncertainty invariably feeds into and increases bellyaching. Clarity starves rather than feeds the whining. Firmly repeat the words conveying your boundary mantra—"Being unsupervised in a house is ***completely unacceptable***"—and once again respectfully acknowledge her feelings—"I am sorry you are disappointed about the play date"— but on pain of wishing that your child came with a mute button, don't you dare qualify, expound, or elaborate. Your child will always seize on this, seeing it as a chink in your certainty, and torture you with moans of protest. (Threat Makers, who forecast consequences that never materialize, and Cavers, who capitulate, take special note of this.)

When you avoid these pitfalls and transmit the strength of your convictions, your child stops whining. Parents with convictions about their well-thought-out limits emit an aura of authority. They practically glow in the dark. Children see it, welcome it, take it seriously, and, best of all, pipe down!

▶**PYB Words of Wisdom:** *The surest way to ensure a crabby kid is to occasionally give in to her demands. Intermittently rewarding your child with indulgence is the strongest possible reinforcer of misbehavior. Just think of yourself as a human slot machine doling out an occasional payoff, and you will understand why your child won't give up until he wins. Don't gamble with that outcome; be consistent.*

Communication Is the Best Discipline Strategy

Clear communication clears up conflict. However, do not wait until you hear the moans and groans of kid resistance to use your *boundary vocabulary.* Let your children hear the rules long before they attempt to break them. Invoking limits when your child heads toward breaking them *is* critical, but delineating them in the first place is an extremely effective discipline strategy. *All* of the No-win Discipline responses invariably fall short in this domain. They are long on reprimands and short on information about limits before they are broken.

Communicate your expectations to your children. Describe to them what you want from them. *Speak to your children.* Talk about limits from day one and see the difference in cooperation. You will have lots more of it *and* far less whining! Why is giving your children the words an effective strategy? Words delivered by a caring parent help children get important values and behaviors into their own heads and hearts.

▶**PYB Words of Wisdom:** *Give words to your children, and you won't have words with them.*

When you use a boundary vocabulary, the voice of your convictions grows into the voice guiding your child in her very own mind. (Of all the No-win Discipline types, Short Fuse parents will see vast improvement in their children if they spend more time talking to their children about limits and explaining specific expectations.) *Setting controls over behavior evolves into your child's self-control.*

Dana, always a *clear boundary-communicator,* actually saw this process in action with her preschooler, Louisa:

"Since she was small, I have told Louisa that 'hands are for hugging, not hitting.' One day Louisa was playing with her dolls, and she looked as if she were about to hit one of them. Then I heard her firmly tell herself the way I might: 'Louisa, hands are for hugs, not hits. Hitting is *unasseptable*. Make nice,' and she stopped and started acting much more kindly to her 'babies.' It was so uncanny, she sounded just like me talking to her."

It is not "uncanny." It is what can (and hopefully does) happen, though not every parent gets to see this in-between step: Dana caught her daughter in the act of making her mother's clear, caring voice her own.

In time, when this conversion is complete, Louisa will not need to repeat this or any other boundary words out loud, she will have them fully set in her mind. She will have developed the all-important quiet "voice in her head" and, with that, a capacity for self-discipline and self-regulation. The stronger that voice is in Louisa's head, the lower Dana's voice will need to be. Shouts of "Loueeza! Don't! Stop!" and other such reprimands become infrequent when your child develops a voice in her head.

> ▶ **PYB Words of Wisdom:** *A child with a quiet voice in her head rarely needs to hear a mother raise hers.*

As parents, we do not always get to see this remarkable advancement, but if we are consistent about using our words, they do eventually become the child's words. Rules migrate from outside in. Once this change firmly takes hold, you and your child are so much better off. Words help children own the limits in their own right, and, best of all, a child who has internalized boundaries does not break them. A child who has the rules in her head and heart now polices her own behavior—she has self-control—and you have a lot less to fight over!

Respond Rather Than React: Taking Steps to Ensure Your Child's Self-discipline

A wise parent starts encouraging self-discipline early. Speak about limits well before your child can understand. Here is my best advice: Use big words even while you have little kids. This often makes parents feel odd. Even if it seems strange to be talking in complete and intelligent sentences to a young child, do so.

If it seems odd to be so verbal with your son, talking with him as if he were an older child, think of it the way you do about the clothes you buy for your small but growing offspring. You get them a size larger than they need, because you know they will grow into them shortly. Children grow into "big ideas" the way they grow into those oversized clothes: fast, before you know it.

When your young child flings her arms about in a moment of angry frustration and thrashes out at you, smacking you across the bridge of your nose (how do they know where it will hurt the most?), do not ignore her behavior, saying, "Oh it's nothing, my little pumpkin," which does nothing to inform your "little pumpkin" about limits. Nor wildly shriek "Stop" or yell "I think you broke my nose," which only serves to put you at odds with your child.

Instead, use your *words* to help them move in the direction of self-control. Try to handle it this way: Firmly but kindly *state the limit,* "We don't hit. Hitting is unacceptable. Hitting hurts," but do not stop here. When it is possible and appropriate, add words to *describe the behavior* you desire to see from your child, and *demonstrate the preferred conduct,* if possible.

You might say, "We don't hit. Hitting is a 'big no no.' Hitting hurts." Then add, "We touch softly. Touch Mommy's face softly," while taking your child's hand and gently stroking your cheek with it. You can even repeat what you have just said ("See, we touch softly") while making this tender gesture, and add, "That feels so nice."

Particularly with very young children, assume a friendly tone of voice. Keep your directions intelligent but also simple and clear. Do not get long-winded, complicated, or stern. This will ensure that a child is not overwhelmed in an avalanche of words and feelings.

Do not minimize this kind of interaction with your child. This is a remarkable parenting strategy—responding with guidance rather than reacting with anger. In this seemingly small moment, you are doing a big discipline job. You are actually *responding* with four specific measures to nurture your child's self-control and instill self-discipline:

These Four Basic Steps to Ensuring Self-Discipline are:

1. **Setting limits** (*no hitting*)
2. **Conveying the impact of the undesirable behavior** (*hitting hurts*)
3. **Helping achieve the desirable behavior** (*gentle touching*)
   - Describing the desirable behavior (*touch softly*)
   - Demonstrating the preferred behavior (*soft stroking*)
4. **Conveying the impact of the preferred behavior** (*stroking feels nice*)

This checklist is a sure deterrent to battles, because all of the steps work toward establishing your child as your partner in the mission of keeping the peace. You are giving your child self-discipline language as well as modeling desirable behavior. Through this firm, clear, and loving verbal and nonverbal communication, you become allies, not enemies in the task of getting your child to adhere to the boundaries and act cooperatively.

"My Daughter Is a Playground Thief": Respond Rather Than React, to Encourage Civil Behavior

Let me give you another opportunity to become well versed in these strategies and to continue on this happy path of remaining your child's ally. Using your self-discipline checklist as a guide, how would you respond to the following disheartening lapse of playground "etiquette" in your preschooler? Here is the scene:

You have been watching your nearly three-year-old daughter, Marcia, on the playground. Marcia has been playing next to her friend Jason, when Jason's baby-sitter comes over and gives him a pail and shovel for the sandbox. Before Jason has a chance to put more than a shovel or two in the pail, Marcia has pulled it away, and Jason does not look too pleased.

Now what happens? Feeling acutely self-conscious, you might want to put a swift end to this baby brouhaha, lunging to grab the pail from Marcia with an embarrassed reprimand, "Marcia, that's terrible of you, give that pail back at once!" But restrain yourself. This reaction should not—if you are following your checklist—even be an option.

▶ **PYB Words of Wisdom:** *When your child misbehaves, breaching a limit, remember to respond rather than react. Your immediate emotional reaction transmits little but your anger, while your deliberate and well-thought-out response teaches your child how to do things better the next time, which helps create a cooperative and resilient kid.*

It will help you to relax if you take kidology into account. Your daughter is not the Al Capone of the playground set and has not begun her life as a thug. At not-yet-three, Marcia does not take something that is not hers out of dishonesty. She grabs because she is still at an impulsive, self-involved stage and doesn't yet know how to act otherwise.

Understanding this, you do not frantically charge across the playground. After all, you want to accomplish more than putting a halt to her undesirable behavior for the moment. You want to respond in a measured way that promotes Marcia's *self-control* and *self-restraint*. As you gently but firmly take the pail, you say, "Please give Jason the pail. It belongs to Jason and he was playing with it." Whereupon you firmly and quietly say, "I know you would like to play with the pail" and then add one of the following *limit statements*:

- "But you are not allowed to grab the pail from your friend."
- "Pulling a toy away from Jason is not acceptable."
- "You may not take a toy from Jason without his permission."

Next, *communicate the impact of Marcia's undesirable behavior.* Depending on the scenario, one of these may accurately capture what you wish to convey:

- "Grabbing the pail frightened Jason."
- "You hurt Jason when you yanked the pail from him."
- "Your taking the pail upset Jason."

Once you tell Marcia the effect of her actions on her friend, continue by helping her achieve a more appropriate behavior—asking Jason's permission—while *demonstrating and describing the preferred conduct.*

"Marcia, the right thing to do is to ask if you may play with a toy. If you want the pail, say, 'Jason, may I please play with the pail,' and in a few minutes it can be your turn to try the pail."

You could easily use this as an opportunity to introduce the desirable behavior of sharing, but do not expect that your child will master sharing until she is of school age. You could also frame this as an opportunity to learn the desirable behavior of "taking turns." It will depend on what strikes you as a valuable limit lesson.

Keep this kidology information in mind: Your child at nearly three is developmentally able to wait a few minutes for her turn. This is an age to introduce delaying concepts, such as, *"soon"* and *"your turn is next."* A child can probably manage this type of delay as early as age two. A one-year-old cannot tolerate the delay of "just a minute, it isn't your turn yet"; it's simply developmentally beyond her.

Finally, give your daughter the last ingredient for building self-discipline: *convey the positive impact of her appropriate action.*

"Jason will be much happier if you ask his permission to use his toy, and it will make it easier for him to give you a turn with the pail."

Once you have done this, you need to stay close by for a few minutes to ensure that Marcia gets a shot at the pail. You might supportively add, "I'll stay with the two of you so that I can help you both take turns with the pail." This response takes Marcia and you through *all* the steps that will help her to master self-control and enable her to become a cooperative child.

> ▶ **PYB Words of Wisdom:** *Mastery of self-discipline takes time. Don't expect your child to get cooperation, sharing, and other social skills right without a lot of practice. You wouldn't count on your dog learning to "heel" after one lesson. When it comes to teaching good behavior, don't ask more of your child than you would of Rover.*

The wild card in all this is Jason. He may not be up to the task of sharing his pail. If he isn't, don't make that offer. Instead, you could try a response set that helps Marcia learn about personal ownership. You might say that the pail is Jason's toy, and that she has her own. Now that you are getting the feel of it, try applying this approach on your own.

▶**PYB Words of Wisdom:** *Did your actions in the face of your child's misbehavior make the problem better rather than worse? If the answer is "yes," you are responding, not reacting, and that makes for a well-behaved child.*

FOUR STEPS TO ENSURING SELF-DISCIPLINE IN YOUR CHILD

(As Applied to Marcia and the Playground Pail Grab)

When your child breaks a boundary, *respond* rather than react:

1. Set the limits: (*you may not yank a toy from another child's grasp*)
2. Convey the impact of her/his undesirable behavior: (*upsets your friend*)
3. Help her/him achieve a desirable behavior: (*ask permission*)
4. Convey the impact of the preferred behavior: (*keeps a friend happier and more cooperative*)

The Joy and Peace of Having a Child Who Has Internalized Self-discipline

It is remarkable to discover that even very young children are quite able to acquire self-discipline. What is also astounding is to witness how discipline, once internalized, not only makes kids well behaved but gives them valuable tools for keeping themselves safe and managing their own lives.

Laurie told me the following story about her daughter, Lana, which shows just how this works: One morning, Lana, who eagerly trotted off to kindergarten every morning, refused to go to school. Realizing that this refusal was unusual, Laurie did *not* insist on the limit routine, but instead took a moment to talk with her daughter and find out what was bothering her. Laurie learned the following: The day before because of bad weather, playground recess was canceled, and instead the whole school watched a movie in the gym. Apparently, not expecting foul weather, the school made a hasty but very poor decision when they selected the movie, and showed the frightening thriller *Jaws* to all the students—even the youngest. This incident was behind Lana's refusal to go to school. After some discussion, Lana told this to her mother:

"The movie at recess was too old for me, it made me feel scared. I closed my eyes when I got scared, but I don't want to see scary movies in the gym. Let's go to the principal and tell her not to show bad movies at recess. Mamma, let's bring my fun videos to school, so that my school has good movies to show us next time during recess."

Laurie and Lana agreed to this plan and, following this discussion, Lana happily left for school as usual.

This scenario and its happy outcome and this heartfelt talk between a frightened daughter and a loving mother is actually a result of Lana acquiring self-discipline. If you carefully analyze what Lana said, you can see that though she is only six years old, she managed this challenging situation at school because she had been taught *and* absorbed the four steps to encourage self-discipline.

- **The movie was too old for me** (*limit violated*) Early on, Laurie had introduced a rule about entertainment: certain movies and TV shows "-were too old for Lana," so now Lana is equipped to identify for herself a breach of this limit.
- **It made me feel scared** (*undesirable consequence or impact of a violated limit*) Laurie had explained that if the limit was broken and Lana saw these movies, there would be an undesirable outcome: they would frighten her. Now Lana has the words to identify and understand the negative impact.
- **I closed my eyes when I got scared** (*protecting herself from the impact of the violated limit*) Lana found a way to cope with the adverse impact of a violated limit; she took charge of the limit-setting and acted self-protectively by closing her eyes.
- **Let's go to the principal and tell her not to show bad movies at recess** (*reestablishing a limit*) Lana made a plan to ensure that the limit would be reset and that she would be safe and comfortable in the future.
- **Mamma, let's bring my videos to school, so that my school has good movies to show us during recess** (*creating an alternative desired outcome to prevent the past negative outcome from reoccurring*) Lana made a creative plan to prevent any future negative outcomes

of this limit violation; she supplied movies to the school that were not too old for her!

One of the many rewards of teaching self-discipline is the joy of seeing the development of your child's capacity for resilience. Lana, as well as your child, can learn to cope effectively with whatever they may encounter in this challenging world.

> ▶ **PYB Words of Wisdom:** *When limit-setting works, it becomes second nature to a child. They do the discipline job for you with creativity and competence. A child with the capacity for self-discipline becomes a problem-solver rather than a problem-child.*

What's Next? Helping Your Child Become Well-behaved in a Challenging World

You can see that the steps for promoting self-discipline on the playground are not essentially different from those for a toddler thrashing in your lap who unwittingly smacks you in the nose. What is different is the increasing complexity that life takes on for you and your child. Working on playground manners, such as sharing, takes more effort than learning to caress mamma's cheek. With maturity and your child's entry into the world of school, the demands on her behavior get even more complicated and challenging than life in the sandbox.

In the next chapter, we will continue to look at the steps for ensuring your child's self-discipline, particularly for your older child. We will see how to expand on them in order to give you additional discipline strategies for your growing child.

Chapter 7

....

Helping Your Child
Get Very Good at Being Good:
Continuing the Development
of Self-Discipline

How to Make Good Kids Great:
The Parent as Teacher

Three-year-old Mikey seems allergic to sitting still. A real handful, he needs limits as well as lots of assistance to get good at being good. And there is no time to waste.

His latest "trick" is block hurling, and his mother, Lynne, has already lost one of her favorite figurines to this indoor "sport." When Mikey hurls his Mickey Mouse blocks across the family room, his mom can apply the four steps for ensuring self-discipline, but she can also draw on additional techniques to make sure that Mikey achieves desirable behavior. As she firmly removes the blocks from Mikey's grip, Lynne can say:

"Mikey, do not throw the blocks. Please, give them to me. Throwing blocks can break something or hurt someone. Blocks are not for throwing. Blocks are for building. Let's use them to build together. Come sit with me and let's see how high you can stack them. Would you like to build a castle or a tall tower? I think that you and I can have fun playing blocks, and you can be a good builder."

What is different about this limit-setting? More than you might think. In our Mikey scenario, Lynne easily integrated three new and very useful self-discipline techniques in response to her son's behavior:

- Teaching
- Redirection
- The Structured Choice

We can go over our block-hurling scene step by step, so that you can see where these three new strategies come into play. Here is what our checklist of *Four Steps to Ensuring Self-discipline* looks like with these additional strategies, all three of which are designed to promote desirable behavior.

1. Setting limits (*"Do not throw the blocks. Please, give them to me."*)
2. Conveying the impact of the undesirable behavior (*"Throwing blocks can break something or hurt someone."*)
3. **Helping achieve the desirable behavior**:
   - **Teaching** (*"Blocks are not for throwing. Blocks are for building."*)
   - **Redirecting** (*"Let's use the blocks to build together. Come sit with me and let's see how high you can stack them."*)
   - **The structured choice** (*"Would you like to build a castle or a tall tower?"*)
4. Conveying the impact of the preferred behavior (*"I think that you and I can have fun playing blocks, and you can be a good builder."*)

Strategy # 1. Teaching: Show and Tell

Surprisingly, many parents caught up in trying to change a child's undesirable behavior omit this seemingly obvious step: teaching desirable conduct. They can get as far as "Don't throw the blocks, you will break something." More often than not, especially in many a no-win discipline pattern, this is where it ends with an exasperated "Give me those things right now!"—which does not bring a child any closer to acting correctly. Parents often take for granted a child's fund of knowledge and assume that their child understands how the world operates, as if after hearing what he ought *not* to do and having been dutifully corrected, he will now understand just what he should and ought to do. For example, a parent might believe, if I tell my son he *should not* throw his blocks, he will now do the right thing.

Reprimands may stop a child's actions, but, on their own, they do not improve, advance, or change behavior, *because you have not taught your child an alternative desired action.* Even if you use kindly expressions, such as "Be a good boy and stop throwing your blocks," children, preschoolers or younger, *do not* have the capacity to understand the virtue of good behavior, much less know how to implement it. So, as much as you scold, you will **not** make a dent in misbehavior, because kids *cannot possibly comply without positive instruction and guidance.* To behave cooperatively, kids require specific directions and information on how to do things correctly. Lynne is doing just that when she instructs, "Blocks are not for throwing, *blocks are for building.*" Lynne is a good parent/teacher, correcting **and** educating her child.

Collecting the Great Discipline Payoff

Guidance does far more than get kids to behave; they become more skillful, competent, self-confident, and self-directed. Just think of a child who has learned, under your direction, to use a knife properly. He will certainly have more respect for the instrument, be less likely to cut himself, and more inclined—because you have shown him how knives "work" and made him feel competent about using them—to try and utilize them as they were intended. And guidance saves time and heartache; for openers, you will make fewer trips to the local emergency room.

Under your supervision, your child might cut up peanut-butter-and-jelly sandwiches into "silly shapes" for his lunch box. Over the long run, he can grow into a self-confident grade-schooler who knows how to make his own lunch, which also saves parental wear and tear.

Think of our little block-thrower, who, with your prompting, has "gotten good" at blocks. Because of your guidance, he will now share your pride at becoming a master builder rather than your anger at being a major pain in the neck. Imagine him running to show you what he has created versus you running to see what he might be destroying. Practically speaking, "oohing" and "ahhing" over a block castle takes a lot less out of you than, say, breaking up a fight with a sibling he has just clobbered.

Guidance improves a child's capacity to be self-directed, self-contained, and a self-starter. If, thanks to you, toys are about fun and pleasure, *not* scolding and punishment, he will be more likely to go to his block pile on his own and engage in imaginative play. Having learned from you how to play, rather than to fight, your child will become a person who is better at occupying himself and far less likely to get under foot. Teaching does create a very big discipline payoff: you get time off for good behavior—your child's good behavior.

GETTING A CHILD ON TRACK: POLICING VERSUS TEACHING

Imagine you are waiting to board a train with your preschooler and are faced with keeping the active little boy safe on a crowded platform. If you are particularly harried and short on patience, you may turn into *police-mom:*

"Don't go near the edge of that platform. You can fall and get hurt. Come here this minute." So, when your son insists, "I want to see where trains come from," you bark at him to retreat, repeatedly, with little effect. Totally exasperated, you loudly exclaim, "Young man, did you hear me? Get back this instant. I told you a million times. You will get hurt. Give me your hand right this second." Then, with your child squirming unhappily, you grab him in tow, pulling him onto the train when it arrives.

If you are having a better day, you are more likely to turn into *teacher-mom*, starting a lesson, not a shouting match :

"Please stand next to me. It's dangerous to go near the platform edge. I know you like to see the trains pull into the station, but you can get hurt if you go too close to the tracks. You must never, never stand near the edge of the platform. Let Mommy show you what a big boy needs to do to keep safe on the platform."

Firmly holding your son's hand, you then walk *toward* the platform edge. Instruction begins: "See this big yellow line on the ground? The trainman painted this line on the ground to keep us safe, and he painted some very important words."

With your toe, you point to the bold yellow warning written on the platform floor and continue: "These words, which you can't read yet, say, 'For your safety stay behind the yellow line.' The trainman wants us to always stay back behind this yellow line so that we are not in danger of accidentally falling onto the tracks where we could get hurt."

(continued on next page)

Then, as teacher-mom, you demonstrate a safe behavior as an alternative to your boy's risky actions.

"Let's keep safe together. Let's move way back from the yellow line and stand near the wall."

With an exaggerated backward shuffle, you and your child move toward the safety of the platform wall, then, when you near the wall, you add,

"Let's try this safety shuffle again," and repeat your little dance.

Only the train pulling into the station halts the fun and the "lesson."

It isn't always easy, but as often as you can, find the patience to be the *teacher-mom* rather than the *police-mom*, because you and your child will have a much easier ride.

Strategy #2. Redirection: Developing a Competent, Cooperative, and Resilient Child

Redirection is a simple strategy, but it works wonders at helping a child achieve desirable behaviors. With redirection, once you have set the limit, you offer your child an alternative activity or action that is *similar* to the undesirable conduct but is acceptable.

"That red truck is your brother's toy. Here is a blue truck for you to play with."

"Try drawing with your crayons on the brown paper, which I can hang up on your wall, not on my antique wallpaper in the living room."

Redirection is a response that takes a negative behavior and reshapes it into a positive one. It has many advantages:

- It is not abrupt or jolting, like grabbing an item from your child. It is a respectful request to modify behavior.
- It provides your child with a sense that he has some control over his behavior. He *can* do something that is acceptable.
- It is not a dead end. It offers a *solution*.

- It encourages your child to become a problem solver and to find acceptable, alternative ways to manage disappointment and frustration.
- It promotes resilience; your child's capacity to adapt, adjust, and bounce back with a smile on her face.

> ▶ **PYB Words of Wisdom:** *Resilience is a quality of character that makes a child a pleasure rather than a handful. A resilient child is optimistic, cheerful, good spirited, and enthusiastic, because he becomes a "can-do kid" instead of a "won't-do whiner." Each and every time you create a solution to a conflict rather than a battle you strengthen this all-important capacity.*

Redirection can also give your child a moment to realize the needs of others: When you give your child another option, you are pointing out *the rights of others*—his brother's right to enjoy the use of his own red truck, your right to preserve the integrity of your living-room wallpaper. Redirection endorses a child's needs and rights but informs him that others have them, too. Of course, when you redirect, you are, by definition, offering an alternative positive behavior. Redirection accomplishes a lot that can improve the mood around your home, to say nothing of the décor.

TRY REDIRECTION FOR YOUR YOUNG CHILD
(Preschool and Younger)

In the following examples, I have emphasized the key "redirecting" words.

1. **Let's try** putting the puzzle together instead of throwing the pieces.
2. The glass horse is fragile. Pease give it to me. Then **come and help me** dust the figurines.
3. I will take those knives from you, because they are very sharp. *I* **bet you didn't** *know that* we could cut sandwiches into funny shapes with this special knife.
4. **Rather** than playing with your brother's clay pot that he brought home from school, you can make your own with this clay.

(continued on next page)

5. You may not use the saw for building, but **look at what you can do** *with* the pieces of wood I have cut up for you.
6. Don't play with your brother's chemistry set. **Did you know that** you could do a real science experiment with these pots and pans?
7. We can **practice** gently closing the door, not slamming it.
8. You are not to ride your bike without a helmet. You can decorate this helmet and **make it special,** just for you.
9. Stop tearing up the papers. **Let me show you how** to make paper planes with old newspaper.

Offering Options to the Older Child

Redirection is not just for crayon-wielding preschoolers. It can certainly be part of your self-discipline-building strategy with your grade-schooler. The stakes will be different, but the technique is the same: you set the limit and then offer an activity similar to the one denied. What *is* different with your older child is that the similar activity *does not* have to happen right then and there. The grade-schooler can wait, because he has the mental equipment to tolerate delay, make plans, and imagine the alternative activity—things a younger child is developmentally incapable of doing.

When your grade-school child wants money for the hottest electronics, you might redirect him from something expensive to a more affordable option, offering a short-term as well as long-term alternative.

"That game is too expensive, but you can go to the store to test out others, and then you can save your allowance and birthday money to buy one."

This redirection, which includes an *immediate alternative* (going to the store) along with *a long-term option* (saving money), will help keep this from becoming a battle. After all, you are not putting the complete kibosh on his dream. He can still make something happen that he wants to happen for himself, even if it is not exactly what he was hoping for. As is always the case with redirection, your child retains some element of control over his life and gets exposed to planning and problem-solving. He is also reminded that his behavior has an impact on others. This purchase is not affordable for his parents, and this fact requires his consideration.

Redirection, a problem-solving strategy, is so much less confrontational than limit-setting alone. Of course, you can't always make such generous offers, and even all the birthday and Christmas money cannot make the unaffordable attainable. If your children know that you do offer an alternate proposition when you can, it makes it much easier for them to tolerate limits, because they come to see you, their parent, as reasonable.

Alex's mother, Barbara, had just delivered to him the bad news—no skateboarding—but without offering any alternatives; she just said, "No, because of my job it won't be possible today." While Barbara often uses redirection, because of her busy schedule, there are no viable options. After a mild protest, eleven-year-old Alex actually defends his mother's limit-setting to his friend:

"My mom says I can't go to the skateboard park today because she doesn't want me to be there with no grown-up around, and she can't come because she'll be late coming home today. But if she could have, she would have figured a way to work something out."

With an older child, redirection helps establish goodwill and a trusting connection, and that goes a long way to helping him develop his own capacity for self-discipline. It makes it easier for a child to accept the disappointment of "No" when, as it happens in life, it just has to be that way.

> ▶ **PYB Words of Wisdom:** *Since redirection offers an alternative, not just the kibosh, kids tend to see parents as firm but not difficult, so they are more likely to cooperate.*

TRY *REDIRECTION* WITH YOUR GRADE-SCHOOLER

In the following examples, I have emphasized the key "redirecting" words.

1. Please give me the digital camera. It's complicated and expensive. **Here is one that you can use for yourself.** You can *also try* a photography class at the "Y," where you can learn to use a complicated camera.
2. **Instead** of you doing your homework in front of the TV, I can sit with you in your room and keep you company.
3. You are not to ride your skateboard without a helmet. **Why don't you** take your birthday money and find a helmet that matches your board, at the skate shop?

(continued on next page)

4. You cannot take your friends out for lunch, but **as an alternative,** you can make them a pasta dinner at home.
5. We cannot afford to get you a DVD player, but **another option** is that we could rent one, so you could get to try it. Then we can talk about saving up as a family to buy one for all of us to share.

Strategy #3: The Structured Choice: Choosing Between a "Yes" and a "Yes"*

The Structured Choice is a simple strategy—follow a limit with an offer of *two* choices, both of which fall inside your acceptability zone. In effect, you do not give your child the option of "No," but instead offer two ways she can choose to say "Yes." This is how you might lay out structured choices with a toddler, but bear in mind that, developmentally, your toddler needs an immediate set of choices, because she is not yet ready to understand or tolerate delay:

"Sophie. Please give me that book. It's Mommy's book for work. You may have the book about Curious George *or* the one called *Eloise.*"

"Jake, you may not bite your sister. You can use your teeth to chew on the cracker *or* a pretzel. Teeth are for chewing food, not your sister."

Each of these examples offers two constructive and acceptable choices. I often hear people suggesting that frustrated kids "should hit a pillow" as an option to replace unacceptable physical aggression, such as biting or hitting. I do ***not*** advise ever making one of your structured choices an activity where children are encouraged to vent their anger aggressively. Studies show that the aimless venting of anger actually makes children more, not less, aggressive.

For a preschooler, a structured choice can sound more conversational and it can be about future, not only present activities, because at this age/stage children have some ability to delay.

"Phoebe, wearing jeans for sledding in the snow is not an option. Do you want to wear the red snowsuit or the black ski pants?"

"Sam, tonight a bath is a must. You are covered in dirt. Would you like your bath before or after dinner?"

*Dr. Haim Ginott, in his classic books on parenting from the 1960s, first introduced these concepts of child rearing. Much of this chapter is informed by his work.

For a grade-schooler, your structured choices can be more sophisticated; you can offer increasingly complicated options and confer greater responsibility. Also the choices for an older child need not be immediate as they must be for a preschooler or younger child, because a grade-schooler can tolerate delayed options:

"You cannot stay at your friend Michael's until eight, Max, it's a school night. Tonight you can stay until six. Saturday, you can spend the day, and I can pick you up at nine, if you prefer to wait until then to hang out with Michael."

"Jill, your lights must be out by nine. Before 'lights out,' do you want to read to yourself or would you like Dad to read to you for fifteen minutes?"

You are allowed to be funny even when you are conveying a serious point. Humor is essential for riding the emotional roller coaster that is your preteen grade-schooler:

"Andrew, I think the Board of Health will be here to condemn your room tomorrow. Will you clean it up before or after lunch?"

"Mitchell, that turtle tank has to be cleaned, otherwise Skipper and Elektra are going to be on the *Late News* to do an exposé: 'Mitchell, the Slum Lord of Turtle Island.' Do you want to clean their tank before or after I book them on the show?"

"Shane, you cannot be late for school. Do you want your brother to come in and wake you with his tuba in ten minutes, or would you prefer five more minutes on your snooze alarm?"

Structured Choice is a way to say one "No" to your kids and come back with two "Yesses." After all, each of the two offered options *is* permissible. Using this technique, you eliminate the undesirable limit-breach and propose two preferred behaviors, each of which falls well inside the zone of acceptability. This encourages the child's independence and emerging decision-making skills; they make the choice, but it also sets boundaries because both choices are within your limits. Once again, what you are doing as a parent is creating that sturdy, safe container for your child, but giving her plenty of room to move around in it.

▶ **PYB Words of Wisdom:** *Life does not come with an instruction manual on good conduct. Kids need parents to provide one. Teaching, redirection, and the structured choice are ways to write an instruction manual of good behavior for your kids.*

How to Talk Your Older Child into Good Behavior

When it comes to taking steps to self-discipline, "start early" is the wisest advice anyone could ever give you. Getting a late start at this—say after your child is five years old—makes the going rougher, though not impossible. While I advocate teaching the steps to self-control early on, I also urge you to continue teaching these steps even as your children mature and seem to master the basics of being well-behaved. Even cooperative children continue to need guidance all through their growing up.

As your child gets to be an older, smarter, and more savvy grade-schooler, he still needs you to lead him down the right path, especially the older grade-schooler, of ten or eleven, who will demand from you more than he is actually equipped to handle. This often confuses a parent. For example, a sixth-grader may ask to spend the afternoon visiting the home of a new friend, Matt, telling you he will be back for dinner or will certainly call if he is late. You naively respond "Fine," and he dashes out the door.

Because he is so able at asking, you let him follow his own plans. You assume he can carry them out without a hitch or without any efforts on your part to reinforce and support his self-discipline. Mistake! Dinner approaches, and there is no sign of your sixth-grader, let alone a call from him saying that he is on his way home. You fume and worry, worry and fume. Then he walks in the door, and you are understandably relieved and understandably ready to pounce. The "You had me worried sick/But I didn't realize how late it was" battle begins.

This scenario could have an entirely more peaceful outcome if every now and again you went through *all* the self-discipline steps with your older kids, especially when you are changing the filter and giving your child more independence and autonomy. We can rerun the previous scenario to see how a peaceful outcome could have taken place if mom and son had a three-minute conversation where limits were revisited. Our replay might go something like this. Mom begins:

"Jonah, you can go out to play at Matt's, but I want us to sit down together for a family dinner tonight and I want you home before dark, otherwise I get concerned. If you are running late, please call, so that I know where you are. I know, when you are playing, it is easy to lose track of time. By the way, you have never been to Matt's before, how much time do you think it takes to bike from his house?"

Jonah answers:

"I guess it will take me a half an hour."

"You can set the alarm on your watch or, as a reminder, I can call you. Jonah, "picks his poison" and sets his watch:

"I'll put my alarm on."

"Please be home on time. I would really appreciate it, it will make me feel more relaxed about your going to Matt's for the first visit. If this is too complicated because it's a school night, you two could have a sleep-over here this weekend."

Jonah leaves, and, in large measure because of this friendly communication of expectations, comes home just about on time or, at the very least, calls to say he is running late, and when he does, the mom adds, "You did a good job keeping to our agreement. Thank you."

You will not have this sort of conversation like a smiling parental robot every time your child walks out the front door. However, because this is a first-time excursion to a new friend's house, this is a good opportunity to walk through the four self-discipline steps with your child. When an older child does something for the first time, it is an excellent time to *revisit* or *revise* existing limits. Always take time to revise and gradually loosen up limits. Remember Mother Nature; the container has to stretch to make room for the more "grown-up" person.

THE STEPS TO SELF-DISCIPLINE WITH AN OLDER CHILD

- **Setting limits:** (*"Be home before dark and don't be late for our family dinner."*)
- **Conveying the impact of the undesired behavior:** (*"I get concerned if you are home after dark."*)
- **Helping achieve the desirable behavior:** *Reaching home on time.*
- **Teaching:** (*"Time is easy to lose track of if you are absorbed in pleasurable activity. You need to plan, so figure out the travel time to this new destination before you go."*)
- **Structured Choice:** (*"Would you like to be fully in charge and use your alarm or do you need some help from me in the way of a reminder?"*)
- **Redirection:** *"You could have a sleepover this weekend."*
- **Conveying the impact of the desired behavior:** (*"I appreciate your coming home on time, I feel more relaxed."*)

MAKE YOUR CHILD A PARTNER
IN PROBLEM SOLVING

To further your child's growth, ask her to join with you in finding solutions to the disappointments and frustrations she faces when you set limits. When she can't go to her best friend's slumber party because it conflicts with her grandparents anniversary, say, "What ideas (alternatives, options) can you come up with?" She will probably surprise you with her creativity and cooperation perhaps suggesting compromises and choices that might not have occurred to you. "Mom, slumber parties go on all night, maybe I could ask for permission to come very late or if not, I could go over in the morning and bring everybody donuts." Make your child a partner in problem solving and she will be less of a problem because she will learn the critical life skills of compromising, finding a middle ground, and negotiating when she faces wishes and goals that cannot be satisfied, which makes all of life a much smoother ride.

Chapter 8

Developing Your Child's
Moral Compass

Raising Your Child to Be One
of the Good Kids

All parents, even the ones you admire, worry about turning out a child who stays on track, who stays one of the "good kids." We worry about misbehavior not only for what it is, but also for what it might become. The fear is that, despite our best efforts, we might raise a child who behaves badly by making poor, or even damaging choices. The greatest source of parental concern, one that I deeply share as a professional *and* a parent, is the possibility that by not picking the right battles we might be left with kids who are "problems."

It is a challenge. Wonderful families sometimes seem to produce not-so-wonderful kids, those virtually residing in the hot zone, Zone III, acting destructively, dangerously, and/or immorally. Even the best parents have their share of "real handfuls." No one is immune. What's more, these problem kids seem to arrive at younger ages. Doesn't your nine-year-old act just as you did when you were a preteen? Isn't your eleven-year-old, especially your daughter, more the sophisticated adolescent than the gawky grade-schooler? Aren't you shocked to discover how much your second-grader knows about sex? Isn't it mind-boggling to see your youngest kid on the Internet when you still cannot make the 12:00 stop flashing on your VCR? Childhood seems on fast forward.

Fortunately, in spite of the fact that everything is happening faster than we might like it to, it is a challenge that we *can* all meet and triumph over. Even in this fast-paced parenting world, *it is possible to raise a "good kid"* and, surprisingly, as you will see, guilt is key to doing so.

Getting Your Child to Live by the Golden Rule

Remember our cat, the one whose tail was nearly dislocated by a curious toddler? When we first looked at the kitty, we used her torment as an opportunity to help a toddler understand the basics: tails are not for pulling. But it is possible to use such an incident as harassing a pet to introduce your child to a profound boundary concept, that of respect for life, or the Golden Rule of "do unto others."

First, when you encounter the misbehavior do as you would always do, *stop the undesirable behavior and set the limit.* As you save your poor cat from harassment, you can firmly say, "Do not pull the cat's tail. This hurts the kitty." Especially as your child gets near the preschool years, and you are interested in developing his or her deepening respect for *all* life, add these boundary reinforcements as they seem appropriate. These are the words conveying respect for life:

- "In our family, we never hurt Nature's (Earth's, the Lord's . . .) creatures. We only use our hands to make a creature feel safe and cared for. Petting your kitty makes her feel safe and cared for."
- "In our family, we only do 'gentle touching' to our pets, because we want to live in a gentle world."
- "We act with respect for all living things, because we want to be treated that way, too."

These expressions take hurting well beyond concern for a household pet and the condition of her tail. These heartfelt comments begin to introduce the idea that this undesirable behavior is part of a larger vision of how you want your child to behave. All of these reinforce the *positive standards* that you set for your child and family. These words introduce right and wrong, values, ethics, and moral concepts (your own *Family Commandments*) and attach them to limits and expectations about appropriate behavior.

Preschool children are ready to hear these more sophisticated words, because they have the beginnings of the capacity to absorb and understand the feelings of others. Though toddlers are not yet equipped to make any moral evaluations, many developmental psychologists believe that you can start moral training early. Some believe that moral development should begin with a child as early as age two. I come down on the side of starting early.

Proud and Disappointed: Creating Healthy or Good Guilt

What is next? As in other situations, continue to demonstrate the behavior you would like to see *and*, in addition, describe the principle it embodies:

- "Let Mommy remind you how to pet the kitten gently" (*preferred behavior*)
- "The kitty feels good and safe when you pet her gently" (*impact of preferred behavior*)
- "Being gentle is the way to be kind, and being kind is the right way to treat a living creature" (*principle the behavior conveys*)

Let your actions reinforce your words and your words reinforce your actions. Next comes the important addition to your boundary-based strategy. Add words and sentiments that convey the critical importance of respect for life:

- "I am *proud of you* when you are gentle, kind, and respectful to living things; it is the right way to behave. I would be *very disappointed* if you did not show respect for living things."

The use of *proud of you* and *disappointed* might come as a surprise to you. These words have fallen into disrepute, since, in tandem, they are *intended* to create discomfort in a child. These sentiments are meant to make a child feel discomfort for *falling short of an expectation, for doing something that is wrong*. Their descent into disgrace comes from the misinformed and misguided notion that somehow being disappointed in your child will make for damaged self-esteem and create a difficult child.

Let me correct this mistaken idea. Damaged self-esteem comes from being uncared-for and unloved, **not** from having a parent who visibly, verbally, *and* lovingly communicates moral and humane standards that he expects you to uphold, that he is proud to see you maintain, and sadly disappointed to see you neglect them.

Standards and expectations, along with the proud and disappointed feelings associated with them, are the very opposite of uncared-for and unloved. Loving expectations bolster a child's self-worth, because they communicate: "I deeply care about you and about your conduct in this family and the world outside your home. I love you and want you to be a decent and loving human being." Do not underestimate the civilizing power of this message. It makes for children who behave thoughtfully and responsibly when they are under your roof or any other one.

> ▶ **PYB Words of Wisdom:** *Loving parents with standards and expectations of goodness and decency invariably raise good and decent kids.*

Used wisely, *"proud"* and *"disappointed"* are critical words for discipline and especially for stopping kids from doing the *"Really Big Bad Ugly Stuff."* Loving disappointment creates a wonderful possibility that, in your child's heart and mind, he will develop the capacity for discomfort, the internal discomfort called *guilt*. Yes, this may surprise you: *Guilt is good.* Guilt is a key ingredient for raising decent, cooperative kids who grow into good family members and good citizens.

> ▶ **PYB Words of Wisdom:** *Healthy guilt inspires a child to behave in his own best interests and in the best interests of others, and to try to make amends when wrong is done.*

Raising a Child with a Conscience: Good Guilt

To see the marvel of raising a child with a conscience, let's go back to those words, "proud" and "disappointed," because that is where it begins. To be more specific, it begins in a parent's loving gaze. When your child looks into the eyes of the person that he loves most in the world—*you*—and sees *loving pride*, he feels wonderful. If, however, he looks into your eyes and sees downcast *disappointment*, he feels awful.

Your child wants to be good for you, and now, looking into your eyes, he sees that he is not. Reflected in your face, tone of voice, and your words, he can see that he is making you unhappy. As you register your loving disapproval of your young child's actions, his inner voice starts to make connections:

- "Uh-oh, I am doing something that makes me lose my mother's approving gaze."
- "Uh-oh, I am doing something that is not good to do."
- And finally over time, the revelation—"Uh-oh, I am doing something very wrong that I should not do."

"Uh-oh" is your child's first rumbling of that discomforting feeling—guilt. "Uh-oh" is the sound of your child's conscience being born out of his deep attachment and love for you.

Here is a remarkable truth: feeling "bad"—the sting of disappointment and the discomfort known as guilt that grows from that—gives your child the potential to be one of the good kids. The "I don't think that I should be doing this" feeling is the first and critical step in a child's developing self-control. It is the start of self-reflection and self-evaluation. It is the start of guilt and a conscience, an internal guiding voice enabling him to make moral and ethical choices. Your loving disappointment in a failed expectation gives your child a great gift, a moral compass.

Guilt is a bad feeling that does a world of good, and the world good. It makes your child grow into a human being who "feels bad" when he transgresses. It is a bad feeling that eventually helps him make good decisions to be a good child. "I will not only not hurt my cat but I won't hurt any other kittens that I meet up with. And even though my brother does not have a tail, I will not hurt him, either."

This brings me back to a fundamental principle for raising decent kids: good parents must have boundaries, limits, standards, and expectations for their children. As a parent, in making rules and then taking the rules seriously, you now see that you are laying the cornerstone of the all-important *conscience*. You *can* start to lay this cornerstone in toddlerhood, but it takes until adolescence for the entire structure to be completed. A child's self-discipline, which allows him to live by the rules, comes from parents who firmly and lovingly set them down in the first place.

> ▶ **PYB Words of Wisdom:** *A conscience is good kid insurance. It assures us a kid who knows right from wrong and behaves accordingly.*

The Guilt Trip: Unfair Guilt, an Unwise Strategy

The strategy you have just learned promotes *healthy* or *fair* guilt. Healthy guilt makes for a cooperative child who *knows* when she is doing wrong and *stops* doing so. As a parent, you cannot ask for more. So don't! Don't overdo the guilt. It is unwise, very unwise. Do not send your children on a continual *guilt trip*, because it hurts rather than helps them, making for high-maintenance kids. Try your very best never to use the following or any version of the following:

- "You can go on your play date, but it means I'll be here in this house alone all day."
- "After all the trouble I went to to make brussels sprouts with cheese sauce, you are not even going to taste *one*?"
- "How can you throw your Teddy Bear like that when some children are so poor they can't afford a roof over their heads, let alone have special toys, like you do."
- "If you are not quiet and let him rest, Grandpa will have another stroke."
- "This bad grade on your spelling test breaks my heart."

The problem with a guilt trip is that it creates extremes and works too well. Display anguish over brussels sprout refusal, and your daughter might actually swallow a bite, even if she hates the thought and the taste. Turn poor spelling grades into a stake your son puts through your heart and he might just try harder and harder. Yes, as a tactic, a guilt trip *can* promote obedience, too much obedience! How and why you get compliance is the problem.

A guilt trip is not fair. It is about provoking guilt in order to obtain something from your child that he might not otherwise have offered, like staying home when he has a play date planned. It robs children of the opportunity to make choices. It stifles personal expression. A guilt trip gets a child to "behave" even if it puts him at odds with his own good and honest motives or personal preferences, like eating veggies smothered in melted cheese when he honestly does not like them. Whatever you may believe, the purpose of a guilt trip is to control a child's behavior. Even if this is not your motive, and you just want your kid to eat healthy food, beware: Kids feel put upon and resent it.

Placing the Heavy Weight of Responsibility on Small Shoulders

Fair guilt conveys a message that a child is failing an important expectation or a valued standard, that he is not getting a behavior right, that he risks doing harm. In contrast, a guilt trip transmits a very different message and a big burden:

- You, my child, are *personally responsible* for someone else's unhappiness, pain, or even welfare.
- It is not only your behavior that is bad, *you* yourself are bad. What's more, you are bad because you are *doing damage* to someone you love. (*You* are responsible for sending Mom to the hospital. *You* can harm Grandpa by being noisy.)
- At it's worst it threatens the frightening loss of parental love.

All of which can create crippling guilt, painful shame, and even self-hate. Children "guilt-tripped" into obedience can become the proverbial "goody-two-shoes." But a goody-two-shoes, while excessively obedient, is frequently frightened, sullen, a perfectionist, highly anxious, and does not easily get along with his peers. He often suffers from crippling guilt, painful shame, and even, at its worst, self-hate.

This sort of child is high-maintenance because he may be:

- beside himself if his spelling-test grade isn't 100
- frantic if his Grandpa looks ill
- frightened to leave his own home
- hysterical if his teddy bear gets lost
- finicky about food
- paralyzed to take chances.

He will be worried that he is bad, unlikable, unforgivable, and unlovable when he believes he is not doing the right thing, which will be a way he often feels. On the day of a spelling test, a "goody-two-shoes" desperately shrieks, "I have a bellyache, I can't go to school today." Alternatively, perhaps one afternoon at your office, your child calls, frantically crying, "I don't care if you have to work late, I'm not having a play date. I don't like to go to other kids' houses. You have to be home with me."

It is plain as day: guilt trips backfire. Whatever compliance you get, you will have a *big trade-off*. In exchange for having your immediate wishes fulfilled, you will have a high-maintenance kid on the long run. He may appear obedient, but he will still have you pulling out your hair.

Too Much Control Leads to a
Child with a Double Life

Controlling guilt also creates guilt overload and secret misbehavior. Parents who make even the most ordinary behaviors guilt-laden transgressions, like health-food advocates who make drinking soda or eating cookies a cardinal sin, will discover that they make their kids so "sinful" that the offending behavior is driven underground.

At seven, Billy was dutifully eating tofu at home, while scarfing down potato chips, chocolate bars, gummy bears, soda, and more of what his parents thought of as toxic waste on the sly. Billy was a junk-food junkie by nine, but only when his parents weren't looking! A diet of guilt trips led Billy to take two paths in life, an overt compliant course and a covert rebellious way. Overused guilt makes defiance go underground, not away, and that is not a trip that you want to go on with your child.

TELLTALE SIGNS OF A GUILT-RIDDEN CHILD

A guilt trip can create a bumpy road for children and parents. Here are some of the signs that you need to watch for in your child to determine if guilt is overused and your child feels burdened by it. Remember, grade-schoolers will ordinarily have some of these reactions. The guilt-ridden child has many of them, and they are intense and long-lasting:

- Extremely sensitive to criticism
- Does not laugh, have a sense of humor, or seem joyful
- Perfectionist
- Irritable, anxious, and worried
- Shows physical symptoms of worry, such as stomachaches, sleep problems, headaches
- Too good, quiet, and/or compliant, or is rarely directly angry or aggressive particularly to parents
- Doesn't say "no" or express negative feelings
- Lies or is sneaky
- Makes up stories to explain away mistakes or misbehavior
- Blames misbehavior on other people (i.e., sibling) or things

Good Kids and the Transforming Power of Love

When you enable your children to develop this internal guardian called a conscience, your children themselves know right from wrong, can restrain themselves from doing harm, *and* can keep themselves out of harm's way. By developing healthy guilt, you have done just what Mother Nature intended you to do: create a safe haven for your child. Only now, thanks to your good work, your children carry it around within them all the time!

Consider this remarkable transformation. Your child becomes his own good caretaker because you wisely expressed your feelings. That is at the heart of your success. You communicated *loving disappointment*, and from this flowers a conscience. No gunfire, no bloodshed, no battles, and you secured the surest road to peaceful coexistence with your child.

CONSCIENCE: WHAT YOU CAN EXPECT
FROM YOUR CHILD AS HE MATURES

It is important to encourage moral development early, which can begin as early as toddlerhood.* Telling a child that her behaviors have consequences is a way to begin that process, but you will have to wait a good while for a conscience to fully flower.

Infant and Toddler

Has no capacity to recognize the impact of behavior on others, so it is impossible for an infant to feel real guilt over hurting someone else. By eighteen months, a child does understand that others exist, but he still has no sense of right and wrong.

Preschooler

Does not yet have empathy, an ability to truly understand another's feelings, but may feel guilty over hurting someone physically; an early preschooler can't make moral distinctions; on his own, he doesn't know right from wrong and is more concerned that a parent might be angry at misbehavior. The late preschooler starts to understand that her behavior affects other people and starts figuring out another person's point of view.

Early Grade-schooler

Abstract thinking arrives, and this enables drawing of moral distinctions, a child can now evaluate right from wrong on her own and feel guilty for not living up to parental expectations or standards. She knows when she has hurt others. She still needs adults to correct misconduct, but she is starting to feel values and expectations on the inside.

Late Grade-schooler

At this age, a conscience sends clear signals (uh-oh!) whenever a child violates what he knows to be right. By the end of this age/stage, a child has acquired the capacity to understand the right thing to do *without* always being told, thus achieving a critical capacity: to be in control of his own urges and impulses, to take responsibility for his actions, and to act and think like a moral human being. A conscience has flowered, though good judgment still takes more time to fall into place, not completely taking hold until late adolescence.

---

*The original work on the stages of moral development was done by Lawrence Kohlberg at Harvard in the early 1970s.

In Praise of Praise:
A Lost Strategy Found Again

Positive Feedback or Approval: Helping Your Child Get Good from the Outside in

With all this talk of self-discipline, self-control, and conscience, I do not want you to lose sight of something important. Kids are good and want to please, especially you, their parents. I am sure you have seen this repeatedly in your family. There is nothing that brings more joy to the heart of a little kindergartner than bringing home that first clay dish for Mother's Day, or the grade-schooler getting his first perfect spelling test score and announcing it proudly at the dinner table. The preteen boy or girl who makes "the team" and wears the sweaty shirt for three days running is thrilled with the accomplishment and eager to share it with you, his mom and dad. The beaming face of your child lights up because he knows those who love him will heartily applaud his achievements, and that makes his day. In fact, your toddler who has just smeared the walls with finger paint is operating on the same wish to please. How could the little Picasso ever imagine you would not be overjoyed at his creation? That is why when you see the mess you go easy on him. He thinks he has just given you the biggest present in his whole wide world, so screaming at him in horror will be a huge blow to his tiny ego.

Once you understand that kids who are loved and valued want to be joyous pleasing machines, you will come to see that there is nothing more effective for getting kids to be well-behaved than giving them positive feedback—otherwise known as parental approval—when they do something well. When given correctly, approval is a strategy that makes kids a breeze to handle. It brings out the best in them. It is the flip side of the disapproval you display to help your child develop an inner moral voice. Approval encourages him to do all the wonderful things he is capable of as well as he can. What a winning combination. Loving disappointment makes him a sensitive creature, while loving approval makes him a capable one.

There is nothing at all complicated about how to do this as part of your parenting job. Your child naturally seeks your approval, and when he does something right, you supply it. He feels pleased (approved of), so he continues his good behavior. He thinks, "Boy, this approval feels nice, I have to try for that again," and he does.

This positive feedback loop starts to swing into motion very early. One major milestone, where you can readily see it in action, is toilet training. Knowing he wants your approval and has a keen interest in getting this right, you buy your child "a big-boy potty chair." Seeking approval, he wants to use this "potty gift" correctly, as his gift to you. He tries hard to make it to the potty chair, and he does. When he does get it right, what do you do? Stand around the gift you gave to him, cheering the "gift" he gave to you. He is all smiles. Approvingly, you call all the relatives to spread the good news, and the result is that he keeps trying even harder. Soon it is on to bigger and better things, like a go at a grown-up potty, a toilet, and everybody is happy. It is a great system. Approval sought, approval won, and your child moves forward, onward and upward in his cooperation and his competence. His seeking approval and your giving it to him shapes his behavior positively.

This is such a good system that it is shocking that it falls by the wayside. As parents, we tend, particularly as our children get bigger and the milestones of development less dramatic, to focus much more on disapproval than approval of our kids, which does not work nearly as well. Disapproval does nothing positive but is used nonstop by most of us. If you want to see this in action, go to your local mall, take a pad and pen and listen to parents and kids. Write down the one column the disapproving comments you hear, and in another, the approving ones.

- "Didn't you hear what I said?"
- "Keep your hands off those toys."
- "Watch where you're going."

The list of critical comments is endless. What about the sounds of approval, how often do you hear them? How many parents with children in tow say:

- "You were so cooperative to put that toy back on the shelf when I said you may not have it."
- "You did a good job putting the clothes back on the hangers in the try-on room."

- "It was so thoughtful of you to pick up that woman's package when she dropped it."

There is no contest. One side of your paper will be nearly blank, guess which?

Find the Good: Notice Your Child Being Well-Behaved

Here is an easy plan that will improve your child's behavior:

1. **Pay attention to the positives and write them down.** Look for them even if they are small or seem insignificant to you. She shuts off the lights when she leaves the room. He puts his socks in the laundry hamper.
2. **Try to let go of some of the small stuff,** at least for a while. Don't get worked up when she doesn't turn off the TV or he leaves a dirty glass on the table.
3. **Acknowledge your child acting well-behaved.** Once you have done the first two steps, start noting the good things aloud to your child and follow these guidelines:

"Do"s

- **Praise small acts of good behavior** Notice a small behavior and comment on it positively, even if it reminds you of all his previous failings. Say, "I see that you remembered to feed your dog today"—*not* "So you finally remembered this morning that you had a dog!"
- **Offer particular praise** Every time you offer praise, be quite specific. The more specific you are, the easier it is for your child to figure out exactly what they have done correctly, and they will, therefore, find it easier to do the approved action next time. "Thank you for taking the glass off the table and putting it in the dishwasher."—*not* a general "Thanks for cleaning up."
- **Praise the effort or the attempt** Even if your children are not completely successful, you can give them credit and encouragement for a sincere attempt to do well. "You studied hard for that spelling test. Next time you will do better."

- **Recognize improvement** Give credit for progress. Focus on the difference, not the deficiency. "You remembered to hang up your coat when you came in today, that was good"—***not*** "You managed to get the coat in the closet, but it looks like it will fall off that hanger in a second."
- **Give gold stars** Young children may do well if they see physical representations of their praise for good behavior; gold stars on a chart that you can both admire are an old and good standby. "Let's put up a gold star because you brushed your teeth by yourself" spurs a small child on but don't over use them and remember to use them for very specific accomplishments and not for "being a good child," for example.

> ▶ **PYB Words of Wisdom:** *Giving a child a present for good behavior probably does more harm than good. It risks tying good conduct to an outside prize unrelated to his efforts rather than internal satisfaction with his actual accomplishments. Sincere praise connects you to your child emotionally, which outlasts any gift you might offer.*

"Don't"s

- **Don't pile on false praise** Do not be a phony and praise something that is not worthy. Kids feel foolish, because they know it's not true. If he has just scribbled for a minute with his crayons, don't lavish high praise, "That's the most beautiful drawing I have seen in my whole life."
- **Don't praise nonexistent accomplishments** Don't falsify your child's talents and abilities. If he is not doing well on a sport team or in school, do not tell him he is a superathlete or a top-notch student.
- **Don't praise without meaning it** Do not treat your child like a pet, giving empty praise every minute until it is utterly meaningless. "Good boy!" "Great job, son! Fabulous!"
- **Don't overidealize your child** Do not make sweeping statements, since these can feel like things your child will never measure up to. "Such a genius!" "What a star."

> ▶ **PYB Words of Wisdom:** *Never reward a child for the good they will do in the future ("If you promise to do your homework on time, you can have a toy"). This will be about*

as effective as giving your puppy a treat before he has an accident. It just doesn't work. Actually, it gives a child a good reason not to alter her actions, since she gets what she wants even though she misbehaves.

This act of paying attention to and praising positive conduct validates a child and encourages him to keep up his good work, but remember, it only works if you find the good behavior. Make it a point to "find the good." Clear away the noisy clatter of the "no," "stop," "enough," and it will be easier for you to hear and see your child being good and able. A good child always wants to be better, and a better child always wants to be good. If you can get in this positive feedback loop, you have it made.

Chapter 9

···

Empathy and Limits in Action: How to Gain Cooperation and Good Behavior

How to Get Out of Your House in One Piece

Thanks to friends who couldn't use their concert tickets, you have the gift of a rare night out. Lucky for you, your favorite band is performing, but that is where your good fortune runs out. Things are not going quite as planned. No surprise; they rarely do.

- You arrive home from work later than expected.
- Your favorite baby-sitter, Sarah, can't make it and sent her younger sister, Laura, who sometimes fills in for her.
- Your son announces that he has a surprise quiz in his least favorite subject, math, tomorrow.
- As if this wasn't enough, he still has his sniffles.

Despite all these daunting challenges, it looks like you will make it. Then, just as you are about to charge out the front door, your eight-year-old fires the opening shot of a potential battle scene. On the verge of tears, he cries, "Mommy, please don't go. Please stay. Puhleeze!" Oh dear, not now. You are so pressed for time, even the smallest skirmish means you will miss meeting your husband and seeing the opening number. What do you do? Here is what you might be tempted to do but shouldn't:

- Sneak out the back door and burn rubber so you are off before he notices.
- Shout loud enough to startle him into silence, "Look, if you don't calm down I will miss the concert and Dad will be furious."
- Beg him to let you go, adding, "You don't have to wait for your birthday, I promise that you can get that new video game tomorrow."
- Feel so guilty about his quiz and sniffles that you say, "Laura, you can go home. I'll call my husband on his cell phone and tell him to go to the concert without me."

Here is the harder but wiser response:

- Walk over to your son, bend down to his height, take him firmly and gently in your arms, make eye contact, and softly say, "I know my leaving *is hard for you*, especially since you were looking forward to seeing Pauline, but I have to go now. The quiz tomorrow probably worries you, too, and I know math is not your favorite subject, so Laura will help you with your practice problems. And having the sniffles *makes you feel uncomfortable*. Maybe making an ice cream sundae with Laura when you finish your studying might be a special treat to help cheer you up. Let me give you a big hug. I love you. I'll call you during intermission to say good-night."

The truth is that, in a moment of desperation any of the first four reactions are all too likely to be ours. These options may seem the easy way out, sneaking out the back door can sound very appealing when your runny-nosed kid is standing sentinel at the front one, but if overused, they make for more, not less strife. Only the last, where our harried mom makes emotional contact with her son but also maintains her boundaries, will prove to be effective. Bringing emotional understanding into parent/child conflict is key. **Empathy balanced by limits is a winning strategy** for making life with your child hassle-free.

Smoothing the Speed Bumps of Life with Your Child: Creating an Emotional Bridge

Utilizing empathy in order to understand your child's emotional experience from his perspective *and* communicating that understanding is calming and promotes cooperation. When mom acknowledges that her harried leave-taking is hard for her overwrought son ("you feel worried and uncomfortable"), she is responding to his distress with understanding, which makes a crucial difference. Empathy smoothes the speed bumps of life and does with words just what Mother Nature does in her container: it bathes a child in warmth, the warm reassuring sensation that "my parent knows what I feel," creating an emotional bridge between parent and child.

> ▶ **PYB Words of Wisdom:** *Empathy is an understanding hug with words*

Empathy is emotional recognition, acknowledgment of another's perspective. It is *not* agreement. "I understand you" is **not** a parental endorsement of a child's wishes and desires, nor is it telling the child that his point of view is right or should prevail. It is a validation that I, your parent, while not feeling exactly the way you do, can still understand what you are going through.

• I can imagine what you feel (pretty miserable)
• Even if it is not what I feel (harried)

Empathy is only part of what this good parent provides. *She offers understanding in tandem with limits.* This parent is compassionate, but she does *not* abdicate her decisions and actions in the face of her child's whining insistence. She does not simply cave to pressure, nor dispense with expectations, such as doing homework, staying with the baby-sitter, and going out as planned. Mom understands, but her reasonable, consistent rules, standards, boundaries, and expectations stay in place. As with Mother Nature, there is a balance, understanding with limits, warm yet firm.

Of course, there are always exceptions. A parent can and should change decisions when and if there is appropriate cause to do so (say, the runny nose was a bad feverish flu, or the substitute baby-sitter was unreliable), but that means a change of plans because of altered circumstances, not a relinquishing of standards.

> ▶ **PYB Words of Wisdom:** *The balance between empathy and limits, understanding and expectations, is a powerful agent in fostering cooperation; with empathy you can raise well-behaved kids without having to raise your voice.*

Empathy Misunderstood: Pseudoempathy

Many of the most misguided approaches to "modern" child-rearing come from misunderstanding empathy. Empathy is not endorsement of or automatic submission to your child's feelings. It is not a way to say to your child, "Your feelings are always right." It is a way to say, *"You always have the right to your feelings."* These are two very, very different messages. The first creates a self-centered child. The latter gives rise to a child who learns to respect the feelings of others.

Not long ago, I saw pseudoempathy in action. A preschooler was walking to nursery school with her harassed-looking mother. She tugged at her mother's arm, pulling her back and refusing to move.

"Mom, I'm tired. I don't wanna walk," she whined.

"I know you're tired, honey."

The whine got more penetrating, the tugging stronger.

"Mom, I'm tired. I don't wanna walk."

"Sweetie, I know you are tired, just walk one more block and then I'll carry you," her bedraggled mother responded.

Before we had reached the corner, the "tired" but hefty little girl, fully capable of walking, had gotten her way and won the whining war— she was aloft in her mother's aching arms. This is pseudoempathy. This mother was not making emotional contact with her unhappy child; bedraggled mom simply agreed with and rubber-stamped her child's feelings (*"Yes, you're tired."*). Then she acted to confirm that her daughter's feelings were the only ones that mattered, by picking up her "tired" daughter who was fully capable of walking but not in the mood to do so. Without any apparent regard to her own needs, mom succumbed to the tugging, whining, and refusal to budge. Unfortunately, mom did not put up a fight.

When a parent allows a child's feelings to run the show, she caves in, and *indulgence masquerades as understanding*. While there is much psychic damage done to children by parents who don't care to know what their children feel ("I don't care how tired you are, just pipe down and keep walking"), indulgence does it own sort of damage. What offspring learn from this is that the only thing in the world that matters is *their* sentiments. It gives children a power that can make any parent miserable. This parental abdication frightens a child, as we discussed, by making him feel that there is no adult in charge.

"I DON'T WANNA WALK"

A Replay with Empathy and Limits: Understand, Hold Firm, and Redirect

A parent capable of empathetic limit-setting reacts like this: She stops, bends down, makes eye contact, and firmly says:

"I see that today you are feeling very tired, but you are also my big girl, and big girls are not carried, they walk to school."

If her daughter whines, she simply repeats herself:

"You are tired and not in the mood to walk, but I will not pick you up, you are too big and too heavy for me to carry, and you are my big girl."

She adds redirection, which offers other solutions while positively reinforcing the limit of "no carrying":

"Sometimes, if you are tired of walking, it can make time go faster and wake you up if we make up a game. Let me time you to see how fast you can run to the corner. On your mark, get set, go!"

The words are very important, but it is the *attitude* behind them that counts most. A parent who takes into account her child's feelings but believes that she, too, has rights, creates an effective balance between empathy and limits.

The Emotionally Literate Child: Developing Empathy in Your Young Child

I am encouraging parents to be empathetic with their children, but parental understanding cannot be truly effective if children are unfamiliar with their own feelings. Indeed, empathy works best if kids have experience with reading their own emotional reactions. Fortunately, if you are communicative and expressive with your children as they grow, they will develop this capacity for self-knowledge and, with it, an ability to respond to your emotional contact. To accomplish this, early on get into the habit of identifying feelings for your children even when you know that they cannot grasp the meaning of your words. Here are some possible parental reactions, which encourage children to discover their feelings and begin the all-important process of giving them "their words."

Encouraging Empathy in Infants

- "Daddy understands that you're very uncomfortable because you don't feel well. Let me rock you to sleep tonight to soothe you."
- "You're fretting because you are very tired."
- "When I sing to you, you smile and feel happy."

Encouraging Empathy in Toddlers

- "Let me kiss the boo boo that makes you feel so upset."
- "Going up so high in the swing is scary and exciting."
- "Your sad eyes tell me that your feelings must be hurt."

Encouraging Empathy in Preschoolers

- "You say you "hate" the barking dog and put your hands over your ears because it scares you."
- "You're crying about being left at nursery school because you are worried that I am leaving you."
- "You want your baby brother to go back to the hospital so that you can have me all to yourself again."

Kids who can tune into feelings are what I dub *emotionally literate* children, because they can *"read"* feelings in themselves and others. Emotional literacy makes children more responsive and cooperative, because they can take themselves as well as others—even their parents—into account. These kids find that happy medium between marching to their own drummer and getting in step with the parade.

Dispelling Common Myths About Empathy: Emotional Honesty *Is* the Best Policy

Parents are sometimes reluctant to be emotionally direct and honest with kids, as if empathy could open up a virtual Pandora's box of upset and distress. They become concerned about talking to kids about "bad" feelings, so they refrain from doing so, worrying that such discussion puts negative thoughts in a child's mind, making him feel worse, not better. This is a myth; the opposite is true. Identifying a negative emotion and expressing it in words actually releases its hold. When a parent says "I think you may be scared of the monsters" to a preschooler who runs from a dark bedroom crying, a child does **not** become more frightened of monsters. Feeling understood and no longer alone with his fears, he calms down and becomes less agitated. An empathetic parent makes an offer no child refuses: "Let me shoulder some of those bad feelings so that you don't have to carry them around all by yourself."

▶ **PYB Words of Wisdom:** *Exploring negative feelings cannot put them into your child's mind. Sharing them certainly makes them lose their power.*

Some parents are also concerned that empathy "babies" a child or keeps him from becoming logical or rational. Once again, the opposite is true: *Empathy helps make reason possible.* When a frightened preschooler cries during a storm, acknowledging how scared she feels is the correct first response, before you start explaining the natural phenomenon of thunder and lightning. The child who "sees" monsters needs you to see the world through her frightened eyes before she can see it as it actually is.

Deal with feelings first; the rational explanation can and will come later, after your child and you have made an emotional connection.

Once a child feels embraced by your understanding, you can read a pre-school sci-ence book to teach her all about storms (in case you need to know, thunder comes from heated air expanding rapidly, which causes sound waves), or the difference between monsters and shadows dancing on her bedroom walls.

▶**PYB Words of Wisdom:** *Empathy is an emotional bridge connecting you to your child. Once you have laid down that connection between the two of you, reason, logic, and knowledge will travel across it in due time.*

HELP YOUR CHILD TUNE INTO EMOTIONS WITH WORDS AND ACTIONS

Pay attention to physical responses, yours and your child's

- When responding to emotions, get close to your child; bend down to her level, make eye contact, put your arm on her shoulder, embrace her.
- Observe your child's body language, then give it words and label the accompanying feelings: "You cried when you heard that loud noise, it must have frightened you."
- Mirror the way your child feels with your own body language; look interested and/or concerned; frown/smile when you see discontent/pleasure on his face.
- Be demonstrative and affectionate when you are making an emotional connection; kiss boo boos, hug, jump for joy, dance, sing.

Don't Burn Bridges: Avoid Disconnecting Emotionally

Some parents react in ways that are destructive to this important process of promoting empathy. When a crying child, disappointed at his own birthday party, hears, "I don't want to hear any of this nonsense about being unhappy" or, frightened at the circus, gets, "You're afraid of the clown? What are you, a scaredy-cat?" this *breaks empathy*, destroying an emotional bond between a parent and child.

There are many ways to disconnect emotionally. Fortunately, being aware of them can help. Try your best to avoid saying such things as:

- *You are such a cry baby*—it mocks a child for her feelings
- *Stop it, nothing is wrong*—it asks a child to deny or doubt her own feelings
- *It's no big deal, you're exaggerating*—it is dismissive of a child's emotional response
- *You aren't cold (hungry, unhappy . . .)*—it asks a child to deny her own reality
- *Falling off a bike wouldn't make me cry*—it makes your reaction the emotional standard
- *Your friends will think you're a big baby for crying*—it creates humiliation over normal feelings
- *I don't care if you're feeling scared, you'll do it*—power trumps a child's feelings
- *You are impossible, nothing makes you happy*—this dismisses a child's feelings, making problems all her fault.

The loving bridge between parent and child is lost in these reactions. These are moments of emotional disconnection when parents lose a golden opportunity to improve rapport with their child.

> ▶ **PYB Words of Wisdom:** *Don't emotionally disconnect; regrettably, it burns bridges instead of building them and prevents a child from understanding or expressing his feelings, which makes for a kid who cannot listen to himself or you!*

Empathy and Limits in Action with the Younger Child

Morning skirmishes over getting dressed are the worst, whether it is over the new pants that "itch" your toddler, or the grade-schooler's new sneakers that are mortally embarrassing since they are—in the space of less time than it takes you to pay the credit card bill—no longer "cool." Fortunately, if you apply empathy *along with limits,* clothing catastrophes, homework hassles, bedtime battles, like so many other potential hot spots, can turn from pandemonium to relative peace.

Clothing Catastrophes (preschool)

Your four-year-old is moaning over the tragedy of his favorite shirt being in the wash. You react, because it is not humanly possible to do otherwise, unless you are a practitioner of transcendental meditation and have learned how to remove yourself from your own body. So, you mutter to yourself, "Oh no, here we go. He's got six clean shirts in the drawer and none of them are any good."

Then you breathe in, a deep, slow breath, saying to yourself, "In with the calm feelings, out with the bad." Counting to ten will also do. Calmed, with a space in your head to **respond rather than react,** you begin empathy and limit-setting.

- *Open with empathy:* "I know that your plaid shirt is your favorite, and it is disappointing not to have it this morning."
- *Next, state the limit:* "But it is in the wash, and you cannot wear it today."
- *Then redirect and offer a structured choice:* "Let's check the closet to find another soft shirt together. Would you like the blue T-shirt or the flannel shirt?"
- *In the face of further protest, you firmly respond with understanding and problem solving:* "Yes, it's frustrating not to have your favorite shirt in the morning, but you will have to wear another one. Which one do you prefer, the red plaid flannel or the blue T-shirt? If you can't decide, I will help and pick one out for you."
- *You can add a loving parenting maneuver, your own **empathetic link** with your child's problem, adding,* "The other night I was going out, and my favorite blue dress was at the cleaners. I was disappointed, but I chose my less favorite pink dress."

BATTLING A CLOTHING CATASTROPHE THE RIGHT WAY, WITH EMPATHY AND LIMITS

Here is a review of the strategic moves in your empathy/limit battle plan:

- **React** (accept but *do not act* on your initial annoyance: *"Why does my kid have six clean shirts and want the only one in the dirty laundry pile?"*)
- **Calm yourself** (Breathe deeply, count to ten, give yourself a space in your head to think)
- **Respond** (by offering empathy and limits)
- **Empathy** (*"I know not having your favorite shirt is disappointing."*)
- **Limit** (*"It's in the wash and you cannot wear it."*)
- **Redirect** (*"Let's choose another soft shirt."*)
- **Structured choice** (*"The blue T-shirt or the flannel?"*)
- **Repeat empathy and limit, only if necessary** (*"You cannot wear your shirt, which is disappointing, but you can choose another."*)
- **Offer an empathetic link when appropriate** (*"My favorite dress was at the cleaners"*)

Empathetic parents are solution seekers, finding loving imaginative, constructive ways for solving problems and navigating the ups and downs of life, all of which makes for a *resilient child,* one able to bounce back instead of one bouncing off the walls.

> ▶ **PYB Words of Wisdom:** *A resilient child who knows how to smooth the speed bumps of life on her own, because you have shown her how it's done, is an easy child to live with. To diminish conflict, there is no bigger favor you can do yourself than raising a resilient child.*

STRATEGIES FOR ENCOURAGING COOPERATION IN THE YOUNGER CHILD

In the chart below are several common skirmishes that you will likely encounter and creative strategies to resolve them once you have been empathetic and set the limits. Every time you assist your child in creating a solution, she becomes resilient, which fosters her cooperative spirit.

Empathy	Limit	Strategies for Resolving Problems Peacefully
"I know that you love to play in the tub, and it is hard to stop having such fun . . ."	". . . but you must finish your bath because it is time for bed."	*{Creating Resilience}* Let's put your toys away and find a bedtime story about the *Three Men in a Tub."* *{Redirection}*
"Walking by yourself makes you feel like a big boy, and you don't want to hold my hand and feel small . . ."	". . . but you must hold Daddy's hand when you cross the street, to stay safe."	"Let's pretend you are a policeman. You tell me when you see the green light and when I may cross the street." *{Kid in Charge}*
"I know that your brother's changing the TV channel startled you and made you mad . . ."	". . . but you need to tell me in a quiet voice what the problem is and not scream."	"Let's go back and talk to your brother to solve this TV disagreement. Talking over problems helps to solve them." *{Using Your Words}*
"It is hard to come to a toy store and buy a birthday present for Timmy and not one for yourself . . ."	". . . but it is Timmy's birthday and not yours this month, so it is Timmy's special time to get a gift."	"After we pick out Timmy's present, we can go through the store on a 'looking trip' to see what you might want for your birthday next month. We can make a list of your favorite toys." *{Looking Trips}*
"I know you are upset that you have to miss the birthday party at the zoo because we have to go to Grandma's birthday . . ."	". . . but Grandma is looking forward to you and the whole family joining her for this special day, and this party is more important to our family than your friend's birthday.	"Next week we can invite a few of your friends to the zoo. We can also make a pretend zoo. You can make the animals out of clay and then make cages out of these shoeboxes. Maybe you would like to make this as a gift for Grandma?" *{Imaginative Play}*

HELPING YOUNG CHILDREN UNDERSTAND THEIR FEELINGS

To assist your younger child in discovering and verbalizing feelings, try these techniques:

- **Drawing** Encourage her to draw what she is feeling, then see what this may reveal. A black crayon scrawled over a page may suddenly make you realize that your child is very angry.
- **Playacting** Encourage your child to use puppets or dolls to act out stories that might depict his innermost feelings. (E.g., puppets that fight may give you a clue to jealousy of a sibling.)
- **Reading** If there is something going on that, you suspect, may be the source of your child's misbehavior, find a relevant book to read together. (E.g., if a child becomes demanding and "babyish" after a new baby is born, a book can help him find a way to express himself about feeling left out.)

Empathy and Limits in Action with the Older Child

Because grade-schoolers spend more time away from you, they are subject to forces and factors that you may be unaware of, such as pressure over schoolwork and difficult social relations with peers. As a parent of a grade-schooler, you will often live with the impact of uncooperative behavior while the causes may well come from people and places outside your home life.

Also, as your child matures, emotions may not be entirely evident from actions. What your child is thinking and feeling may be a veritable mystery to you—and to her. It is not uncommon to have a frightened grade-schooler who looks and acts like an irritable pain in the neck, or to have a whiny, weepy child on your hands every morning as you leave for school who is actually feeling left out and socially rejected by his classmates. Before you can offer your child understanding, you need to shed light on just what emotions are roiling around in your older child, to uncover unexpressed emotion.

▶ **PYB Words of Wisdom:** *As you attempt to decipher your child's emotional state, bear in mind his developmental stage. Grade-schoolers, as you will recall, are very sensitive, full of self-doubt, self-critical, hyperaware of their peers, as well as moody, all of which is often, very often, at the root of misbehavior. Kidology can give you empathy clues.*

Procrastination (grade school)

Even though she went to her room hours ago, your eleven-year-old dawdling daughter is not finished with her homework; it is almost her bedtime, and you are stressed, just craving some "down time" for yourself.

With an older child, offering empathy is now considerably more complicated, because you need to get to the feelings behind your child's procrastination, which may not be as easy to discern as with "the favorite shirt" skirmish.

Open with "You seem to be having a hard time settling down to do your homework," and watch your child's reactions, verbal and nonverbal. You may well get a hint about her feelings right here. If she is very agitated, you might sense, for example, worry, fear, or fatigue. Then you can help by asking a *few* additional open-ended questions, being careful not to come off sounding critical or your child will shut down.

> *"Is there anything on your mind that's making it hard for you to work?"*
> *"Do you have any bad thoughts that are making it difficult to concentrate?"*
> *"Does the homework feel like too much for you?"*
> *"You seem upset. Are you worried about something?"*
> *"Are you worried about doing well in school?"*
> *"Do you feel that you aren't up to doing the work?"*

This is what you might uncover if you listen sensitively and pick up *empathy clues.*

- *"I don't want to show my science project in front of the whole class."* Your child might be frightened and full of self-doubt. Self-critical, self-conscious thinking *is* par for the course for a grade-schooler, and he is paralyzed by fear, so he doesn't start his project.

- *"I'm not good at spelling anymore, because now the words are so long."* You may discover that schoolwork is suddenly feeling harder, so he is too anxious and tense to practice new words.
- *"Everyone is better than me at math."* Delays settling down to homework may actually relate to his competitiveness and the worry that he can't achieve like other kids, so he can't buckle down to attack the problems.
- *"No one will want to be my friend if they see that I am such a dumb loser."* Your procrastinator may actually be afraid, paralyzed by potential shame, embarrassment, or fear of failure, so he can't even bring himself to begin to try.

Armed with emotional insight, you say with compassion:

"Now that the work feels harder, you are worried that you might not be able to do a good job. That can make it hard to even face your homework."

Then you follow with the limit-setting:

"I see that you are worried, but you need to spend the next half an hour trying to do your work, and then get ready for bed."

You then proceed to *problem-solve* the immediate emotional difficulty—fear—*and* the practical one—incomplete homework. Using a structured choice, you say, "It can sometimes feel less upsetting if you are not alone with your homework and all these bothersome thoughts. Dad or I can sit in your room while you are working. Sometimes listening to music with a headset on can help quiet troubling thoughts in your head and help you focus. Would you like to try the music, or would one of us sitting in the room be better?"

Following this on the spot problem solving, you can also lay the groundwork for any *long-term resolution* that might be necessary, saying, "Tomorrow we can have a family meeting and find other ways to help you with solving this homework problem and with being so upset about how hard school has become."

During this talk, it fosters cooperation if you add your childhood war story, which is another way to show how you emotionally identify with your child's plight. A big dose of physical affection also works wonders.

"You know, when I was in fifth grade, I got such a bad grade on one math test and was so embarrassed that I ripped it up in tiny pieces and tried to get my dog to eat it! Come, let me give you a hug."

Empathy, limits, problem solving, laughter, and a hug are the sure road to a resilient and cooperative kid.

It does take a few minutes of talk-time to connect with your kids emotionally, but it beats a long, drawn-out night of homework hassles and bedtime battles.

BATTLING PROCRASTINATION THE RIGHT WAY, WITH INSIGHT, EMPATHY, AND LIMITS

Here is a review of the strategic moves in your expanded empathy/limit battle plan for your grade schooler:

- **React** Accept but do not act on your initial disappointment. ("Why did she have to dawdle all night, especially when I am desperate for some down time?")
- **Calm yourself** slow down, count to ten, and breathe deeply.
- **Uncover your child's feelings** To gain emotional insight, ask open-ended questions, watch for verbal and nonverbal clues, listen, identify feelings underlying the behavior, take into account kidology and stage-related struggles, look for empathy cues.
- **Respond**
  - **Empathy** (*"You are worried that you will not do a good job."*)
  - **Limit** (*"You need to work for a half hour, then go to bed."*)
- **Immediate strategly for resolving the problem** Offer a structured choice. (*"Dad or I will sit with you, or you can listen to music on a headset."*)
- **Long-range strategy for resolving the problem** (*"We will have a family meeting to work on your homework problem."*)
- **Offer your war story, your empathetic identification** (*"School was hard for me, too. I even got bad grades that embarrassed me."*)
- **Give affectionate reassurance** (*"Let me give you a hug."*)

Your Grade Schooler and Empathy-based Limit-Setting

Here are some all-to-common melees you will encounter and how you can resolve them amicably.

Fussing Over Missing Out on Fun

"It's no fair that I can't go."

Empathy
"I know you are upset that you have to miss your class trip to the planetarium. It feels bad to be left out of such fun with all your friends. I wonder if being left out feels as bad as missing the trip?"

Limit
" . . . but, unfortunately, you have strep throat and you are still contagious, so you can't go to school."

Strategies for Resolving Problems Peacefully {Creating Resilience}
"Let's go online, to the planetarium Web site. We can look at their schedule and buy tickets online for the star show this weekend, maybe with a few of your friends."

{This parent *creates a second chance* for her son's inclusion and being part of the gang. She also acts as a *social lubricant* to get her child back in step with his peers.}

Unruly Friends' Fracas

"Can't you leave us alone, we're just having fun."

Empathy
"You girls are excited about having a slumber party. It's fun to be together and put on makeup and listen to music. None of you want to stop . . ."

Limit

". . . but you are making too much noise and keeping us up. You need to turn out the lights, get into bed, and calm down. I am very tired, and you need to show me that you can respect my wishes, so that you will be able to do this again."

Strategies for Resolving Problems Peacefully {Creating Resilience}

"See if you can try and help each other get quiet. It helps if you all whisper really softly to each other, then, gradually, you will fall asleep. Try to see if everyone can use whispering voices. If it is too hard for you to settle down, you can leave the family room and break up into small 'sleeping' groups. I'll give you fifteen more minutes to settle in. If you can do it, I can get a good night's sleep, and then I will make pancakes in the morning as a treat for everyone."

{Recognizing that group pressure makes it hard to resist misbehaving, this mother does not get angry or single out one child for reproach. She (1) enlists the group as a whole—"try and help each other get quiet"; (2) offers a structured choice—whispering or breaking up the large group; (3) offers an incentive for group cooperation—pancakes in the morning and future slumber parties.}

Refusing-to-Practice Ruckus

"Don't make me practice, it's so boring."

Empathy

"I know that you find practicing the piano boring. Having to do the same thing over and over again is not very exciting. Piano exercises are no fun at all . . ."

Limit

". . . but in order to play real songs, you have to do a lot of the boring stuff first. It's like a ball player. You have to practice your throwing over and over again before you can pitch in a game. There isn't any way to get good at piano without the tedious stuff."

Strategies for Resolving Problems Peacefully {Creating Resilience}
"Perhaps you could break down your practice into three fifteen-minute sessions and take a break between each. I can give you my kitchen timer so you can do that. There is also a new computer program designed to help kids with piano practice. We can look it up online and see if that might help. Your father also hated practicing, but he's glad he stuck with it and knows how to play."

{Mom's solution *breaks down the task, uses technology*—timers and computers—and makes an *empathetic bridge* between son and Dad.}

Sibling Scuffle

"She keeps bugging me and poking me because I won't let her use the computer."

Empathy
"I realize it can be hard to share a computer when you both have important things to do on it."

Limit
". . . but teasing and annoying one another are both unacceptable. There is no reason, no math test or science project, that ever makes it OK to behave in this rude way toward each other. This is my firm voice; this behavior must stop immediately."

Strategies for Resolving Problems Peacefully {Creating Resilience}
"I am not going to play the judge and decide who started this argument or who is right and who is wrong. I will not take sides. I am not going backwards, I am going forward to try and solve this problem now. I will only react to what I can observe, and what I see is that both of you are behaving badly.

"Since you two are not able to cooperate, I will have to do the cooperating for the two of you for the moment. Tonight I will make up the computer schedule, and it will only be enough time for each of you to complete your schoolwork. Tomorrow, when you are both calmer, I am confident that the two of you can sit down and make your own schedule together. If you can, we will follow your plan; otherwise, I will continue to make the schedule until you can find a way to work together on this problem and I will continue to make the computer hours limited to schoolwork until you can come up with your own cooperative plan."

{This parent's approach is to create a solution, not adjudicate a quarrel, which never stops siblings from fighting and arguing. Any parental decision about who is at fault only prolongs sibling conflict. Instead of falling into the *trap of "holding court"* in the middle of a squabble, this parent *temporarily enforces cooperation*. She then gives the solution of *creating cooperation* to her kids and a *vote of confidence* in her children's ability to work things out. She also indicates that her schedule will be stricter than the one her kids will devise, to *give them a good reason to work together.*}

Supervision Skirmish

"I can, too, walk to school by myself. Everyone else gets to do it."

Empathy
"I know it seems that a lot of people in your grade are walking to school alone, but Mom and I decided that you could go by yourself next year, in fifth grade. I'm sorry that it makes you feel angry. I wonder why you feel so annoyed? [Here is where you listen attentively and ask some open-ended questions] Oh, it's because your friends call you a baby. That must feel very embarrassing to you."

Limit
"This is a decision we made because we think it will keep you safe. With all the traffic in town, we would worry if we did not take you to school."

Strategies for Resolving the Problems Peacefully {Creating Resilience}
"I wonder if we could make a plan that helps you to walk alone and feel grown up and that helps Mom and me not to worry? I could walk you to school but stay on the other side of the street while you walk, or I could drive you and drop you off a few blocks before the school. Once we have a chance to see how this new system works, Mom and I can consider other changes."

{Dad's solution is to find a *compromise*, which he then offers as a *structured choice*.}

Changing the Filter: Loosening Limits

In this last example, the father's wise solution takes into account a very important aspect of parenting, *loosening up the limits as children grow*. This dad sees his son's frustration as legitimate, because he knows that, as a parent following Mother Nature's lead, he has to relax his protective hold as his child matures. Dad's creative solution, *finding a halfway point* (walking across the street or dropping his son off), which will make both child and parent satisfied, is a step toward changing the filter while still keeping the container safe. Limits should not be a way we hang on to our children and keep them from becoming their own persons. That restraint causes conflict. This is why dad even entertains the prospect of reconsidering his limit. Limits are crucial, but they are only effective and positive if they allow children to grow and take on more of the world on their own terms. Compromise, adapt, and rethink your decisions period-ically. The filter needs to be changed.

Using Empathy, Limits Setting, and the "D" Scale to Stand Your Ground with an Older Child

Clothing Confrontation (grade school)

"It's not too tight or too short, every girl in my class wears clothes just like this. I have to have this. I have to. I'm not going to school if I can't have it."

Empathy
"From the way your are talking it sounds like these clothes feel very, very important to you. Does it make you feel cool and popular to come to school dressed like this?" What do the girls say to you if you come in your usual clothes? I remember when I was in sixth grade that girls were mean about what you wore and how you looked. Once a girl was so mean to me that I cried, I bet it is still the same. I know that it's exciting for you and all the girls to look like those models and singers that you see on TV and in the magazines . . ."

(This mother voices *no* objections to her child's choices to avoid falling into the no-win trap of engaging in a fight. Instead, she stays focused on uncovering hidden feelings. Mom uses her child's insistence as an empathy clue. Understanding that excessive peer pressure can make a child adamant, this mother encourages her daughter to talk about her preteen longing to fit in. She also uses her own "war story" to help her daughter see that her mom can understand the pressure.)

Limit

". . . but I am not comfortable having you go to school in them because they are very tight and skimpy and seem more appropriate for older girls at parties than for a girl in grade school. This is something that you may not be able to understand entirely but it is not good for young girls like you to be under such pressure to look so grown up and sexy. I think that you need time to grow up and TV, magazines, and social pressure push girls to grow up before they are ready. It's my job to keep you safe and part of the way I will do that is by letting you take all the time you really need to be a child and not encourage you to grow up too fast, which can create problems. It might make you very annoyed with me but you may not have this outfit."

Strategies for Resolving the Problems Peacefully {Creating Resilience}

"I think that many parents not just me, see that you girls are being pressured from many directions. I am going to talk to other parents and your principal about this to see how we can help all of you girls to not have to grow up too fast. Some schools make rules about what kids can wear— like no tight shirts that are above the belly button—and that helps calm things down. Even if the school does not make this policy, we parents can make it among ourselves. I am also going to talk about what we grown-ups can do to stop girls making fun of each other's clothes."

{This parent uses the school and community to help support what she feels are critical safety limits and starts to address another underlying issue, girl's social bullying."}

Empathy Revisited

"I recognize that saying 'No' is not going to make it easy on you and I'm sorry that you will feel unhappy because of it. But when it is comes to keeping you safe and sound, I am willing to take on your unhappiness because I want to make the right decisions for you. This is always a hard moment for both of us when I do my best to make a decision that I feel is right but it is not the one that will make you happy. As your mom, I like to make decisions that make you happy but only if I know they will also keep you safe." [Mom "revisits" her daughter's frustration and the bind they both are in because they have different roles and goals. But she stands her ground; she does not give away parenting power to her child but calmly revisits her resolve to be a responsible guardian, which—over the long run is reassuring to a child.]

Mom has done her pick your battles homework. She has a well thought out concept of the limit she is setting and she has assessed where this battle falls on the **"D" Scale.** Though at first it might appear to be over a matter of taste, in this family, it is not. This mom sees herself as safeguarding her daughter from the pitfalls of a hurried or lost childhood where girls feel pressured to be sexual at a young age, which makes this a **Zone III** battle, not one about differences in personal taste (Zone II). Clarity about where this limit falls on the "D" Scale gives parents the needed resolve to maintain the limits they set and decide that this is a battle worth picking. Even if she protests, her child gets the important message—my mom is not stopping me from dressing the way I like, she is trying to keep me safe. Confident that she is wiser than her child, this mom acts accordingly, making it clear that she is not afraid of child's potential anger when enforcing the limit creates frustration. **Warning:** *Only pick this battle if you sincerely believe that it falls into Zone III. If your concern does not measure up to this level of seriousness, you are picking this battle for the wrong reasons and it will not end well. Review the "D" Scale in chapter 5 to clarify the boundary issue.*

> ▶ **PYB Words of Wisdom:** *Do your parenting homework. Especially when you are facing a serious confrontation, analyze your motives and determine the genuine boundary issue, where it falls on the "D" Scale. This clarity will help you pick the battles that you need to go to the mat for and give you the resolve to navigate them with composure.*

> ▶ **PYB Words of Wisdom:** *Handled with empathy, limits, and creative problem solving, every conflict can be an opportunity for growth, showing your child how he can competently take on his world. This is a gift that will last a*

lifetime making him a happy and well-adjusted human being.

MORE STRATEGIES FOR ENCOURAGING COOPERATION IN THE GRADE-SCHOOL CHILD

In the chart below are typical clashes that you will encounter with your older child and creative strategies to peacefully resolve them once you have been empathetic and set the limits. Enabling your child to create her own solution to conflict creates resilience that fosters her cooperative spirit.

Empathy	Limit	Strategies for Resolving Problems Peacefully {*Creating Resilience*}
"It really feels terrible to be picked last for soccer . . ."	". . . but you signed up for the team, and they are depending on you, so you will have to go to practice."	"David, our neighbor, plays the goalie on the high school soccer team. Maybe you could practice with him so you could get good at that position." {*Finding a Mentor*}
"I know that your brother is annoying to you because he always tags after you . . ."	". . . but you have to play with him when I am making dinner, because that is your responsibility on Thursdays when I come home late from work."	"If you need a break from him, you can let him watch a video for fifteen minutes." {*Using Technology*}
"I know that spending time food-shopping with me can be a pain . . ."	". . . but I am not comfortable leaving you alone when I am not going to be in our neighborhood for a whole afternoon, so I will need you to come along."	"Make a list of things that you like to have in the house. Then you can be my shopping assistant, fill your own cart with these items, and go through the checkout line by yourself." {*Making a Child Your Assistant*}

Empathy	Limit	Strategies for Resolving Problems Peacefully
"I know that you and your sister like to feel grown-up and wander around the mall . . ."	". . . but it does not feel safe to have you off on your own unsupervised, so, if you come to the mall today with me, we will have to shop together."	{"Your eleventh birthday is in two months. Would you like a walkie-talkie as a gift? By then I would feel comfortable having you on your own, and we could stay in touch over the handsets." {*Readjusting the Limits and Using Technology*}

I'm Just a Kid Who Can't Say, "Yes.": Using Empathy and Limit Setting with the Challenging Child

There are days when a child is in a bad mood, which makes him extremely uncooperative: "I don't want to go to bed now; I'll finish my homework later; I'm not going; I don't like to do this; Leave me alone." Then there are kids who seem as if they were born "No" machines as if they are missing the words, "Yes, mom/dad" in their vocabulary.

Kids are intermittently or chronically uncooperative for a variety of reasons, some of which you have already encountered. Reaching them depends on assessing the emotional underpinnings of why they cannot be more agreeable and then communicating this emotional insight to your children. Kids are disobliging because:

They are ready for more autonomy: Our young man who insisted on walking to school himself was not just being willful, he appeared uncooperative but he was actually chafing for more autonomy. He was ready to spread his wings and his cranky complaining was actually a disguised request for more freedom. A parent who recognizes a child's appeals for independence and responds empathetically and reasonably to them advances cooperation.

They are acting out a developmental struggle: Whether it is the two-year-old who insists on feeding himself or the preteen who demands to dress like a teenage rock star, developmental issues often come into play making a child look uncooperative when they are just trying to navigate the pushes and pulls of their own young lives. The quickest route to cooperation is using your kidology expertise to zero in on the emotional basis for their apparent opposition or defiance. Once you adopt this informed and empathetic stance, it stops you both from digging in your heels, instead you and your child work as allies in getting them and you through this age/stage problem.

They have a temperament that makes it challenging for them to cooperate: A child's personality style may make them slow to take on new situations, to make transitions quickly, or to focus. As a result, they may look habitually unaccommodating or resistant when you request things of them. They are not. Adding this insight to your approach ("I know it takes you a little while to get your toys back in place, let me help you" or "I realize that organizing your homework can be tough for you.") makes both of you more relaxed and gets things accomplished with less tension.

They may be under stress: Too little sleep, too little attention, or too much school pressure are just a few of the stresses that may undermine you child's capacity to be obliging. Identifying a child's source of tension ("Studying for your first finals puts you under a lot of pressure.") lightens his load and yours and frees him to be more accommodating and you to be more patient.

They are overcontrolled: Kids who constantly balk at parental directives are often unwittingly balking at feeling overcontrolled. In your effort to "raise him correctly," you may be giving your child "orders" not actually asking him to cooperate. If you find this might be your pitfall, you can reduce tension measurably by empathetically identifying the problem. ("I think that you are not feeling so cooperative because you feel I make too many demands on you.") If you are brave enough to say that and ready to give up some control, you will foster cooperation. Your child will be less resistant as you allow yourself to loosen up.

They are unknowingly acting out a conflict that is actually a reflection of parents differing discipline styles: Kids who are chronically uncooperative are sometimes this way because their parents have very different discipline styles; one is permissive and the other is controlling. By refusing to follow rules and directions, a child is acting like the laissez-faire parent and challenging the controlling one. If you have this spilt in your parenting you must work with your partner to find greater parenting consistency. This split gives a child far too much power.

If you take up this challenging task of trying to be better balanced in your parenting styles you can offer this emotional insight to your child, "I think that you are often uncooperative because you get mixed signals on what we expect from you. We are going to work on being more consistent because it is not good for you to be contrary." **Warning:** *Don't offer this candid empathy unless you are ready to become more aligned. Otherwise, a child will unwittingly use this knowledge of your differences as a wedge between you, which creates the risk that he will pit you against each other, making him more, not less, cooperative.*

The family has unwittingly identified one kid as the "difficult child:" One of the prime reasons for a chronically oppositional child is the splitting that families can establish between siblings: One child in the family acquires the label—"difficult child"—in contrast to another sibling who is anointed the "good one." This splitting is disastrous. It pigeonholes a child into one role, a bad one. Everything she does is seen through this negative assumption about her so that no matter how hard she tries, she can do nothing right; in a fight with the "good" sibling, she is always to blame or if the dog barks, she must have been mean to him. The utter hopelessness of ever doing anything right makes her throw in the towel, then she ends up fulfilling the role of the "bad seed." Unconsciously she feels, "Since you see me as oppositional and difficult, well I guess that is the role that I will take on, permanently. And since I have no way to succeed at making you pleased with me I will get very good at being very bad!" This child is in a bind. It can create an endless cycle of misbehavior, since she comes to act as her parents predict, negatively, thus confirming their worst views of her.

If you hear yourself or your other kids using names to describe one child—tough, pigheaded, stubborn, mean, not nice, the "bad one"—you may be at risk for this family problem. Empathy can help but it is only the beginning. ("I think sometimes we are too hard on you and see things you do in a negative light.") This family injustice needs correction. If splitting is well entrenched in your family, you would do well to seek family therapy to rebalance this family dynamic. **Warning:** *If you do not address this early, you will have hell to pay since this child will invariably become a very difficult adolescent.*

Revisiting Misbehavior: Second Chances and Do-overs

A happy outcome is not always possible at the very moment when the road to cooperation is feeling bumpy. It takes a pretty calm, cool, and collected parent to pull this off. If tempers are high and nerves frayed, walking through these steps when your child is in the middle of having a hard time may be beyond you both. If you cannot get past *reacting* badly in the moment, there is still something to do. Go back to the behavioral mishap. Do not let the problem calcify. Unaddressed, it only gets worse, especially if there is an underlying unexpressed emotion, such as fear, driving it, as in our grade-school procrastinator. Every day that a procrastinator delays homework, makes the next day's homework harder to face. Revisit the "scene of the accident," because it can prevent you from clashing with your child the next go-round. Cindy, who "blew it" with her daughter, Katy, one early morning (mornings are a rough patch for many families), was able to get things on track by the time evening rolled around. She sat in my office telling me about her *second chance* with Katy.

"My daughter is something else. The other morning, it was the usual mad chase to get both kids, Katy and Willy, to their different schools on time. We usually do OK, but this morning, I waited at the foot of the stairs for Katy and she was nowhere in sight. I called for her. No answer. I yelled to her to get a move on. No Katy. She finally appeared at the top of the stairs as if she had all the time in the world. 'Get moving,' I snapped.

"Then, as if she took my words as a challenge, she actually slowed up, and came down the stairs one step at a time, deliberately stopping on each before she would take the next step. She glowered at me in silence. It drove me crazy. I could see she looked irritable and out of sorts, but I was fried. I thought, 'This girl is just trying to get my goat.' I lost it and yelled, 'Katy Anne, get in the car this second.' I was fuming, and Katy was sobbing. That was how we started our day.

"At night I realized that I needed to apologize for losing it. I also thought about Katy's irritability. Maybe something was going on. It wasn't like Katy to be so fussy in the morning. She loves school. I decided to take your advice and 'revisit the scene of the accident.' At bedtime, I went into my daughter's room and said, 'This morning you looked grumpy, but I think you were upset. What's going on?' Then I listened. That was all it took. Katy replied without hesitation: 'There are five things bothering me.'

"She went through several small disturbances and then came to her real heartache, which brought tears to her eyes. Her best friend, Rebecca, had ditched Katy for another girl, Mandy. The two girls had been leaving Katy out of their games, and no longer sitting with her at lunch, and they were now, as my daughter tearfully reported, carpooling to school together. This was the final blow to Katy.

'Mommy, now that they come to school together, their moms know each other, and they will have lots of play dates and time to talk in the car rides and really be best, best friends, and I'll be all by myself.'

"When she finished, I finally got it, and said, 'I guess it was hard for you to go to school today, **especially** because you weren't in the car pool with Mandy and Rebecca and feel so left out. You wanted to be in the car with them, not with William and me.'

"My Katy nodded in agreement and looked as if a big weight had been taken off her small shoulders."

Once Cindy realized the real issue, she offered loving support, an emotional boost, to help problem-solve with Katy—*motherly intervention*. Cindy offered herself as an emotional ally and facilitator in Katy's friendship struggles.

"Tomorrow I am going to call the girls' mothers and talk to them about joining the car pool. They probably thought that because I drive you and William to school, I would not be interested in a car pool, but I will tell them that we are."

"There was no question that we cleared the air. I said to Katy that I was sorry that she was unhappy driving to school with me, but that tomorrow she would need to be on time. I kissed my now-much-happier daughter good-night.

"I'm so happy we got it straightened out. But boy, I wanted to kick myself. If I had just been a little more understanding that morning and said, 'Katy, you look upset. What's wrong?' we wouldn't have fought, the kids would have gotten to school on time, and I could have helped Katy with her friend problems."

Cindy is right. Understanding would have made a difference. No fighting, crying, ill-will, lateness—and, without all that turmoil, maybe even some quiet time to help a young girl's hurt feelings. Even if it comes a little late, getting into our children's heads and hearts is always a winning strategy for raising well-behaved kids. Raising cooperative kids can come with "do-overs" and second chances. If you don't get it right the first time, give empathy, limits, and your loving ingenuity another shot.

▶ **PYB Words of Wisdom:** *Walk in your child's shoes, and she will be less likely to step on your toes.*

More Good News About Empathy: The Gift of Understanding

You are sitting in the family room, reading the paper, when your older boy tussles with his younger brother, who wants to play Chutes and Ladders but can't yet play by the rules and "ruins" the game. Here are two possible but not equally preferable outcomes:

- In exasperation, the older brother calls his sibling a fat baby whom no one wants to play with. Your little one, who thinks that "big bro" is a demigod, looks crushed. In a minute, there will be a torrent of painful tears and more fighting.
- The older brother says, "I know you really want to play with me, but it makes me mad when you mess up the game. Let's go do something else together that we both like. Do you want to go outside and play ball?"

This second outcome is the payoff you reap from raising kids with a well-balanced approach to discipline, empathy, limit-setting, and creative problem-solving. If you hear your child talking to other children in this way, if your child sounds well, a lot like you, he has incorporated the essentials of social cooperation. He is a child who has internalized a sensitive approach to others. He tunes into feelings. He is emotionally literate, which makes him a child who will get along with you, your family, and the rest of the world, and that should make you a very proud and happy parent. Empathy is the gift of understanding that you give to your child and that he gives back to you and the world.

▶ **PYB Words of Wisdom:** *Empathy and conscience-building are closely related: Moral behavior depends on*

knowing the impact of bad or injurious behavior on oth-
ers. Empathy is the capacity to understand another per-
son's perspective, how they feel. The more empathetic
your child becomes, the better developed his conscience
will become.

Chapter 10

Getting Good at Getting Angry: Discovering the Positive Power of Parental Anger

The Power of Positive Anger

Here is a quick review of what *not* to do to get kids to behave: shout, yell, threaten, reprimand, criticize, whine, nag, explode, blame, lecture, take it, moan, curse, swallow, wail, cry, or stew. Gnashing your teeth, muttering under your breath, flying off the handle, wringing your hands, having a fit, and pulling the hair out of your head are also not on the list of winning discipline strategies. Of course, all of us do one or all of the above at one time or another. We may be parents, but we are only human. To make discipline work for you rather than against you, getting good at getting angry is essential.

What Is Anger?

- Anger is a completely normal feeling
- It is our emotional response to things not going as we want, or expect them, to go

- It is a feeling experienced when a goal is blocked or our needs are frustrated
- It is our natural response to displeasure and disappointment, which is why parents are frequently in the throes of being angry

Routinely, kids do not do what we want, expect, or need. We *want* them to sit down. They stand up. We *expect* them to say "thank you," and they run off without a word. We need them to be quiet, but they make a ruckus. Our goals of getting them to school on time, doing their homework, or picking up after themselves are regularly thwarted, despite our best effort, and it makes us mad.

Constructive Versus Nonconstructive Anger

Having an angry feeling is a normal emotional state (anger is as valid a feeling as love), and it is not a problem in itself. How we *react* to this emotional state is the source of trouble. If we allow anger to unleash aggressive behavior, such as ranting or, even worse, spanking, we are not only feeling angry, we are *acting out* on our angry feelings. This is not only unhelpful but might prove to be destructive.

Depending on how it is managed, anger can either foster communication, strengthening our connections to our children, or block its flow altogether, creating ill will as well as more anger in them and in us. Constructive communication of anger alerts children to your needs, expectations, and goals, thereby creating an opportunity for response, support, reconciliation, and amends. It transmits facts and feelings rather than attacks. When you say, "I am very angry that you did not lock your new bike as you said you would and now it is stolen. You will have to go to the police station and file a report, and you will have to work to repay us for the cost of it," you are conveying information—you *expected* your child to lock his bike and be responsible for his possessions. You are also giving him the opportunity to feel the *consequences and cost* of his lapse in responsibility, and act constructively—to file a police report and pay for his stolen bike. Constructive anger gives children a chance and a way to be better behaved.

The nonconstructive expression of anger has the opposite impact. It stops your children from caring about what you ask of them and increases their desire to respond in equally hurtful ways. Rather than encouraging change and improving behavior, it promotes more anger. Shouting. "You're so damn irresponsible. You are never getting another bike and you can forget about going to the hockey game Saturday, too, for that matter," and stalking off in a rage neither informs your child about what you want from him nor keeps the communication flowing between you. Feeling under attack, when you act out your anger, your child will inevitably respond with anger. Can't you just see our bikeless boy furiously stalking off and slamming the door in reply? Ironically, the very point of the conflict—the stolen bike and responsible behavior—is lost in the rising tide of anger.

> ▶ **PYB Words of Wisdom:** *When you constructively communicate your angry feelings, your child's response is more likely to be an apology than a slammed door. Constructive communication of anger keeps doors open— literally.*

Parents are not the only rightful owners of anger in a family. Kids have needs, expectations, and goals, too. Routinely, theirs are thwarted as well, creating their own brand of disappointment and frustration. A child dying to stay up to watch the end of the seventh game of the World Series and prevented from doing so with a parental admonition "It is a school night even if the Yankees are your favorite team," will *not* be a happy camper. No matter what your good intentions are, your baseball fan will be frustrated and angry. Whether or not this encounter mushrooms into an all-out fight or leads your child down a path to cooperation will depend upon the way *you* manage *his* anger. How you as a parent respond to your child's anger is as crucial to your parenting success as how you manage your own. Knowing how to do both well puts you and your child on the same winning team. (In the next chapter you'll get help learning how to respond appropriately when your child is angry with you.)

Seven Steps to Getting Good at Getting Angry

Following these seven steps will produce winning discipline. The first four steps (and the focus of this chapter) will help you manage your child's misbehavior.

1. **Respond rather than react.** Acknowledge that you *are* angry, then calm yourself.
2. **Assess the boundary breach.** Ask yourself is this a Zone 2 or Zone 3 misbehavior? This evaluation helps calibrate your anger.
3. **Be empathetic with yourself.** Develop personal "anger insight" and let yourself know why you are feeling disappointed and frustrated.
4. **Share Information about your angry feelings with your child.** Verbally communicate this "anger insight" so that it becomes information, which lets him know the impact of his behavior on you, and precisely why his conduct has angered you.

Then, by mastering the first four, you can accomplish these three additional steps, (the subject of the next chapter) which will enable you to use anger constructively in the service of implementing effective discipline.

5. **Discover your child's perspective on his misbehavior.** Listen to your child and work toward his view of the boundary he crossed or the limit he violated.
6. **Respond to listening with limit settings and problem solving.** Harness anger to reassert limits that have been violated.
7. **Carry out no-nonsense discipline through the strategy of consequences and cost.** Use your anger constructively to create effective discipline, which corrects your children's misbehavior and prevents it from reoccurring.

When You Get Angry with Your Child: Managing Your Own Anger

Let's start with a child's misbehavior and your anger. For the moment, it could be anything from a minor but annoying infraction—an empty milk carton left yet again in the refrigerator by your seven-year-old—to a more serious transgression—your eleven-year-old lying about a failing grade on a math test. While these are hardly moral equivalents, even a seemingly small offense, like no milk for your morning coffee, can make the steam come out of your ears. Whether your anger originates from a small misdeed or major disobedience, there are seven steps that can help you manage your anger, and they involve using some skills with which you are already familiar.

Step 1. Respond Rather Than React

Your child misbehaves, and it drives you crazy. When this happens, control yourself! Do that deep breathing I have been recommending, or count to ten or more. Talk to yourself. Say "*I will not react, I will respond*," which is an indispensable parenting mantra that helps keep you centered. Work hard to get that space in your head, which enables you to respond rather than react. It is essential to exert self-control and create a place in your mind for reflection.

Slowing down an anger reaction can be helped if you are sensitive to what sets you off in the first place. Not all misbehavior makes us fume. Some things get to us the way other things do not. If you look carefully, you will discover that most anger reactions between parents and children have *trigger points,* hot spots around which anger flares up.

Try to see where your hot spots lie by taking your ***Anger Inventory:***

- What in the course of the last week made me angry with my kids?
- When and where did it occur? Who was involved?
- What triggered the anger and how did it make me feel?
- What was my nonconstructive anger response?

When you complete the inventory, you will see a time, circumstance, and/or an issue that makes you more vulnerable to acting out on your anger. Knowing this will help you to gain control over any outburst you might be inclined to have. By discovering that early-morning fights are your vulnerable "what, there is no milk?" moments, you can forewarn yourself that you are entering a potential hot zone. As you walk to the kitchen, you can remind yourself, "I'm tense in the mornings, so I need to work in *emotional slow motion* before I even walk in for breakfast."

If it was the shock of finding you could not trust your child, this is likely to be a hot spot for a good while, until his school problems are resolved. Figuring this out can help you keep your cool as you grapple with what might be a serious and long-term problem. Preparing yourself for the long haul can reduce the likelihood that you will constantly be flying off the handle over poor grades.

Step 2. Assess the Boundary Breach. Is Misbehavior an Everyday Lapse (Zone II) or Serious Violation (Zone III)?

When you are angry yet give yourself space for reflection, you can consider whether your child's misbehavior is an everyday lapse that falls into Zone II, or whether it goes over the line and represents the breach of a critical rule, which is intolerable and falls into Zone III.

Look at the **D Scale** again:

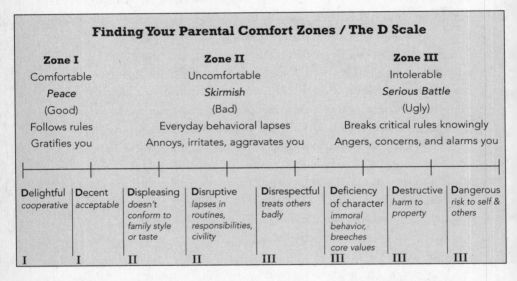

In a heartbeat, you can see where a milk carton catastrophe lands. At its worst, it will only fall somewhere to the left of **d**isruptive. On the other hand, if it turns out that your eleven-year-old deliberately trashed that failed test, lied to you about it, and is not doing his schoolwork, buckle up: you are in Zone III. You have to be concerned about **d**eficiencies of character, or, if this proves to be part of a larger pattern of intentional dishonesty, perhaps **d**angerous behavior, where he is putting himself at risk. When you consider this possibility, keep your mind open until you learn all you need to know about the incident. Later, you may change your perception about the boundary violation: It is all too common for some transgressions to look far worse than they prove to be once you know all the facts and feelings involved.

This assessment is a crucial step in managing your anger. It does not eliminate your anger but it helps you to calibrate it, allowing you to know whether you are just involved in a momentary skirmish or whether you need to gear up for a major battle. This boundary assessment lets you know if you are over- or underreacting and just how far to run with your anger. The offending seven-year-old milk-gremlin warrants a response mode different from that for an eleven-year-old who might be headed for some serious trouble in school and, perhaps, elsewhere. But remember, even when your test-taker looks like he may be going off the deep end, you will stay angry *with* your child. Mobilizing your anger can save your eleven-year-old from harming himself, and, as you know, protection is at the core of your and Nature's parenting approach.

> ▶ **PYB Words of Wisdom: What a Difference a Word Makes** *Do not say "I am angry **at** my child." Instead, say, "I am angry **with** my child," to remind you about the goal of constructive anger: to stay connected, so that, even in the heat of fury, you remain "with your child." It reminds kids that even when angered, you are on their side.*

Step 3. Be Empathetic with Yourself

One positive result of an *Anger Inventory* is that you begin to identify your own emotions when you get angry with your child. This helps significantly with your next step in anger management: being compassionate toward yourself. We have covered this ground, but it needs reemphasis when it relates to anger. In that space in your head, have an inner dialogue where you acknowledge your own feelings.

Look into your heart and figure out what the impact of your child's misdeeds is for you. Be an emotional detective; uncover your own feelings. Even if you cannot do this in the moment of the mishap, be sure to work on developing *personal anger insight*. Reviewing your no-win discipline pattern can also offer you help. Ask yourself open-ended or general questions, which can open the door to personal understanding.

- What is the impact of my child's behavior on me?
- Why am I so angry?
- What is it stirring up in me?
- Why does it get to me?

This is another sort of inventory, but this time you want to develop insight into your *emotional trigger points,* the sensitivities that your child's misbehavior gets to in you. Here are some very common *emotional trigger points* for parents. Perhaps one or more lies at the root of your anger toward your child's misconduct:

- I feel worried, anxious about my children.
- I feel disrespected, not appreciated, or taken for granted.
- I doubt my parenting skills and worry that I have failed my children.
- I feel helpless, out of control, overwhelmed, pulled in too many directions.
- I feel ignored or disregarded by my family.
- I feel foolish, embarrassed, or belittled.
- I feel criticized, hurt.
- I try so hard to do the right thing, but I still get accused of the doing the wrong thing.

From this added self-reflection, you will discover more information about the impact of the offending behavior. Perhaps this is what you might discover:

- With your child who scarfed down the last gulp of milk, you arrive at this insight: *"I really get offended when I work so hard for my son and he doesn't seem to show me consideration. I work in and out of my home, and I do not feel appreciated."*
- When you consider your child's unreported test failure, you come to this insight: *"Nothing makes me more disappointed than discovering my son did something dishonest. I worry about my goal of raising him with a good character. Maybe I have failed as a mom in this crucial area. This worries me."*

Think of this inner reflective dialogue as *self-directed empathy.* Once you come to this understanding and give voice to it in your own mind, it works the way all understanding works—you will feel soothed. Thoughtful compassion toward yourself is an emotional tranquilizer and especially effective for getting anger under control.

▶ **PYB Words of Wisdom:** *Remember, empathy is an understanding hug with words, and you deserve that "hug" as much as your child does. You, like your child, will find it soothing.*

Step 4. Share Information About Your Angry Feelings with Your Child

Do not keep your emotional understanding—your *anger insight*—secret. Share with your child this information about how you feel. *Let him know the impact of his actions on you.* Conveying the impact of his behavior is a crucial component of *all* aspects of raising a cooperative child, especially managing anger. You are a person, not just a caregiver. Your child needs to know and make room for your needs, expectations, and goals as you do for his. Life is a two-way street.

Once you have the words, use your words. Describe your reaction and your angry feelings utilizing "I" statements that reflect the insights you have developed about just how and why you are upset. Don't attack your child with your fury; instead communicate, in the first person, your own emotional reactions to your child's misbehavior. Why use this technique? This is true emotional exchange and communication. Every feeling statement that begins with "I" reinforces the idea that you are not accusing but rather sharing information, your view, your perspective, your expectations, your needs, and/or your sentiments.

- "I" statements say: "This is *my take* on this situation that we find ourselves in together right now."
- "I" statements suggest that there could be another side to the story—your child's side—and leaves room for that view to be heard.
- "I" makes room for "you," the other person, and keeps communication open.
- "I" statements promote a dialogue, not a monologue.

But, most important,

- "I" statements come from your heart, not your fury, and they are never mean-spirited. This is why your child can be open, hear what you have to say, and take in your feelings without feeling defensive.

To do this, first describe the event from your point of view. Then describe your emotional response to the event. Also, add what you expect to happen, since this leads the way to better behavior.

In response to the milk carton problem, you could say:

"When I found the empty milk carton in the refrigerator, *I felt* very annoyed. I have told you many times that *I need* a bit of milk in the morning for my coffee, to get me going for my busy day. That small bit of milk is important to me. So, when I reach for the carton and it is empty, *I feel* as if what I need is not considered, which is why *I feel* especially angry. Please, when you are through with the milk next time, throw out the carton and write on our family shopping list that we need milk, so this does not happen again." Through this "insight" exchange, you have given your child vital information about who you are in relation to him.

In response to the failed and discarded test, you might communicate your anger in this fashion:

"When *I found* your test in the garbage, *I felt* very angry. You said that you did not get it back and did not know your grade, yet here is your paper with a failing score. When *I see* this test with an F on it, and you told me something so different, *I feel* all stirred up inside. *I feel* disappointed by this apparent dishonesty, but *I* also *feel* worried about problems you may be having in school. Now that you know something about how I feel, we need to talk about this further, so I can work to understand *you*."

This emotional communication may feel awkward, especially if your family is used to heated verbal exchanges when there is conflict. If that's the case, don't be put off, think of it as learning a new language, the peace-promoting language of empathy and connection.

▶ **PYB Words of Wisdom:** *A parent who has a mind full of insights is always mindful of how he treats his children and is a better parent for it, especially when it comes to handling anger and discipline.*

KEEP THE DOOR OPEN: AVOID OBSTACLES TO COMMUNICATION

When you are sharing your anger information, here are some pitfalls to avoid:

Do not use accusatory "you" statements. Do not say, "You are so irresponsible for losing your bike." Instead, say, "I worked hard to earn money for that new bike, and the fact that you don't even know what happened to it makes me feel that my hard work is taken for granted, and that makes me very angry." "You" statements can feel like accusations and an attack, which only serves to make a child feel defensive and close down. "You" statements cut off communication rather than foster it.

Do not kitchen-sink. Do not throw every gripe and grievance into the conflict you are having. Do not say, "Not only did you leave an empty carton in the fridge, but you didn't clean your room or walk the dog this morning."

Do not make condemning generalizations. Do not say, "You are *always* leaving things where they do not belong. You *never* show consideration." Keep to the specific event in the here-and-now. Hint: If the sentence starts with the word "you," it is more likely that you will fall into this trap.

Do not give a history of misbehavior, which indicts your child's character. Do not say, "Ever since you were nine, you have been acting in this inconsiderate and lazy way. You've always been a selfish kid." Stay current, focus only on what is going on with the present mishap, and don't assassinate your child's character.

Do not ask questions when you know the answer. Do not say, "Was it you who left the carton in the refrigerator?" or "Listen, remember that math test, did you ever find out how you did on it?" when you already know the facts. This is entrapment, and it isn't honest. Do not expect to get honest answers from a child if you do not ask honest questions. Only ask questions that are genuine efforts to get a grasp on the situation.

Do not overload the emotional "I" statements. Do not issue a laundry list of your injured feelings. You risk overwhelming, confusing, or burdening your child with too much information and guilt. For example, if you grew up poor and never had enough to eat, *do not* include your painful feelings that an empty milk carton reminds you of those terrible days when you were poor and went without food. That's overdoing it.

An Important Reminder to Parents
Who Cannot Express Anger

A slew of parents have anger problems, but it is not about controlling unleashed anger. On the contrary, Deniers short-circuit anger, doing everything and anything to keep fury at a distance. They unwittingly bury anger, so it goes underground and seems to disappear from view. Since anger is an effective parenting tool, these parents need to be encouraged to let the anger out of the bag. Then they can use it in the service of raising cooperative kids. ***Do not fear your anger! Remember, anger is only a feeling***. Anger is an emotion, which will help you become a better parent. What's more, here is the good news: anger put into words creates outcomes completely different from anything you fear; it makes loving bonds between a parent and child stronger because children feel cared for and safe.

What You Should Never Say or Do When
You Are Angry

Anger used well is a wonderful agent of change in families and the world. Just think of anger at injustice, which leads people to better the lives of others. Child labor laws, for example, came into being because people harnessed their anger constructively to make our country safer for our children. Mothers Against Drunk Drivers (MADD) uses anger to make the roads safe for our families.

Unfortunately, some parents are so overwhelmed by their anger that they cannot get to this point. They react to their children in destructive ways. Take a look at the destructive discipline responses that follow, to ensure that you steer very clear of this bunch!

Shame: Some parents lose it when they become angry—belittling, ridiculing, or humiliating their children. They lash out, calling their children dumb, lazy, and/or stupid. They make demeaning comparisons: "Your sister wouldn't be greedy enough to take the last of the milk." They undermine competence, saying, "Your manners are disgusting, let me feed you." These reactions result in shame and an overall feeling of worthlessness. A shamed child not only feels bad, he comes to believe he is bad.

Name-calling: Some parents act out by labeling their children. When they are angry at an active child, she becomes a *demon*; a quiet child becomes a *slug*; or a non-competitive kid becomes a *loser*. Calling a child names nibbles away at his self-esteem and often creates a situation where he believes this to be true and acts accordingly.

Making your children and their misbehavior bad: Unfortunately, there are parents who do not separate the child from the misbehavior. In reaction to a child breaking a glass at the dinner table, this parent does not say, "I can't stand it when you drop things." Instead, he shouts, "*I can't stand you.* You're so clumsy." It is as if they cannot separate the child from the misdeed—a bad action means the child is bad—which makes children feel unlovable.

Mean-spirited or sarcastic talk: A father angry at a window broken by a stray baseball might impulsively snipe, "So, you think you are such a good baseball player, Mr. Smarty Pants?" A mother dissatisfied at her child's efforts to keep her room clean, might snipe, "This is what you call a clean room. You have to be joking." Both may believe that they are just ribbing their children, but poking fun hurts and leaves a child feeling incompetent.

> ▶ **PYB Words of Wisdom:** *From time to time, all aggravated parents have harsh thoughts in their heads. Keep them from coming out of your mouth.*

Nasty threats: Making wild threats that they have no intention of keeping can happen to parents overwrought with anger: "I am sending you to the orphanage if you don't start getting good grades." "I have had enough. I'm going to divorce Dad and leave you both with him." Threats filled with ill-will or frightening prospects are *very* damaging, even when they stand no chance of happening, making a child anxious, uncertain, and generally insecure. This parent is probably too overwhelmed to find constructive ways of keeping her child under control, and the threats are a misguided attempt to stay in charge.

Excessive guilt: Some parents let their anger go overboard by making their children feel excessively responsible for anything that they do wrong. Regrettably, they may say to a preschooler who accidentally swats a playmate, "You hit your friend. How could you do such a thing?" Excessive guilt may paralyze a child. Every move they make feels as if it will cause damage or injury. This parent may be highly anxious and unwittingly uses guilt to keep anything bad from happening.

Icy rejection: Angrily acting out can take the form of withdrawal of affection. Parents may get emotionally cold, stop talking to a child, or cease being physically responsive and affectionate, as if this is a way to show the child the error of her ways. It doesn't; instead children feel abandoned and terrified.

Abandonment: There are parents who feel so helpless and overwhelmed by their anger in the face of a child's disobedience that the only thing they can do is to escape. When their child has a tantrum at the mall, they may throw up their hands and just leave the child wailing, perhaps having the misguided notion that "this will teach him a lesson." It doesn't. It frightens a child and gives him no guidance on how to get anger and frustration under self-control.

Revenge: The parent who furiously retaliates has gone over the edge into unacceptable acting-out and loses control. Angry at his child for breaking his radio, he goes into his child's room, smashes a toy, and shouts, "Now let's see how you feel when your favorite thing gets broken." This is completely unacceptable, since it is cruel and models destructive behavior as if it were an appropriate response to anger, which it never ever is!

Verbal abuse: Some parents are verbally abusive, spewing curses and vulgarities at children when they are angered. When they are highly distressed, it is the only way some parents know how to talk, and it is totally unacceptable.

Physical abuse: We all know the sad fact—too many parents hit their children in a fit of rage. These parents have tempers and little control over their impulses. The position I take is that *it is always wrong to hit a child*. The only way a mother's or father's hand should be on a child is for gentle, affectionate contact. Physical abuse models the most destructive form of acting out. ***This problem does not go away without help, such as anger-management training and/or psychological treatment.***

> ▶ **PYB Words of Wisdom:** *A blow delivered is remembered for a moment by the parent and forever by the*

child. Long after the bruises on a child's body fade, the bruises on the heart and soul endure.

Emotional abandonment: There are parents who unwittingly resort to emotional blackmail when overcome with rage. Their child behaves badly, and they say, "I don't love you anymore." Unconsciously, these parents make the disobedience into a measure of a child's love for them. If you, my child, loved me, you would be well-behaved. Since you do not behave well, you are showing me that you do not love me. So the parents lash back with "I don't love you, either." The problem here is that these parents feel insecure and personalize their child's misbehavior as if it is a message about love rather than a simple misdeed.

▶ **PYB Words of Wisdom:** *What you won't do to a stranger's child, don't do to your own. Keep this in mind, especially when you are furious and feel as if you're about to lose it.*

Help for Those Parents Who Have Severe Difficulty with Anger Control: Finding a Way to Stop Losing It

Unfortunately, there are parents whose anger gets quite out of hand and they use these dozen destructive responses routinely. These reactions, especially if they are rage reactions, can cause serious problems. Their children often develop the very same kind of behavior, turning a family into a war zone. It does not have to be this way. Anger does not have to be a legacy parents pass down from generation to generation. Getting hold of anger happens if a person recognizes its hold and takes appropriate action to change.

Working over the years as I have, with so many parents trying so hard to be good parents, I can assure you that I have never met one who *wanted* to act out destructively. It is just a sad fact of life that some of us do not develop the skills we need to use anger fairly. Is it hard to imagine? Of course not. Beaten as a child for wrongdoing, how could even the most well-intended parent learn to manage anger constructively? Called a "fool" or a "bum" for making childish mistakes, where would he find the model for good anger when he has his own children? Destructive anger is a sad legacy that too many parents bring along with them from their first family into their own parenting.

Understanding is **not** a substitute for changing destructive behavior. Even if a parent has reason to believe his or her past contributes to present difficulties, it is not a reason to continue acting out. Wherever or however these negative reactions came to be part of parenting does not get a mom or dad off the hook. You are responsible for your actions. I am not issuing an *abuse excuse*. If any of these acting-out behaviors are recognizable as your own, you must stop them and make a commitment to learn the positive model of managing anger I am offering here. To do this, professional help or *anger-management training*, both widely available, are an absolute necessity.

> ▶ **PYB Words of Wisdom:** *Your own suffering never gives you a pass to behave destructively to your child. Never! Understanding does not get you off the hook for bad behavior. It is a call to stop the harmful behavior immediately, take responsible action, and change.*

Though no decent parent means to do it, when a mother or father transforms anger into negative, destructive action, a child comes to these conclusions about herself:

There is something wrong with me.
I am a mistake.
I am worthless.
I am no good.

Acted out, parental anger has only one sad outcome: a hopeless child who does not know how to fix things when they go wrong and who will find herself struggling with out-of-control anger as she grows. By contrast, anger that is fairly used tells your child, "You have done something wrong, you have made a mistake, what you did was not good." This reaction allows anger to be the beginning of a new possibility, the possibility of better behavior, which is the direction all good parents want to go.

▶ **PYB Words of Wisdom Using the Gift of Power:** *As a parent, you can use your power to extend your child's reach or you could use that strength to hold him back. The first is using the gift of power and passing it on, the latter is misusing it. As a parent, you should use your greater power to raise a child, not raze him.*

Chapter 11

....

Implementing
No-Nonsense Discipline

Getting Down to Business When
a Child Misbehaves

Getting good at getting angry allows you to get down to business with your child—the business of getting him to behave well after he has done something wrong, when he has crossed the line breeching a significant boundary or violating a serious limit. Now that you have learned how to manage your anger positively continuing with the next three steps (introduced in chapter 10) will enable you to carry out no-nonsense discipline—effective discipline that actually puts an end to objectionable behavior.

▶ **PYB Words of Wisdom:** *Implementing no-nonsense discipline is the surest way to avoid falling back into any of the eight no-win discipline patterns. No-nonsense discipline harnesses the positive power of parental anger transforming you into a take-charge parent. No-nonsense discipline is winning discipline!*

Having first made your angry dissatisfacation over misbehavior clearly known to your child here are the remaining steps for implementing no-nonsense discipline. (After a brief review of these steps, I will guide you through them in more detail.)

5. **Discover Your Child's Perspective on His Misbehavior: Listen to Your Child.** Make a point of talking with your child to gain his view on his poor behavior or misconduct—even if it is a major boundary violation. Listening can uncover hidden reasons for misbehavior.
6. **Respond to Listening with Limit-Setting and Problem-Solving.** With a full understanding of your child's real motives for misbehavior, use your newfound parenting skills to reassert boundaries that have been violated, as well as to find solutions to the problems that you have uncovered.

But now, in the face of a broken limit, be absolutely certain to:

7. **Carry Out No-Nonsense Discipline Through the Strategy of "Consequences and Cost."** Whatever the reason for its appearance, misbehavior demands appropriate repercussions as well as follow-through. The power of positive anger can be used to accomplish this and improve behavior by holding children accountable for their actions and responsible for making amends.

> ▶ **PYB Words of Wisdom:** *Make your child accountable for his misbehavior, and it will eventually add up to your having a very well-behaved kid.*

How to Implement No-Nonsense Discipline

Step 5. Discover Your Child's Perspective on His Misbehavior: Listen to Your Child

Even as you remain appropriately angry about misbehavior, make time to hear out your child's perspective on his transgressions. You will probably uncover reasons and motives for the misdeeds that you and your child might not have fully understood.

Once you have constructively expressed how your child's misbehavior has made you angry, open up a dialogue.

- **Do not attempt to talk when you are furious.** A dialogue should not take place in the heat of the conflict, because you need quiet time for getting angry *with* your child. Tell your child, "I am very angry, but I do want to hear what you have to say. I will be a good listener when I have an opportunity to collect my feelings."
- **Arrange a time just to listen.** Before leaving your child, make a specific arrangement to meet in order to listen: "We can meet tonight at eight P.M. after I put your little brother to bed." This commitment to listen to his feelings, his side of the misbehavior story, communicates a critical point: Anger does not stop our relationship from going forward. We stay connected and work together even when our feelings are stirred up.

How to Be a Good Though Angry Listener

- **Assume the best of your child even at the worst moments.** Assume that you have raised a good child despite the breach of conduct. Good kids, like good people, make mistakes, sometimes even serious ones, but it does not mean that the bottom drops out and all is lost. Happily, most children's bad behavior is a lapse, not the beginning of the end. Even though you might discover more disheartening news (the failed test your son secretly discarded may be a sign he is doing very poorly in all of his subjects), your child is still lovable. Starting with this frame of mind will help you to be a good listener.
- **Convey your dual emotions: anger and concern.** Let your child know that you can hold two sets of feelings toward him when he misbehaves, anger *and* concern. You might say, "I was very angry this morning and I still am very upset about what has happened, but I am also concerned and want to listen to your feelings. Tell me what is on your mind." Recognize and acknowledge your anger but do not let it interfere with your empathy skills.
- **Listen actively.** Active listening means hearing not only what your child says but also helping him to explore his behavior fully. It means enlisting your child in the job of figuring out and gaining insight into his own behavior. To foster this goal, apply techniques with which you already have some familiarity:

---

*This is the way therapists listen.

- *Use neutral prompts:* Only *make nonjudgmental comments or ask open-ended questions, which encourage him to share his thoughts, feelings, and perspective. "Tell me more" is a good, nonjudgmental therapist's prompt.*
- *Mirror comments.* Listen to your child and echo his statements. If he says, for example, "It was a really hard test," repeat his feeling, saying, "So the test felt very difficult for you." If he says, "My teacher hates me, that's why I failed," mirror that, too. Do not deny your child's feeling, even if it sounds absurd. You know his teacher does not hate him, but, at this moment, it describes his feelings. Mirroring makes a child feel safe and understood. In this climate, he will keep talking and you will gain more information about the boundary breach.*

Listening Leads to the Best Discipline Responses

Getting an accurate picture of external reality is *not* the goal of active listening. You want to get a picture of your child's *internal reality*, his perception, which will help you decipher the emotional rationale for his actions. This insight will ultimately lead you to take the best and most effective discipline measures.

For instance, you may learn from your child's act of dishonesty that some area of learning feels very hard to master. Your "dishonest" child may have hit an academic and/or social speed bump and imagines it to be a veritable Mount Everest. The result is that in the typical self-critical mode of a grade-schooler, he may be mortified about his own shortcomings and freeze in his tracks at the prospect of studying. Listen empathetically, and you may find out that the discarded test was about his wanting to *hide his shame*, not mastermind a plot to pull a fast one. In fact, discarding the test in a way that allows you to discover it (he left it in his bedroom wastebasket) may well be a sign that your child wants his problem detected and is asking for your help.

This may not be the scenario that you uncover. I guarantee, however, that your listening date will be illuminating. Once you gain your child's perspective on the misbehavior, you might find yourself reworking your initial assessment. A liar who is being dishonest delib-

---

*Dr. Carl Rogers developed this technique in the 1950s and based his therapeutic approach on this. Now it is generally used as a technique rather than a form of therapy.

erately and repeatedly, evokes parental anger entirely different from that reserved for a worried child who is lying because he is ashamed and disappointed in himself. There is a good chance your anger will shift from fury to something more manageable, leading you and your child on the road to addressing the problem that motivated the dishonesty.

Step 6. Respond to Listening with Limit-Setting and Strategies for Resolving the Problem

Discovering your child's perspective along with his emotional motivation **does not** mean that you endorse your child's dishonest behavior. The shame is understandable, but the behavior—lying—remains unacceptable. Even as you lovingly accept his feelings, do not forget your anger, yet do not be controlled by it, either. Reassert the limits while working toward problem-solving the way you have learned earlier. Clearly restate that dishonesty is *not* a behavior tolerated in your family, nor is it a constructive way to deal with personal problems.

Then be helpful. Try giving him an idea that shifts his view of himself to a more positive light, which can give him a broader perspective on his personal unhappiness and direct him toward constructive action.

"There is no place in our family for dishonesty. I'm sorry that it makes you feel so ashamed to fail a test, but it is not right to hide a failure by lying. It also does not solve your problem but makes it worse. Let's plan to do something right that also solves your problem with schoolwork." Then add a practical problem-solving approach:

"Now that I know that school is so hard for you, we can work to make things better. I have an idea or two. Your school has a club of older kids from the high school, 'Homework Helpers,' who meet with younger kids after school and help with schoolwork; this might be a good club for you to join."

No matter what solution you offer, be certain to balance understanding with a firm, clear message about boundaries. Above all, you want to be certain that your son will learn from this episode and change his ways. To make this change a certainty, you must also implement **consequences and cost.** Introduce this discipline step at the conclusion of your listening date:

"I am sorry that things are tough for you right now, but being dishonest breaks a vital family rule, the trust we share. Lying is never an acceptable way to solve this problem or any other you may have. Since you did something unacceptable, broke our trust in you, there will be **consequences and cost** for your misbehavior."

Step 7. Carry Out No-Nonsense Discipline
Through the Strategy of "Consequences an Cost."

Thoughtful talk as well as empathy about behavioral lapses is crucial, but there does come a point when talk is *not* enough. To learn responsible, boundary-based behavior, children need to experience **consequences** when they go over the line and break a limit. If they have acted badly, they need to see and feel the **cost** of these negative actions. Used correctly, consequences and cost are powerful teaching tools. *They change behavior for the better.* If your child has broken a limit, especially if it falls into the intolerable range—destructive, dangerous, or a deficiency of character—this is a critical step. Since most parents are used to meting out punishment rather than implementing consequences, let me explain what consequences and cost are all about.

We can use a clear though painful and, hopefully, avoidable example of the instructive power of consequences and cost. A child touches a hot stove. The *consequence* is that he feels pain and learns, "Do not touch a hot stove!" The *cost* of pain from the *action*, touching what he should not go near, changes your child's behavior. He learns from the safety limit he has broken. Stove-touching is eliminated. This is an example of a *direct* or *inevitable* negative consequence.

This is a clear example, but a bad one, too. While consequences and cost are a great way to teach, they should *never* put a child at risk. If misbehavior or a broken limit leads to a lack of safety, stop the action. Remember Mother Nature's cardinal rule: Safety first!

> ▶ **PYB Words of Wisdom:** *The closer and more directly your child's misbehavior connects to his experiencing the consequences and paying the cost, the more likely it will be to be an effective form of discipline.*

An Illustration of Utilizing Direct Consequences and Cost: Mom to the Rescue? No!

Imagine that your child has been disorganized, left his book report at home, and is in danger of getting a poor grade for not having it in on time. You could run home from your office during lunch, grab his report off the hall table where he left it, and run to school to deliver it, muttering as you meet him in the hallway, "How could you be so careless about your schoolwork," but this only teaches your disorganized child one thing: "Mom is a bit like our dog. Call her, and she will fetch." Rescuing, which eliminates consequences and cost, does not change irresponsible behavior. If anything, it reinforces the misbehavior, because your child knows that your anger means little and he gets what he wants even if he errs or violates a rule.

But, suppose, you were on track and managing your anger well enough to allow for the negative consequences of your child's misbehavior. What would you do? Let the misbehavior run its natural course. So now, when you get a frantic call at work about the forgotten book report, you *resolutely, but without rancor*, say, "I will not bring the report to school. Since you were not responsible about managing your homework, I guess this will unfortunately **cost** you a lower grade for handing in your report late." There is a good chance that having to face his teacher without his homework and having his grade adversely affected will be considerably more effective than your lecture about his lack of responsibility and organizational skills.

▶ **PYB Words of Wisdom:** *Steel yourself against protecting him from the costs in his young life. There are important consequence lessons of childhood that will keep him from future, more serious failures. Paying the price now can save a costly mistake in the future.*

Creating Consequences That Are a Reasonable Fit

Not all misdeeds fit so neatly into this framework of direct consequences and cost, but you can still use the basic concept. Sometimes you, as a parent, need to intervene and play a part in creating or inventing consequences and cost when they do not happen spontaneously. When you must intervene, try your best to be reasonable, logical, creative, and kind, and keep the cost in line with the violation.

What if the misbehavior was an infraction of your household rule—"Everybody takes care of his/her possessions"? Suppose your daughter did not follow this rule and neglected her clothes, CDs, or even her hamster. Here are some *creative negative consequences and cost* that are a reasonably good "fit" with the misbehaviors:

- **Condemned by the Board of Mom** Make your daughter's messy room off limits. "Since you do not take care of your belongings, the consequence is that this is not a habitable space, and the cost is that none of your friends can play in your room until it is cleaned up and livable."
- **Fashion Disaster** Let your daughter discover that poorly cared for clothes get messy, and that this is the way she will have to wear them. Or remove her clothes from the floor and her room and leave her with one outfit to wear each morning. Revoke her privilege of choosing her own wardrobe as a cost of her misbehavior. Grade-schoolers are fashion forward, so this can be a highly effective cost.
- **Disappearing Act** Remove uncared-for possessions. If she is tossing her CDs on the floor, remove them. "Since you are not taking care of your belongings, I am taking them out from under your care as a consequence of your not respecting your possessions."
- **Mom on Strike** Do not pick up after her or do any cleaning, dusting, vacuuming, or laundry. Let her take responsibility for the chores that you usually take on. (This is only appropriate for a child who is capable but unwilling to do her chores.) "Since you do not clean up, and expect

me to do your chores, the result is that I feel exploited, and I am going on strike for the next week." This is a fair consequence and cost for taking advantage of a worker, namely, Mom.

- **Out of Business** Do not buy her any new personal possessions, clothes, CDs, or treats. Nix the new. The mall may be available, but act as if every store in it has gone out of business. Let your child know the cost of her disregard: "Since you do not take good care of your possessions, I will not give you any additional ones to take care of."

- **Litter-bugged** Do not clean her hamster cage. Tell her, "Since you are not cleaning the cage as you said you would when we let you get the hamster, you will have to live with the unpleasant results of your neglect until you find time to clean it up." If this still does not work, the cost she must pay is regularly supervised cage cleanings.

- **Foster Care** Perhaps she is very neglectful, not giving food or water to her hamster. You say, "You are not keeping your pet safe, and this is intolerable. It will have to go to a temporary 'foster home' until you can prove you are ready to take good care of it." Give her hamster to a friend as a "foster caretaker" until she is prepared to take responsibility. Let her have "visitation rights," where she gives food and water and cleans the pet's cage at the home of the foster caretaker and demonstrates a change in attitude and behavior. Be sure to indicate that this is a temporary situation, which will end as soon as she shows a consistent change in her actions.

> ▶ **PYB Words of Wisdom:** *One of the great advantages of consequences and cost over punishment is that a child can come to know what to expect if and when he misbehaves and alter his behavior accordingly to avoid paying the anticipated price. Punishment offers no such useful information.*

Taking Swift Action: Immediate Consequences and Cost, not Punishment

Sometimes a child's misconduct calls for an immediate and stern response:

- **Misbehavior** You're playing Scrabble when your child starts fussing and won't stop, angrily protesting over everything you do, until he ruins the enjoyment of the game.

- **Immediate Consequence and Cost** "Your behavior is making this no fun at all, and I don't want to play under these unpleasant circumstances. I feel aggravated, and I will not play with you any longer, so I am putting away the game for another time, when this can be enjoyable."

Or

- **Misbehavior** You are about to head for the movies, when your child speaks to you rudely, using foul language.
- **Immediate Consequence and Cost** "The way you are speaking to me is offensive and unacceptable. It feels very unpleasant to be with some-one who is insulting me. I'm angry and I do not want to share my after-noon with you, so we will not be going to the movies."

In both these instances, the cost of misconduct is the immediate loss of a pleasure or privilege—Scrabble and a movie. But this is *not* punishment, since anger was not uncontrollably vented. Instead, a parent's calm but angry resolve conveyed that the child's actions caused dismay, and that con-sequences follow:

- *Treat others poorly and they will not be inclined to give you of their time or effort.*

Delivered with this measured response, a game that ends and a movie that is canceled can each stand as an instructive discipline lesson, helping kids understand that there is a cost for unacceptable behavior.

> ▶ **PYB Words of Wisdom:** *Consequences and cost work only if you say it when you mean it, mean it when you say it, and are never mean while carrying them out.*

BY-LAWS FOR IMPLEMENTING CONSEQUENCES AND COST

Let the consequences and cost fit the "crime"

- **Be Fair-Minded Even as You Make Your Child Feel the Cost** If he breaks a window while playing ball, his paying to repair the window and spending a brief time without his beloved softball can work. Expanding it to include banning all sports, or canceling attending a professional team with his dad the following month, loses a sense of balance and proportion.
- **Follow Through** Consequences and cost work only if you act consistently. If your child has watched more TV than you permit, make the cost no TV for one week and stick to it. Longer stints are not reasonable and not enforceable, so do not set yourself up for failure. Create consequences that are reasonable for both of you.
- **Don't Ever Include Humiliation as a Cost** For example, if you will not allow your daughter's friends in her room, do not tease, embarrass, or shame her in front of them.
- **You Can Use Humor but Not at Your Child's Expense** A sign on her door "Condemned by the Board of Health" is playful but helps make the point. Make sure that your humor does not belittle your child.
- **Never Make a Cost Hurtful or Cruel** If a child is uncooperative at the dinner table don't send her to bed without food or force her to eat food she finds objectionable.

Paying the Cost When Trust Is Broken: Give Your Older Child the Job of Repairing the Damage

When your child has broken a serious limit, oftentimes the result is "broken trust." In order to "pay the cost" for damaging confidence, a child must take on a job—*the job of repairing the broken trust*. Let him know that "Repairing our trust in you will take time. You need to restore it *piece by piece*. We will give you help in planning how to rebuild our trust in you, but doing it is going to be *your* responsibility."

Giving your child the "job" of repairing broken trust is a powerful discipline tool. Join your child by guiding him toward change, but give him the responsibility for doing it. It is appropriate to use this approach with an older child, since one assumes he can understand the concept of trust.

Breaking Curfew, Breaking Trust

Here is an example of how this "repair job" can work. Suppose your child broke a rule about staying away from home—he was out on his bike all day, you did not know where he was, and, by nightfall, you were frantic. You could use this approach of creating a job plan to repair trust.

1. "Right now we feel that we can't trust you to obey our rule to keep us informed about where you are and to come in when expected."
2. "Here are the consequences and cost for your actions: Since you used your bike in a way that was not responsible and broke this rule, you may not ride it for two weeks.
3. "To rebuild our trust, this is your 'repair job.' For the next week, we will expect you home immediately after school. That will mean no after-school play dates."
4. "For the following week, we expect you to be home one hour after school, no matter what. You need to wear your watch every day to make sure you can gauge the time. I'll also put a reminder on your bathroom mirror, so you will see it when you leave for school in the morning."
5. "After this two-week job of working to repair our trust, we will have a family meeting to see how well you are doing your job."
6. You can also ask your child for input: "Are there any ideas that you have about how you can do this repair job? Do you think there is any way we can help you do this job well, because we want you to succeed?"

Soliciting your child's advice as to what he thinks he can do to make things "right" makes him part of the solution rather than part of the problem. Children who have room to fashion their own consequences and cost can come up with creative ideas: "My friend's mom beeps when she wants him to come home. Can I get a beeper?"

You might consider this option if you feel your child really needs help with time management, not just the rules.

Adding your child's input makes room for compromise.

Your child might say, "Could I go out one afternoon for a play date and show you that I can get home on time?" One way to respond to compromise is to say, "I can consider this as a possibility once you have worked on repairing our trust and we see your behavior going in the right direction."

▶ **PYB Words of Wisdom:** *To be effective when repairing trust, consequences and cost must follow a sequence or plan. Take time for this; it is worth it and it works.*

THE JOB OF REPAIRING BROKEN TRUST FOR THE DISCARDED TEST

Monitoring Is the Cost

The child who has lied about failing schoolwork pays with losing his right to make his own homework schedule, as well as with restricted activities, supervision, and monitoring at home and in school.

1. "A part of your repair job will go on at home. You will not be permitted to be in charge of your homework schedule. You will not watch any TV on school nights for the next two weeks, since you need all your time to catch up on schoolwork. Either Dad or I will sit in your room to supervise you when you are doing your homework."

2. "A part of the repair job will involve your school. I will ask your teacher for help. During the first two weeks of the mending, you will have to bring home your work signed by the teacher, so that I can see that you are completing your assigned schoolwork. I will also ask her to call me if you do not hand in your homework, because, as a *consequence* of your dishonesty, I cannot trust your word."

Taking a Parenting Time-Out

Setting up orderly steps that your child follows to rehabilitate your relationship is, in my experience, the only approach that works. It takes the infraction seriously but stays focused on the goal, i.e., reestablishing trust and getting your child back on track. The consequences and cost are reasonable, respectful, and helpful. They are also proportional to the breach of the limit. This is not an endless punishment, but neither is it a quick fix. It takes time to rebuild trust, and the consequences and cost need to reflect that factor. It is clear that Mom and Dad will have a lot of extra work, but they must do it. Grade-school children who do not get this measured, thoughtful, embracing response risk getting lost, especially as they move into middle school, where they are harder to keep track of. This is important work. **Take a "Parenting Time-Out" for this one.** Take time out of anything else you are doing in order to embrace and guide your child.

▶ **PYB Words of Wisdom:** *Constructive anger makes you calm, clear, determined, reasonable, and above all effective when disciplining your child. If this is how you feel you are implementing no-nonsense discipline.*

Avoid Inflicting Punishment: Suffering Does Not Encourage Good Behavior

Here are several discipline reactions that I find noninstructive.

Time Out to Rethink Time-Outs for Kids

Sending children to their room alone when they are misbehaving is not necessarily a good tactic. Leaving a child alone to think of how he has acted badly is not effective; he learns nothing, he develops no problem-solving skills. He may feel abandoned or even grow to hate his own bedroom and/or being alone. A "listening date" following misbehavior is a tool; a time-out is not.

Sometimes children do need a *geographic cure*. Your daughter may be so agitated from fighting with her big brother that it is appropriate to change her locale and separate her from her sibling. However, if animosity and fighting are so bad that a geographical cure is necessary, *parents should take time out from whatever they are doing to try to help an overwrought child*. Staying connected to your child when she is acting badly is very important. In the middle of an outburst, kids desperately need you, so don't leave them alone.

WHEN YOUR CHILD IS MISERABLE TAKE A CONSTRUCTIVE AND LOVING TIME-OUT: "EMOTIONAL REFUELING" LESSENS IRRITABILITY AND IMPROVES COOPERATION

More often then not, an irritable, cranky, or uncooperative child is in need of a "time-out" to be *emotionally refueled*, to reconnect with her attentive, warm, and loving parent. At moments when your child is trying your patience, try your level best to spend a bit more nurturing time with her rather than resorting to banishment or isolation. This warm interlude will bring out the best in her and you, replenishing your child's good mood and restocking her storehouse of good behavior and your patience. Joanne found emotionally "replenishing" her child saves untold aggravation.

Joanne left for work in the morning with her preschool daughter, Jill, sniffling and moaning, "Mommy, puhleeze stay home." That night Joanne came home to a long-planned dinner with her in-laws and a daughter who now sat at the dinner table in her all-time crankiest mood ever. Fortunately despite her daughter's award-winning performance of "grumpiest child of the year," Joanne caught herself getting worked up but managed—despite her embarrassment—to restrain the impulse to reprimand her daughter. Instead she said, "Jillie, I can see this isn't working. I think you need some help since you are in a bad mood and can't stop complaining. Let's go into your room together to see what we can do to make this better. Please excuse us for a few minutes."

Once there Joanne did not scold Jill, instead she said, "I think that you are irritable because you did not have enough time with me, which is especially hard today because you aren't feeling well and we missed our usual together-time when I come home from work. I think it might make you feel more comfortable if we take a few minutes to read a book." Ten minutes later a far more relaxed and cooperative Jill returned to the table with nearly a smile on her face.

Grounding and Extra Chores

These tend to be punishments, which parents throw at children in the heat of anger and frustration. "You're grounded until you're thirty!" Often they are broad and do not bear a direct relationship to the misdeed. If you fail math, having to stay home for a month after school does not make a whole lot of sense, while having to do an after-school tutorial with "homework helpers" promotes change and is an appropriate consequence. What makes these punishments particularly ineffective is that most parents do not enforce either grounding or extra chores very well.

Tough Love

Tough love, the idea that your child needs to "learn the hard way" is a *terrible* punishment strategy. Locking your child out of the house when he comes home late, selling his pet because he does not take care of it, shutting him in his room to get him to bed, are cruel and unloving responses to misbehavior. They should **never, never** be used as part of your discipline strategy. Tough love is not love at all; it's mean.

> ▶ **PYB Words of Wisdom:** *Consequences and cost instruct, while punishment inflicts suffering. If you achieve the former, you are using anger constructively in the service of true and effective discipline.*

What to Do if Your Kids Are Really Not Nice

"Today is your twenty-first birthday. Over these last twenty-one years, I have been your mother. Through twenty of those years, you have been completely delightful and for one you have been an absolute impossible handful. Fortunately, that one year was equally dispersed over the other twenty."

(Marion's toast to her son, Aaron, at his twenty-first birthday)

You know what Marion says is true. Sometimes our children are not nice. On occasion, even good kids break the rules embodied in our Family Commandments. For example, they are unkind or even cruel, and we get very angry, as well we should. Fortunately, these breaches are rare. You know that kids have the capacity to be mean, but such behavior as teasing, exclusion, or fighting usually does not make its appearance until third grade—yet arrive it does. This is when you start to hear:

"I'm glad my little sister is crying because she can't play with my game. I can't stand her."

"I purposely didn't invite Hannah to join our club, because she's a
　big baby."

"He pushed me first, so I pushed him back."

"I took the air out of my brother's bike tires because he's so mean
　to me."

"He's a big cry baby who just can't take a tease."

When a child's behavior gets dicey this way, it requires an anger
response different from that at other times. This is because your child
intentionally directed his misbehavior at someone else and caused harm.
Intentional harm toward another human being requires this consequence and cost: *your child must make personal amends to the individual injured.* The harm may have been with words, such as teasing,
or actions, like a playground-shoving match. Whatever the infraction, if
your child intentionally or willfully brings harm to others, you must add
the following consequences and cost to any other you plan to take.
Remember, these steps are *in addition* to everything else you will do (for
example, creating consequences for harm he caused a friend, such as
suspending play dates for a period of time).

The Three "R"s of a Real Apology

You must help your child to learn to apologize in a way that makes
amends, rights the wrong, and heals. This is the moral, humane thing to
do, and this is one of the highest purposes for discipline, to raise a
decent and humane child. Use your angry parenting resolve to guide
your child through the following three steps, the Three Rs, which make
for a genuine and responsible apology: *Remorse, Restitution, and
Reform.*

1. Remorse
Help your child develop a sense of genuine regret over his behavior.

- **Guilt** Encourage him to feel internally disturbed by his misdeed; in
  other words, to feel appropriately guilty. Strongly convey your disappointment: "I am angry and ashamed that you could act so thought-
  lessly": "This act of unkindness is absolutely unacceptable and makes
  me profoundly disappointed in you."

- **Empathy** Encourage him to feel empathy by reminding him of the impact his hurtful actions have had on others and of how he would feel if it were done to him: "Hannah must have felt sad and hurt when you kept her out of the club. I am sure that if this happened to you, your feelings would also be very hurt." Or, "You would feel very angry and upset if a friend hit you."
- **Amends** Insist that he assume *personal responsibility* for making amends. Help him find a way to go to the person he injured and apologize for his deed. Be firm but never mean, because this is a humbling but vital character-building experience. When they are genuine, apologies sound something like this:

"I am sorry that I did not let you join the club. I know it feels really bad to be left out, and I was wrong to do this; it was mean."

"It was not right that I shoved you when I got angry, it made things worse and it's not good for you or me to fight when we are mad; it just makes us madder and doesn't solve problems."

2. Restitution

Let your child know that he must find *specific* ways to make up for his behavior to the person he has actually injured, and that the best form of restitution is the one that comes closest to redressing the wrong. Buying her a candy bar is not an act of apology for meanly excluding a child from a club. Inviting her to join, is. Candy may be a peace offering, which can have its place, but your child needs to remedy the situation he created. Ask your child to come up with ways he can make up for his misdeeds, and offer your guidance as well. Following an apology, he can make amends by:

Including the excluded child in his activities
Playing with his sister
Pumping up his brother's tires and lending his bike while his
    brother's is unusable
Speaking kindly to his friend and eliminating teasing
Behaving respectfully to his classmates
Using words, not actions, such as shoving, to express his anger to
    a friend

Having committed a wrong, your child must do his very best to right it.

3. Reform

An apology is only meaningful and valuable if your child—or any person for that matter—does not repeat the same action. All this work is meaningless if your child goes back to school and finds another child, not Hannah, to tease. Let him know that a responsible apology involves a commitment to do things differently in the future, and you will expect that from him, otherwise his apology is hollow. Help him work on ways to avoid repeating this behavior, which is something you and he can do using the many discipline tools, particularly consequences and cost, which you have now acquired.

> ▶ **PYB Words of Wisdom:** *If there is the unlikely possibility that your child's behavior is intentionally dangerous, and he is undisturbed by it and unrepentant, this suggests a serious problem, which may be greater than you can handle, so seek professional help.*

BULLYING: WHAT TO DO IF THE PROBLEM IS SERIOUS AGGRESSION AT SCHOOL

If your child is very aggressive, or is the victim of any very aggressive behavior, you should consult your school about starting a program on the problem of bullying. "Thirty percent of U.S. students in grades 6–10 are involved in bullying—as the bully, victims, or both."* The time to start tackling the bullying problem is in grade school, before it takes hold.

Trading Places: When Your Child Becomes Angry with You

In the last chapter (chapter 10) when I first introduced the *Seven Steps at Getting Good at Getting Angry*, I said that parents are not the only rightful owners of anger in a family. Kids at every age and stage have needs, expectations, and goals that are routinely thwarted, creating their

---

* "Student Survey: 30% Are Bullies, Targets, or Both," Christine Kilgore, *Clinical Psychiatry News*, June 2001, p. 9.

own brand of disappointment and frustration. They, like you, get angry. And often, yes, very often, your child's angry frustration is directed at you—their parents—even when you may have little or nothing to do with the cause of his unhappiness, say when he doesn't make it into the finals of the spelling bee. At other times you will be at the center of your child's misery and he will let you know then as well, trust me. Whether it is something unavoidable, like missing your daughter's final soccer game because you had a flat tire on the way home from work, or something intentional, like setting a limit on TV watching even though your son is dying to watch the NASCAR races, you will most definitely make your kids angry and hear about it!

Whether or not any of these encounters erupt into an all-out fight or lead your child down a path to cooperation will depend upon the way *you* manage *his* anger. So now that you have the tools to use your own anger for effective discipline, the next step—and it is a big one—is learning constructive responses to your child's anger when it is directed toward you.

> ▶ **PYB Words of Wisdom:** *It takes resolve, patience, and skill to weather the angry storms that are the natural tempests of childhood. But once you learn to navigate these challenging waters, it will be smoothe sailing for you and your child.*

Here's what you can typically expect. Your child *will* become angry with you, because:

- You have endless demands on your time, such as work and other kids which force you to make hard parenting choices. (*You miss the class play because of a business trip.*)
- You ask things of him when he is in a bad mood. (*He's cranky from lack of sleep.*)
- You brush up against his sensitivities. (*You beat him at checkers.*)
- You touch on an emotional or psychological trigger point. (*Divorced, you've invited the new man/woman in your life to decorate the family Christmas tree.*)
- You are human and make mistakes. (*You forgot the cookies for the bake sale.*)

- Your efforts disappoint. (*You didn't buy the present he wanted most.*)
- You are subject to the vagaries of life. (*You are late picking him up from school because of a traffic jam.*)
- You did nothing—at least nothing that you can immediately figure out. (*Her friend did not invite her to a party, and she is taking it out on you.*)
- You ask for cooperation and/or compliance. (*You insist he give his sister a turn with the TV remote control.*)
- You set limits. (*You don't let him go to the movies until his social studies report is completed.*)
- You carry out no-nonsense discipline. (*You cancel play dates as a consequence of misbehavior.*)

Whatever your intentions, at one time or another, you will hear, "You're so mean, you're no fair, and I hate you." In the face of this inevitable onslaught, here are the things you should and should not do when your children make you the object of their frustration.

- **Tolerate being an object of your child's anger but only if it is expressed appropriately.** Do *not* tolerate any behavior that is unacceptable, aggressive, or abusive, but children desperately need to know that there is room in your relationship with them for them to feel angry feelings toward you.
- **Permit ambivalence.** Give your child room to feel love *and* hate toward you. This helps him learn to live with ambivalent or contradictory feelings, and to discover that he and everyone else is a package deal, a source of pleasure *and* frustration to each other. Learning that it is normal to have a full range of feelings toward you, negative and positive, allows a child to accept in himself the things he loves and the things he does not like.
- **Always encourage your children to put feelings, especially anger, in words.** Give them the words to make anger a source of information about the way they feel, as you have done for yourself.
- **If you have done wrong, apologize.** Being a parent does not exempt you from saying that you are sorry and asking for forgiveness.
- **Don't get defensive.** Apologize and, if it is appropriate, add an explanation: "I am so very sorry that I was late. It was not my intention to be late, but sometimes in life things stop us from doing what we planned. Today, for me, it was a traffic jam."

- **Express interest in finding out more about your child's anger toward you, so that you can both learn from it.** "I understand you are angry at something that I've done. It was never my intent to upset you, but I want to hear from you about your feelings. I can't go back and undo whatever has made you angry, but we can go forward and do things differently. It will help me and you if I can learn more about your angry feelings."

- **Listen to your child's angry complaints even when they feel unjustified or unfair.** Permit your child to tell you the impact of your actions on him even if this means that you must listen to his anger and disappointment when you have done your level best to make him happy. This is really very, very tough on parents, but expect that you will be a source of frustration to your child even if and when you have tried your hardest to be a good parent. You may be trying to be very sensitive to your older child after a new sibling enters your family but still come up short—*from his, little boy perspective.*

  ▶ **PYB Words of Wisdom:** *When your child gets angry, never permit her to behave badly toward you. Instead try to become an emotional shock absorber, respecting her right to be angry and helping her find the words to express her unhappiness, which is especially trying when it feels completely unjustified, unfair, and unwarranted. This willingness to listen without getting defensive will go a long way to reducing the intensity of your child's frustration and is an astonishingly effective tool to stop conflict from escalating.*

- **Do not let your child's anger frighten or intimidate you.** When your child is angry, do not back off, stay centered and clear. Don't give up your parenting authority just because your child is angry. You can change your mind about limits, but *not* under fire. Revisit your decisions, for example about consequences and cost, when you and your child are not in the heat of battle.

- **Be careful that your own guilt or self-doubt doesn't throw you off in the face of your child's anger.** All mothers question their mothering and feel guilty about not measuring up. Working mothers in particular, torn by the demands of job and children, can feel especially tormented when they face a child's angry disappointment. Just know that whatever you do or don't do, it is natural for kids to get disappointed.

- **Do not believe your child's bad press about you.** You are not a mean, hateful monster. He just hates to be frustrated. When he screams with the angry conviction of childhood, "I hate you," this is a tough moment, but just remember: he's wrong, you *are* a good parent. Frustration clouds his vision, so he can't see the loving you temporarily.

> ▶ **PYB Words of Wisdom:** *Don't make your child's bad mood a contagious disease. When your child is flooded with anger, do not react in kind, act kind. Your quiet voice is most loudly heard.*

- **Don't let embarrassment keep you from effectively dealing with anger.** If your child acts up in public, remember, this is a momentary situation, which *all* parents encounter. Try not to let embarrassment keep you from responding appropriately rather than trying to save face.
- **Be an empathy detective.** If there is enormous frustration toward you, there is frequently an underlying meaning. Kids who seem to be overreacting to a situation are frequently grappling with something more than the problem immediately at hand. Help him uncover the feelings behind the anger he displays. You may discover that your child is not just having a problem sharing a TV remote. Perhaps he is struggling with a more fundamental problem, feeling abandoned because a new sibling has "taken his place" which may be the root cause of his intense anger.
- **Consider that your child's anger may be an alert notifying you that you need to institute change.** The anger that your child is expressing may be a sign *you* need to compromise or change. Perhaps in a family with a new baby, an older child's fury may be "telling you" he needs more of your attention, so give it.
- **Frustration may come from too much control.** Your child may be balking under restrictions that are too severe or no longer developmentally appropriate. Change the filter if your child's anger is a sign he needs more control. Don't hang on to your child; he has to be delivered into the big world.

- **Help your child make an important discovery—*there is love after anger.*** Make certain that whatever anger there is between you and your child never, ever gets in the way of your love for your children. Communicate to them that no anger that they feel toward you, or that you feel toward them, can undo the love you have for each other. Tell them, *"No matter how angry I get with you or how furious you get with me, we will always love each other. There is always love after anger."*

SURVIVING A TANTRUM: RESPONDING CONSTRUCTIVELY TO YOUR CHILD'S ANGRY MELTDOWN

Tantrums usually appear around age two and can continue to appear through grade school, but they are more of a preschool problem. A child with a sensitive temperament may be more vulnerable to tantrums, as might a child without language or delayed speech. If your child has a tantrum:

1. Ensure your child's safety. Make certain that your child is not at risk for hurting himself, others, or property.
2. If he is at risk, do a *geographic cure*: remove him from danger.
3. Stay calm. This is especially trying, since tantrums often occur in public and can be painfully embarrassing. Just try to bear in mind that it happens to *everyone* at one point or another.
4. Attempt to embrace or hold your child, not with force but with firmness. It can help her feel more contained, which is calming, since kids are often scared by their own loss of control during a meltdown.
5. Do not raise your voice; speak in a particularly quiet and measured voice. Whisper soothing words of reassurance, "You are going to be OK and I will help you find out what is frustrating you so badly."
6. Some books I have read on the subject advises parents to walk away if the child is safe. I do not. Your child is suffering, even if it seems unreasonable to you. Respect the suffering even if the reason seems perplexing, and offer your help in calming him down.

(continued on next page)

7. If your child uses abusive language or acts mean-spirited during a tantrum, do not give up your role as a limit-setter. Say, "I know that you are extremely upset, but you may not use bad words even if you are very frustrated and angry. You must always try and use your words to tell me that you are upset."
8. If your child is being physically aggressive, hold him gently but firmly and say, "I will not let you hurt yourself or let you hurt me."
9. After the tantrum, assess the trigger. Often it is the result of excessive stress: frustration, confusion, exhaustion, hunger, or overstimulation (I have seen more tantrums per square mile at Disneyland then any other place). Sometimes kids with delayed speech are more vulnerable, since they do not have "their words."
10. After the tantrum, schedule a "listening appointment" to try to decipher why it happened.

What Getting Good at Getting Angry Accomplishes

It is evident what constructive anger accomplishes. It gives you a resolve of purpose. It moves you forward in responding to your child's misbehavior. It is a force for good, helping you develop good conduct and moral behavior in your child. This is really the true goal of discipline. In fact, "discipline" means "to teach." In harnessing compassion and anger, you have become a loving teacher to your child. You have managed your anger civilly, put it in words, and then conveyed your heartfelt feelings to your child for his own good and personal betterment. You are accomplishing the goal of all discipline—instructing for the good.

▶ **PYB Words of Wisdom:** *Anger put into words does not cause harm, pain, suffering, or injury. Anger put into words of feeling, makes your child a decent person and the world a safer place.*

ANGER FOR ALL THE RIGHT REASONS

Constructive anger is anger for "all the right reasons." You are angry because your child has missed getting behavior right, and you are going to help him get on target. Constructive anger is a positive force in your parenting. Here is a recap of the reasons why. Constructive anger:

> Gives you the resolve needed to carry out your plan of consequences for your child
> Allows you to communicate your frustration in words
> Allows you to be firm
> Allows you to be clear
> Allows you to be consistent
> Allows you to follow through
> Allows you to be just
> Allows you to be loving while angry
> Shows your child that you care
> Develops your child's resilience as he sees he can correct even his worst wrongs
> Gives your child a positive model for managing his own anger
> Above all, it shows that there is love after anger

NO-NONSENSE DISCIPLINE: DECIDING IS NOT ENOUGH

Three frogs are sitting on a lily pad in the middle of a pond. One decides to jump in. How many are left on the pad? Three. Surprised by the answer? Then consider this: It isn't enough to decide; to get off his bottom and that lily pad, the frog has to take action and jump in. Whether you are a frog or a parent, resolve is *not* enough. To break the bad habits of no-win discipline and make no-nonsense discipline effective, you must take the plunge and actually implement these strategies. Don't just make up your mind; put no-nonsense discipline into action, and you will have a better-behaved child for sure.

Chapter 12

Getting Through a Day:
Winning Tactics for Surviving
the Hassles and Headaches
of Everyday Life

Parents spend most days living in Zone II, struggling with the everyday hassles and headaches of kids and family life. Homework, car rides, mealtimes, chores, money, bedtime, and sibling rivalry are causes of our would-be battles. From the time we open our bloodshot eyes until the time our children finally close theirs, we face one possible skirmish after another, but we do not have to get bent out of shape in the process. You can take the aggravation out of daily encounters by using these four winning tactics that build on much of the skills and knowledge you have acquired:

- Joining
- Step by Step
- Positive Reframing
- Giving Notice

Winning Tactic #1: Joining

Use what you know about your children and their development to *join rather than fight them*. You can join your child's imagination, his playfulness, or even his dreams, to help you negotiate every battle, from bedtime to mealtime. Joining makes for smoother relations with your child, you become an ally rather than the enemy.

Transitioning Turmoil

Discipline Goal Getting a younger child to give up an activity or play peacefully.

No-Win Reaction "I will count to three and you had better be in that car!"

Winning Tactic Joining your child's imagination.

Your preschooler is not "uncooperative"; he is caught up in the magical world appropriate to his age/stage, and, when he is in this imaginative world, the real world ceases to exist. Play is his work, and he takes it seriously. He is a playaholic, just as he should be. Let's use the illustration of a child so immersed in pretending to be on a motorcycle that you can't pry him loose from a playground jungle gym.

- **Pretend along with him:**
  1. "I can see you are driving really fast and that you are a big, strong, and brave policeman chasing a bad man. Let's drive motorcycles together and catch him."
  2. Make motorcycle noises—"vroom, vroom"—just as he would.
  3. "Let's drive our motorcycles this way, to the car, and chase this bad guy all the way home."

Playfulness gets him off the monkey bars without your needing to pry his body parts loose, because you are permitting him, sensitively and gently, to leave the playground without wrenching him from his imaginary world.

Mealtime Melees

Discipline Goal Fostering good behavior at meals with a distractible preschooler or toddler.

No-Win Reaction "You are not leaving this table until you have had a proper meal!"

Winning Tactic Joining through imaginative games.

For a preschooler, there can be so much going on at the table—chatting, laughing, arguing—that the purpose of dinner—eating—gets lost. Preschoolers are not yet great at concentrating and may still need your undivided attention for a few minutes at this busy time to help her get on track.

- **Play "mouse in the house":**
  1. Tell your preschooler that there is a mouse in the house and that it is stealing all the food from hungry children.
  2. Then put food on a fork, hold it near your child's mouth, and dramatically lament, "Oh my, there is a mouse in the house and he is eating all my Sophie's food and she will go hungry. Where can that mouse be?" Turn away from your child as you "look" for the mouse.
  3. Your child will get her part. She will "steal" the food off the fork. Then you can say, "Oh my, the mouse ate the food. I will have to try and feed my poor hungry child again."
  4. You can repeat this endlessly, as preschoolers never tire of "fooling you." This quick game allows your child to become a "hungry mouse" instead of an uncooperative kid.
- **Airplane or locomotive:** Food on a fork destined for your toddler's mouth can become an airplane flying into the hangar, or a train rushing into the tunnel. Accompanied by the proper sound effects and your enthusiasm, this also does the job.

If these tactics don't work, go on to utilize other techniques with which you are already familiar:

- **Structured choice:** Bear in mind that children go through temporary stages of food preferences. If playfulness does not work, you might try a structured choice. Would you like mashed potatoes or rice? Encouraging autonomy about food makes kids more interested in eating.

- **Legalize food:** Studies have shown that the best and most balanced eating habits develop if children actually eat when they are hungry. Don't force your child to eat if she is doesn't have an appetite. Experts on eating disorders call relaxing control around eating "legalizing food." They find children raised in this fashion have fewer eating problems once they become preteens or teenager.*

Supervision Skirmishes

Discipline Goal Finding acceptable ways to let your older grade-schooler out on her own safely.

No-Win Reaction "Over my dead body are you shopping at the mall alone."

Winning Tactic Joining your child's wish or desire for independence.

Here is the way to peacefully navigate through a request for unsupervised shopping time:

- **Don't start with "no."** Ask your daughter to tell you all about the day that she would like to have without you. Your willingness to entertain her "big plans" can calm the waters and gain her cooperation.
- **Join her wish for independence.** "That sounds exciting and fun, to think about doing things on your own. How would you spend the day?" Let her give you all the details. Bite your tongue. Do not say anything critical or judgmental. Give her the space to try spreading her wings in your conversation.
- **Don't automatically fight her proposal,** even if she describes activities for which you are not yet ready to confer permission. She is just imagining aloud what this adventure might be like. Become her ally, interested in discovering the ways she would like to spread her wings.

---

*The term "legalizing" foods is from the book by Jane R. Hirschmann & Lela Zaphiropoulos, "Preventing Childhood Eating Problems. A Practical Positive Approach to Raising Children Free of Food and Weight Conflicts."

- **Give her room to express all of her desires,** then you do *not* back her into a corner where defiance is her only way out. If you take the challenge out of the proposal, an immature child, who is not ready for independence, will frequently lose her drive to go. Just talking about it is often enough for the time being, and her desire will lose its urgency if you are *accepting* of her ideas. Before you voice your objections, give her time for her own second thoughts. Grade-school kids often come up with lots of big ideas but are not determined to pursue all of them—until forbidden to do so. Do not categorically forbid forays into independence, especially as your child moves into adolescence, or you will have hell to pay.

On the other hand, if you hear her out, you might have a shift in your attitude and need to employ other tactics:

- **Changing the Filter:** Perhaps you will begin to hear, in her description of her day at the mall, that she *is* maturing. Maybe she *is* ready to take some new steps, which may mean there is some work you must do to reset boundaries and limits.

  Consider these options:

  - **Compromise:** *Honor a request for unsupervised shopping, partially. Take her group of friends to the mall and allow them an hour on their own while you have a coffee. Let another mom do this next time, so that your daughter has a chance to feel what it is like to be without you nearby.*
  - **Agree to revisit the limit in the future:** *At a family meeting, discuss your feelings about future timing for greater independence. Don't fall into the trap of setting an exact date, but make it clear that the time* will *come when all of you are ready to handle it. Teach her that, in your family, independence must be earned and is not simply conferred.*

CHANGE THE FILTER IN A TIMELY FASHION TO AVERT FIGHTING ABOUT CONTROL AND AUTONOMY

Here are two tactics that encourage autonomy but allow a parent to remain in charge:

My House Rules

Look at several areas of his life—for example, hygiene, chores, play dates. Using a structured choice, let him decide on the rules he will need to follow. Together you may come up with something like this:

two play dates a week
one sleepover every other week
one bath or bedtime refusal a week*
one special day off every three months

By allowing your child to create the rules that his life runs by, you allow him to gain autonomy and competence. He will also balk a whole lot less, since these are his rules, not yours. His general mood will improve, because he won't be feeling overly controlled.

*Right of Respectful Refusal

Select some requirement of his daily schedule that he can choose not to do on occasion, but make sure it follows a rule, for example, the right to refuse bedtime and ask for fifteen more minutes may be exercised only once a week. Perhaps she may be allowed to refuse a bath one time a week in order to read a bit more before bed. This makes kids more likely to be cooperative than making them give up their routines does, because in return for respecting their choices they'll respect you.

Bedtime Battles

Discipline Goal Getting your frightened preschooler to bed without a fuss.

No-Win Reaction "Don't you dare come out of that bedroom one more time. Those aren't monsters, they're shadows."

Winning Tactic Joining your child's magical thinking.

Think about this: Your child sees monsters, and you are trying to ask him to be sensible and reasonable. Sensible and reasonable is *not* what monsters are all about. A child of this age cannot tell that monsters in the dark are not real. While you should reassure him that they are not and that he is safe, you will first need to *join his magical thinking* to win this battle. Empathy must precede reason. You can try one or all of these:

- **Scare the monsters away.**
  1. When he calls out in fear, go into his room and say, "I am sorry that these monsters are scaring you. I am very angry that they are both-ering you, so I am going to chase them away. See, they are afraid of me."
  2. Then knock on the walls and sternly say, "Monsters, get away and stop bothering my boy, right now!" As an alternative, open the win-dow and chase the monsters out of the house, or use a broom to "sweep" the monsters out of the closet, then leave this monster-chasing equipment in your child's room for safe measure.
- **Magic "weapons."** Create a *"magic lance"* that he can keep by his bed. Buy or make a "sword" (a glow-in-the-dark one might be good). An action figure, such as Superman or Wonder Woman, can also serve this purpose. Conduct a ceremony in which you say magic words that give the sword the power to frighten monsters away. A spray bottle filled with water and labeled *"Monsters Away Spray"* may also do the trick.
- **Make your child more powerful than the fear.** Tell your child that the monsters are very afraid of him and that is why they only come out at night. During the daylight, they are afraid to appear, because he will catch them, so they hide in the dark. Give him a flashlight and let him shine it to scare away the "scaredy-cat" monsters.
- **Throw away the monsters.** Have your child draw a picture of the monster and then crumple it up, or tear it in little pieces, and throw it away.
- **Shadow game.** Darken a room and shine a flashlight behind your hand, so that funny shadows appear on the wall. Let your child do the same, so that she feels in charge of the scary shadows.

Monster fears, which can start at three, recede once a child is about five and he learns the difference between the real and the not real, so be patient and understanding. However, fears are not over; at the next age/stage, scary animals and people fill a child's vivid imagination.

Bedtime Battles (continued)

Discipline Goal Getting a frightened nearly grade-schooler to sleep without protest.

No-Win Reaction "You are just making up stories about robbers outside your window so you can stay up later. You're a big boy now, there is nothing to be afraid of."

Winning Tactic: Joining with magic rituals, lullabies, equipment, technology, and training/instruction.

Your child wants to stay up late, not to manipulate you, but to feel safe. Though your child is past the monster stage, he now faces new fears that more closely resemble reality. These invade his waking imagination and his dreams; kidnappers, murderers, terrorists, physical harm, and death will follow him until about age seven.

Try to "quiet" these anxious and noisy thoughts echoing in your child's mind:

- **Create a magic ritual.**
  1. When you say your final good-night, tell your child, "It is hard to fall asleep with all these troubling thoughts filling your head. I am going to pull the bad thoughts out of your mind and put good thoughts in."
  2. Make a whooshing noise next to each ear as if you are drawing them out.
  3. Follow this by "sprinkling" good thoughts in each eye and sealing these in with a magic kiss on each eyelid.
- **Give your child a magic chant or poem:** Make up a few lines that your child can repeat to herself that can "chase" bad thoughts away. "Bad thoughts go away, bother me another day."
- **Sing to your child:** Families often pass down favorite lullabies, sometimes in languages from ancestral countries. If you do not have one in your family, start this tradition. Many easy and lovely songs are available on tape. Singing is a gentle way to "drown out" troubling thoughts. Tell your child to sing this song to himself when you are not around. (These refrains are ways to *lull* a child into saying *bye* to his day.)

- **Make a nighttime toolbox:** Let your child select "equipment" to put in a "bedtime toolbox." He might choose a flashlight, a night light, a favorite stuffed animal, a storybook, a music tape, and his reliable magic lance, now upgraded to keep the bad guys instead of the monsters at bay.
- **Utilize technology.**
  1. Relaxation audiotapes especially made for children, where the soothing voice of an instructor talks the child into a deep state of self-relaxation, can be valuable. You can even make one yourself; the sound of your voice might have the most calming effect.
  2. Other technology aids, which serve to "drown out" or muffle anxious thoughts in a child's mind include: white-noise machine, heartbeat-or heart-sounds pillow, music playing softly through a headset, TV droning quietly as background noise.
- **Provide relaxation training/instruction.**
  1. With instruction, a child learns cognitive techniques to envision good images to replace the bad ones his imagination generates. This helps a child gain control over her own thoughts. In his book *no more monsters in the closet*, Dr. Jerry Brown provides excellent suggestions for teaching children how to channel their own imaginations to calm their fears.
  2. Yoga is an excellent way to help people learn to control their bodies, fear, and stress reactions, such as rapid shallow breathing, jumpy stomach, rapid heart-beating, and nervousness. Suggest that your school introduce it as part of the gym curriculum for early grade-schoolers. Learning yoga can help you become your child's relaxation coach.
- **Consider that your child's temperament may be the problem.** Not every child who resists bedtime is frightened of scary things. Due to their temperament, some children just can't bear letting go of the day and refuse to close their eyes for *fear of missing out on something*. Anxiety about loss is their "monster." Some of these tactics, such as relaxation tapes, singing, yoga, and/or a favorite stuffed animal can help an active or restless child relax and let go of her day.

> ▶ **PYB Words of Wisdom:** *Above all, join your child's magical world rather than fight it. Take her monsters seriously, learn to tell time her way, make up stories, be playful, and be silly. The more you can access the whim-*

sical, playful child in yourself, the less you will be battling your child.

Winning Tactic #2: Step by Step

In her wonderful book *Bird by Bird*, the writer Anne Lamott tells how her young brother once felt paralyzed by a science project in which he had to write about many, many birds. Seeing his son's procrastination, their father suggested, "Just do it bird by bird," which freed the boy to do the daunting assignment. Children are more cooperative when you help them take small steps from one activity to another, or break an activity down into individual tasks. When a parent "just asks" a child to stop playing and come to dinner, there is a bigger gap than you might realize between what you want him to stop doing and what you want him to do next. Setting out tasks step by step *bridges* this gap.

Homework Hassles

Discipline Goal Getting homework completed in a timely manner.

No-Win Reaction "How many times have I told you to stop playing and start your homework."

Winning Tactic Step by step, to make daunting schoolwork doable.
   Break down your general request to "buckle down and work" into small steps. Try this approach:

1. **Assist him with a transition** Give him a warning that he will need to stop his play in a few minutes, then say, "Playing time is over. Please put away your ball and mitt. Let me go with you to your room to help you settle in to do your homework. I know that sometimes sitting down to do homework can feel hard. I think you will manage your work better if I help get you on track."
2. **Lay out steps for homework readiness** "Let's go through a step-by-step checklist of things you need to do to get ready to do your math homework." (Write down this checklist and post it near his desk.)
   - Clear your desk.
   - Take out a pencil.

- Check your assignment pad.
- Take out *only* one book (a pile of books on a child's desk can make homework look insurmountable).
- Use a bookstand to keep the page open.
- Take out your subject notebook.

3. **Break down the homework itself into manageable pieces** When he is ready, add this: "Now let's help you focus on just your math homework, step by step."
   - "Clear your desk, check it on the list, and only then go on to taking out a pencil."
   - "To help yourself focus on one problem, put this ruler across the page in your math book."

4. **Initially stay close by a to keep an eye on things** "I can sit here for a few moments to get you started on your list." If your child is energetic, you can also add, "If you need to, get up and stretch after two or three problem."

5. **Give him room to try his skills** Once you see that he had completed several problems, say, "When you are all done with your math, call me and we can see what schoolwork you have to do next."

   Bear in mind kidology and the characteristics of this age/stage A grade-schooler is not a good manager and is not yet analytical. He is not a good task completer. His self criticism also gets in the way of settling in to work. Step-by-step technique gives him the responsibility for doing his tasks but respects his need for organizational support that adults may forget he still requires.

> ▶ **PYB Words of Wisdom:** *As with so many other strategies acquired in childhood step-by-step is a useful tool for getting through grade school and all of life. Giving strategies to your child is a gift for now and forever.*

HELPING HANDS: SMOOTHING
THE ROUGH PATCHES

Perhaps your child is having a very tough time with schoolwork. He gives it his best shot, yet still struggles, and so suffers acutely. He sulks, cries, or, at worst, feels frantic. A cardinal rule in parenting, as in all of life, is *not to stand by idly and let people suffer*. Help your child if he is in a tight spot not from misbehavior but from being overwhelmed. It does not ruin a child for life to relieve his suffering, which is different from doing his homework for him. At your child's darkest hour, offer your *Helping Hands:*

• Tell him if he is ever stuck with something, that he finds daunting Mom or Dad can use their "helping hands" to lift him over the obstacle. Indicate clearly that you are not going to do the work for him but that sometimes, when you come to a high wall, you need a lift.
• Let him know that he can ask for a helping hand *only* if he has already tried hard himself, and that it is *not available* if he has left his work to the last minute.

When children encounter learning obstacles offer "helping hands" to avoid continual tension-conflict.

Anxiety and/or panic interferes with learning. Identify and empathize with his problem: "Keeping those new words in your head can be hard, especially if you are anxious." A "helping hands" response would be to make him *flash cards* and work with him to show him how they can be memory aids. Forcing him to study longer, or a note asking his teacher to excuse him from the test, would not be.

A lag in a specific skill interferes with learning. Children develop skills unevenly, one might become a particular obstacle, causing him overwhelming frustration and making him "feel stupid": A child may be a slow reader, which interferes with his otherwise adequate math skills and his morale. A "helping hands" response to this struggle can be: "I know that you find the reading part of the math problems hard, maybe I could read them aloud for you. Then you can concentrate on the math."

A learning disability (LD) interferes with learning. Some children with LD have a glitch in one area. For example, they may not have

(continued on next page)

good auditory skills and find it difficult to take in what is said in class. A helping hand would be to acquaint the teacher with your child's best learning mode, perhaps asking that she write his assignment down rather than give it to him orally.

A helping hand to child in an area of deficiency or developmental lag is especially critical for children with Attention Deficit Disorder (ADD) or Learning Disabilities, so that they do not come to believe that they are stupid.

Supervision Skirmishes

Discipline Goal Assuring that outings away from home are in your acceptable comfort zone, especially regarding safety.

No-Win Reaction "I don't care if she is the most fun girl in the school; you are not having a sleepover at a perfect stranger's house."

Winning Tactic Step by step toward creating a safety comfort level.

With a grade-schooler under your roof, I think that making "Bird by bird" your family motto would not be a bad idea. Your grade-schooler always wants to take on more than she can manage, especially when it comes to going off with friends.

- **Do not veto the idea out of hand.** This would crush any third grader with a new friend, especially one having her social ups-and-downs. Indicate that you *are* willing to say "Yes," but gradually. Your daughter will not balk the way she would if you just jumped to a quick and absolute "No." Say this: "I am not comfortable sending you to a stranger's home. Sending you on a sleepover will feel like a good decision if we take time and do these three sleepover steps":
  - **Step 1. Arrange after-school play dates:** "I will talk with your friend's mom. We can invite Anne and her mom over for a visit here. Next time you can go to her house, I'll pick you up and meet her mom then, if she can't come to our house."
  - **Step 2. Schedule an "almost sleepover":** "On the weekend, you can play together in the afternoon and have supper at her house. Your friend can come here for a long weekend play date, too. That way you can have lots of time together and even spend the evening with your new friend at her house."

- **Step 3. Schedule a sleepover:** "Then, as we get to know her family and they get to know us, we will consider a whole-night sleepover."
- **Establish "Step by step" as a family rule.** To avoid future conflicts, at the next family meeting tell your daughter that this step-by-step approach will now be the family rule about new activities, particularly those not under your supervision. The next time you encounter this sort of dilemma, you will have even less of a struggle.

Clothing Catastrophes

Discipline Goal Ensuring that your child is tidy and takes good care of his possessions.

No-Win Reaction "If you do not pick up the clothes on your floor, they are going into the garbage."

Winning Tactic Step by step, games, and humor to make clean-up possible.

Assume that your son knows as much about being tidy as you know about nuclear physics. Draw on your creative talent and playfulness to teach this challenging subject.

- **Laundry Basketball:** Tell your son that you are going to hold tryouts for a new sport—*laundry basketball.*
  1. Show him the goal—to get the laundry into a hamper—and how to score points: by making his clothing land in the laundry basket.
  2. Have a bell sound when he scores, and make appropriate whooping calls when he does; it can add a measure of silly fun to this.
  3. Start the same thing with papers and trash that are lying around.
  4. Once your child gets the hang of this sport, relax. Do not nag. Every so often, knock on his door, go into his room, blow a whistle, and call "game time." Then let him "pick up the ball."
- **Wind-up his cleaning motor:** Come into your child's room with a big key (you can cut it out of cardboard), put it gently on his back, and tell him, "I can see your cleaning engine is stalled, let me crank it up to get it moving." Grade-schoolers respond better to silly, playful encouragement than stinging criticism.
- **Remember, if these tactics do not work, you can utilize Consequences and Cost, with which you are already familiar, to correct the misbehavior:** If the clothes do not reach the hamper, they are not

where they need to be in order to be cleaned, so ***do not do his laundry!*** When he complains, restate the limit and the impact of his misconduct: "You must be responsible for putting your clothes and trash in the proper place. I work hard, and so do you. I will do my share to take care of this family, but you are expected to pull your weight also." A few weeks of paying the cost with no socks for gym or wearing wrinkled shirts will have an impact. Even boys like to look well dressed.

Transitioning Turmoil

Discipline Goal Promoting patience and eliminating pestering.

No-Win Reaction "If you don't stop pestering me, we are not going to the zoo next Saturday."

Winning Tactic Step by step, as you join your child's sense of time.
    Telling her in advance is not necessarily a mistake if you add a step-by-step followup to your announcement. Your young child does not measure time the way you do, so the gap between the promise and the reality are huge for her. Even on a Friday, Saturday can seem like a lifetime away.

• **Begin with empathy:** When your child pesters you with "Is it time yet?", respond, "I know that you are excited about the trip, but we will not be going for a few days yet, which feels very far away for you. Let's see if we can find a way to help that time not feel so very far."

Once you acknowledge her frustration, break time down into concrete measurements that a young child can actually understand:

• **Clothing Clock:** Say, "There are three more schooldays until Saturday. Let's put out the clothes you will wear each day until Saturday and take out your favorite pink shorts for the trip to the zoo. Then, each day, as you get dressed, you can see how close you are getting to the day when you will wear your favorite shorts to the zoo."
• **Water Clock:** Take a large measuring cup and fill it to a level corresponding to the days your child has to wait—four cups for four days, for example. Let your child pour off a cup each evening before bed, so she can see the *"flow of time"* until her big day.

- **Breakfast Cereal Clock:** Take small cereal boxes corresponding to the number of days she must wait. Let her choose her favorite cereal for Saturday, the zoo day. Line them up on the kitchen counter and have her *"eat up the time"* at breakfast each morning.

(These tactics are also useful if you must leave a preschooler for a few days, say to go on a business trip.)

Winning Tactic #3: Positive Reframing

Putting your child and his behavior in a positive light can make family life a good deal more peaceful. In fact, it is possible to reframe or recast many parent/child conflicts positively so that they virtually disappear.

Sibling Struggles

Discipline Goal Appropriate behavior of an older sibling with a new baby.

No-Win Reaction "If you go to your baby sister's crib and annoy her one more time, I will not let you near her."

Winning Tactic Positive spin to help a child adjust to a major life change.

- **Positively spin the loss of babyhood into a gain in status and privileges:** "You are no longer the only child, but your sister's arrival made you into the 'big brother' in our family. You are now the oldest and biggest child. Because you are such a big boy, if you like, you may have the *special job* of helping me rock the cradle."
- **Special treatment for "big brother":** Ask others to help you acknowledge your older child's gain in status.
  1. Politely ask people closest to you that they bring your son a *"big brother"* gift when they come to visit the new baby—a new piggy bank where everybody gives him a little "big brother" good-luck money, a T-shirt that proudly says, "I Am a Big Brother Now."
  2. Ask others to spend *special time* with the "new big brother." Grandparents can be a real help here if they give extra TLC to their grandson.

- **Apply your knowledge about empathy. As you work to have a child reframe his sibling rivalry, always respect and make room for the negative emotions:** Do not ignore negative feelings or force your child to reject them in favor of the positive. If he bumps into the crib, firmly set the limit and acknowledge the ill-will, which is entirely normal, saying, "No, it is *not* acceptable for you to be rough with your sister. I know you wish she would get sent back to the hospital but she is going to be part of our family, just the way you are." Do *not* say anything like "I know you really love her and think she is wonderful, and you did not mean anything by shoving the crib, because you are her big brother."

    Permit an older sibling to acknowledge the hurts and disappointments about losing his status before you point out the good. Allow ambivalent feelings of love/hate, excitement/sadness. If you do not make room for ambivalent feelings, you are asking him to reject, bury, or hide negative emotions, which always puts a burden on a child and makes sibling rivalry worse. The "power of positive reframing" only works if there is room for the full range of emotions.

Temperament Tiffs

Discipline Goal To bring out the best in your child's personality even if he has a challenging, active temperament or personality style.

No-Win Reaction "Sit down in your seat this instant, you are bothering everyone. They'll think you're a brat."

Winning Tactic Positive spin to develop a good view of your child's personality.

- **Positively reframe your and your family's current negative view of your child's personality:** Accept her temperament and think of her in glowing, *not* critical terms: "My daughter is an energetic, outgoing, friendly, active little girl who likes to keep on the go." Help her (and yourself) understand her own personality, learning to work with her temperament, not against it.
    1. List all of your daughter's qualities in the negative, then draw up a list of affirming adjectives to replace each one. Spirited, energetic, lively, can-do, vivacious, full of life, are a few first-rate words.

2. Make a point of using these words daily:

"Today you are in such high spirits."

"You are so full of energy it is hard for you to sit down for a long time to concentrate on your math problems. Why don't you shake some of that extra energy out of your body, so you can sit more easily?" Let her wiggle or do jumping jacks for a while.

3. Do not allow other family members, especially siblings, to use negative labels (e.g., brat, pest, devil, troublemaker, nuisance) to tease or name-call.

• **Positively reframe potentially negative views of your child's personality for others:** Let people who have contact with your daughter know about her personality in advance—with a positive spin, of course.

1. Before a play date, tell her friend's mother: "My daughter is really athletic, she prefers playing outdoors rather than being inside doing arts and crafts. Rollerblading, or tag, or soccer is right up her alley."

2. Alert the person sitting near you in a public place, e.g., an airplane: "My daughter is a bundle of energy. I thought I would tell you in case you are not used to an active, outgoing child." With your advance notice, he might be able to change his seat.

3. Work with the teacher to reframe her idea of your child:
   • Once a teacher starts to regard her positively, she will respond more favorably, and your child will not run the risk of getting a reputation as a "difficult kid," which can dog her through school and spark endless conflicts. As a rule, kids labeled "difficult" do poorly in school.
   • Instead of reprimanding your child to "sit still," the teacher can give her a job, like collecting papers and books, that will show your daughter constructive ways to channel her high energy.

Teachers are very resourceful at this, so get their help.

• **Put a positive spin on your child's future:** Parents often come down hard on a child's active temperament or personality, because they fear it spells doom and gloom for her future. This stops them from seeing that an active child whose energy is channeled and harnessed can turn into a real go-getter, *provided that is the way you see her and she sees herself*. Be realistic: she will not be the neat little girl in the smocked dress sitting quietly in a church pew, so don't insist on that goal. But she could be the best climber and gymnast in her grade—which is pretty terrific (for less aggravation, dress her accordingly). Remember her active temperament can lead her to a career in adulthood that requires this sort of personality, from politician to mountain climber to soccer coach. If you see her personality in an optimistic light she will mature into a productive adult and find her place in the world.

- **Identify successful active adults:** To reinforce this positive spin, find ten active, energetic, outgoing people in various fields of endeavor whom you admire, and then imagine your child's future as one of them. Maybe even a president or an Olympic star.

CHECK YOUR CHILD'S TEMPERAMENT

Many of your child's sensitivity issues could be laid to rest if they are related to his *temperament*. If you have not done this already, go back and make a temperament assessment of your child. Then you can readjust many of the things you do to better suit his temperament and make life smoother. The more you know about his behavioral style, the more you can work around it.

Please Do Not Disturb

Let your child construct a wheel that indicates whether he is ready for company or not. Let him post it on his door, the way you might in a hotel. Respect his right to decide if he wants to be alone, unless you feel he is at risk, i.e. that he is doing something dangerous in his room.

Mood Wheel

Let your child make a wheel that indicates his mood, from "sunny" to "stormy," and post it on his door. This is especially good for a child with a sensitive temperament who has siblings. It can help others be sensitive and respectful to his emotional state.

Chore Wars

Discipline Goal Gain cooperation and participation in tasks around the house.

No-Win Reaction "You are the laziest bunch of kids I have ever seen. You don't do a thing around this house to help out."

Winning Tactic Positive spin; using games so kids *want* to help around the house.

- **Chores into games:**
  1. In the fall, ask your children to come out in the yard and make the most gigantic pile of leaves they ever saw, instead of demanding that they "just pick up that rake and get moving." You can even turn "leaf piling" into an annual "sporting" competition.
  2. In the winter, after a snowfall, ask, "Who can take all the snow off the sidewalks and make it into a funny snowman on the front lawn?"
  3. For spring cleanup, try announcing, "Who can find ten pieces of trash on our property?" instead of "Pick up all the garbage in the garden."

       Award "litter-buster" prizes to each child.

  Take this tactic indoors, as well:

  4. "Pick your clothes up off the floor" can change into a fun activity—"Can *we* make all the clothes on the floor disappear?"
  5. Beat the clock: take a timer and set it for three minutes. Then challenge your child to see if the two of you can put away all the toys and blocks before the bell rings.

WHAT A DIFFERENCE A DAY MAKES: POSITIVELY REFRAMING YOUR CHILD'S MOOD

Each of these tactics can make children feel special and important, which helps put them in a good frame of mind. Remember, if they don't fall into your comfort zone, don't use them.

Personal Days

Institute a personal day off. Permit your grade-school child to stay home from school for her own personal reason. A personal day can

(continued on next page)

restore a child's mood and make her less irritable. It can also provide a time for more attention, which reduces tension. To make this effective and not playing hooky, create a system for this "day off." The conditions are:

1. One personal day every three months.
2. Never before or after a weekend.
3. Planned, not last minute.
4. Not permitted if test or project is due or if special activity is planned in school.

The rules make it important and serious, and not just a way to avoid school.

Only-Child Days

Give each child an opportunity to have your undivided attention for a day as if she were your one and only child. This helps ease the sibling rivalry, if your child knows that she can have your undivided attention for a time.

Self-Control Catastrophes

Discipline Goal Encourage your children's self-control of their voices, bodies, and actions.

No-Win Reaction "Quiet down, I've had enough of you for one day."

Winning Tactic Positive spin; pretending and games to improve compliance with your requests and/or instructions.

Kids listen better and behave better when they hear good supportive words, just as losing teams often improve if they have a buoyant cheerleading squad and supportive fans. Reframe requests or instructions with an encouraging twist rather than a reprimanding snap. Try to shift from telling your child what *not* to do to *what to do* **Don't fall into the trap of becoming the "No" Monster.**

- **Still as a mouse:** Rather than shouting, "Stop running all over the place like a wild man," say, "Come stand with me and let's see how very still you can be." Or say, "Can you be as still as a quiet little mouse hiding from a cat?"

- **On and off buttons:** Preschoolers like pretending to be machines or robots. To get him to settle down, tell your child he has "on" and "off" buttons, and turn him "down," or "off," by touching his switch, which might be his nose, for example.
- **Marching like a soldier:** Some children respond to the idea of marching in step, "like soldiers," while others that find moving in rhythm, to a gentle beat, or even slow dancing, are positive ways to gain calm and control.
- **Putting on your brakes:** If an out-of-control activity is dangerous (he is running toward the street), you may have to grab your child for his own safety, but you do not have to shriek "Get here right now" when snatching him out of harm's way. Instead, offer a firm, positive reminder that "We put on our brakes when we come to the street," to reinforce this positive behavior of coming to a halt.
- **Red light/green light:** Play this classic street game with your child and his friends. Line them up in a row and tell them that they may run to you when you say, "Green light," but they must stop instantly when you shout, "Red light." A child must sit out if they run on the "red" command. The last child standing is the winner.
- **The stopping game:** To teach an active child not to run into traffic, start by firmly stating, "We always come to a halt at the curb, because it is dangerous to run into the street, you can get hurt. You may *not* cross the street without holding my hand." Then suggest that you play the "stopping game" together, to practice learning to stay safe.
  1. Take your child's hand and run animatedly to the curb, saying the words "Go, go, go" as you head for the corner. As you get to the curb, say, "Stop," and come to a dead halt. You can even pretend to be a car or motorcycle and make your "brakes" screech as you stop.
  2. Do this repeatedly, praising your child, "You did it. Let's try again."
  3. After you feel sure that your child knows the rules of this "game," tell him, "Now it's your turn to do it all alone." Go to the corner and have him run to you and stop at the curb by himself. Be sure to remind your child that even though you are playing, this is a very serious game, and going across the street with an adult is a rule until he is bigger and has learned to do it safely on his own.

A FEW WELL-CHOSEN WORDS CAN PUT A POSITIVE SPIN ON SEEMING MISBEHAVIOR

Young children do not deliberately misbehave or not listen. More often than not, in the excitement of the moment, they lose sight of good and safe ways they need to act. Positive reframing gives them a needed reminder of what you expected of them not where they have failed.

Reprimand	Positive Reframing
"Be quiet."	"Please hold all those feelings inside for a minute, until I am done talking."
"Stop sulking."	"Can you show me what a big cheerful face can look like?"
"Put on those pants this instant."	"Let's see if your leg can wiggle into that pant leg and peek through that hole at the end."
"Don't go near that china cabinet."	"I bet you can make an invisible fence around the cabinet and never ever step over it."
"You didn't hear a word I said."	"Please turn up the volume on your ears."
"Shut up."	"Can you press your pause button so that I may speak?"
"I don't care if it is your gift money, you are not spending another dime."	"I think you can be a smart consumer if you save your money and then buy things that you really want."
"Sit down this minute and get to work."	"Please bend over. I have a jar of special homework glue that I am going to put on your bottom to help you stick to your work."

Winning Tactic #4: Giving Notice

Giving children warning can help negotiate peacefully many a parent/child conflict. Adults get this assistance all the time. Children, even more than adults, need time to collect themselves when making transitions. Add this technique of "giving notice" to your repertoire.

Transition Turmoil

Discipline Goal To make transition in a timely way.

No-Win Reaction "You move like a snail; hurry, we are going to be late again."

Winning tactic Giving notice, joining, positive reframing, and step by step to keep kids on schedule.

- **Count down to launching time:**
  1. Announce, "We are going to our church/synagogue/mosque this morning. Our family will 'take off' from our launching pad in one half hour. Would you like me to give you the countdown every ten minutes or is every fifteen OK?"
  2. Then come to his room at the designated time, knock on his door, and say, "Attention all passengers. Countdown is beginning. Fifteen minutes until we launch this vehicle for church."
  3. As you reach the last few minutes, make your "countdown" announcements more frequently, until you say, "Blast off!"—and "rocket" your child out the door.
  4. It may be helpful to have a younger child draw a rocket. Every time you enter his room, he can move it closer to the lift-off position, finally taking his rocket along with him as he "lifts off" for church.
  5. You might give your son small steps along the way, telling him just what he has to do to get from his room to the car in *launching stages*, rather than one big and general request.
     - "At the start of countdown, turn off all electronic equipment to prepare for take off."
     - "At the second announcement, go downstairs and head for the car, to be in 'ready' position for takeoff."

- ▪ "At liftoff, please be in the back seat and securely buckled up by blast-off time!"
- **Utilize a timer** To help a kid keep track of time—especially if he cannot yet read a clock—place an egg timer or an hourglass in his room. Give your son a ten-minute notice and set the timer for a five-minute interval. Announce, "When the bell rings (or when the sand runs out), I will be back to see if you are getting ready to leave." Return to his room to reset the timer for the next five minutes, and say, "When the bell rings this time, I will come back to get you and we will be leaving." Put a large, happy-looking clock in your child's room from early on, to help him get used to the day when he will use it to put himself on notice. If it makes him proud, buy him a watch even before he's up to telling time.

TIPS ON GETTING YOUR CHILD'S ATTENTION AND COOPERATION

To gain your child's cooperation, use the techniques of a good teacher. Let your behavior underscore your intent and your words.

Approach Your Child Draw near your child when you want her to listen. Bend down to her level. Put your hand on her shoulder.

Make Eye Contact Use your eyes to connect with your child, send a message with your gaze of approval, disapproval, and/or expectations.

Use Lively Facial Expressions and Gestures Nod, smile, wink, frown, tilt your head, use hand signals and even your whole stance to beckon a response.

Modulate Your Voice Use an inflection in your voice as a signal. Lower your voice when you want to be heard; it attracts a child's interest. Reserve a certain tone when you are seeking immediate cooperation, and give it a name, e.g., "This is my serious voice."

Manners Mayhem

Discipline Goal To stop rude or inappropriate behavior.

No-Win Reaction "Take that finger out of your nose!"

Winning Tactic Giving notice with private family words and signals.

Some children need help focusing on or remembering what is expected of them when it comes to manners, or behavior suitable to public versus private places. Making up family signals can be a way to draw a child's attention to an offending behavior without a reprimand or shame.

- Use colors to signify behaviors that are not acceptable. Call a "code black" for a child's bad habit—say, picking his nose in public.
- Make up family words to alert a child that she may be stepping over an acceptable line. Decide that greedy behavior at a table will be called "three," as in "three little pigs." Then, if a child has grabbed a big piece of cake at a party, quietly say, "three," as a reminder that the behavior has gone too far.
- Make up a family signal, so that tapping your nose means "stop," as if to symbolize a pause button. Then, instead of telling your child, "Be quiet and stop interrupting me," simply press the secret "pause button" to signal what you expect.

FOUR WINNING DISCIPLINE TACTICS

Post this list on your refrigerator to help you keep your cool.

Joining Use what you know about your children and their development to join rather than fight them.

Step-by-Step Create a step-by-step bridge for your children between what you ask of them and what they must do, so that they are able to do as they are told and to follow instructions.

Positive Spin Use positive reframing, which transforms negative attitudes into positives and fosters the spirit of cooperation.

Giving Notice Develop techniques to assist your child in making changes and transitions, which ensures compliance.

Chapter 13

....

Encouraging Cooperation in Kids: Using Practice Tactics

We need our children to do so very many things to help the family run properly. There are things they have to do routinely: going to sleep, brushing their teeth, or going to bed. Then there are things that we ask of them that fall outside of the daily requirements of life. Sometimes we ask them to try something for the first time, like going to the doctor, which is a big and not a daily routine. Sometimes we ask them to do something for the first time, like brushing their teeth, which starts out as novel but which will become part of everyday life. Occasionally, we need them to cooperate for an unusual venture, perhaps a plane trip. There are also events that ask them to stretch their maturity, like sitting quietly at a formal holiday dinner. Occasionally, they join us in a required activity, like a trip to the supermarket or shopping at a mall. The following tactics help you peacefully navigate the not-so-routine requests that you make of your child.

Practice Makes for Cooperative Kids

When we ask our kids to take on new tasks or ventures, we often neglect to offer them this much-needed option—practice. Asking children to do a job without allowing an opportunity to try out or run through their skills is an obstacle that gets in the way of kid cooperation all the time. These four techniques are ways to help kids practice, providing tryouts and trial runs and eliminating fights.

Practice tactics are:

1. Pretend Play
2. Visitation
3. Rehearsing
4. Role-playing

Winning Practice Tactic #1: Pretend Play

Children love to mimic. By drawing on this, you can get them to acquire all sorts of reasonable conduct without having to push them into compliance. Think of using a toy telephone when your child "calls" you for a talk, it works far better than instructing a child on proper telephone manners.

Pretend play can allow them to stretch to a new level of proper or more mature behavior without being at risk for failure. In the world of pretend, there is no failure, because it *is* play. When children know how to play, they become cooperative.

Encouraging Manners Through Pretend Play

There is a bottom age-limit when you can expect to make your child part of a dinner party, where he will be required to sit in his chair and act like a young prince. Nonetheless, you can get very young kids to be polite, provided you start early. Manners are the way we make it easier to get along with other people. Manners are social rules, agreed upon so that life runs smoothly. You don't grab the food; instead, you say, "Please pass the sprouts," and that keeps mealtime from turning into a food fight. You can start practicing these rules of civility very, very early.

Please, May I, and Thank You:

Even with your toddler, it is never too early to start with the basics, practice "please" and "thank you," but make sure to *model* this behavior, not just demand it. If you knock on his door, even when he is two years old, and say, "Excuse me, may I *please* come in," you are starting the job of good manners. "Please" and "thank you" are serious and important words, which actually transmit a very valuable message to your child. They say, "Remember, the things you need and want in this world come from others." These polite words acknowledge the part other people play in making our lives work. Realizing this purpose will help them take manners seriously and not just see them as arbitrary or silly rules.

To keep kids on track, model socially appropriate connecting behavior. If you are not the "politeness pro," they will not know what to do. If you need to tell your child something, don't shout across three rooms. Walk to his room, knock on his door, and ask for his attention. Use your child's name when addressing him. "John, I am sorry to interrupt your homework, but please stop what you are doing for a moment so that I may ask you something." Wait until he makes eye contact, before speaking, and only then go on to talk. When you are through, thank him for his time. Adding what seems like a bit of formality to your family interactions will go a very long way toward making your son fit for the company of grandparents, neighbors, friends, and the occasional king or queen with whom your little prince might dine. An entire family that practices respect, regard, and courtesy for one another gets along amiably and is very nice to be around—every day and at formal holiday dinners, too.

Tea Parties

- Have your child invite guests to a tea party. "Invited guests" can include stuffed animals, siblings, and you.
- Together set a table with napkins, silverware, and all the trimmings.
- Offer a few pointers about placing a napkin on his lap, chewing with his mouth closed, and refraining from grabbing in favor of requesting that food be passed.
- Read a children's book on etiquette with him, which can provide some helpful hints.
- At the tea party, pretend to be royalty, kings and queens, and exaggerate all the polite manners you want from him.

- Go through introducing yourselves by name to one another, even the teddy bears! In a high-pitched voice, say things like, "My delightful young man, would you be such a dear as to pass the jelly sandwiches?"
- Make sure that the tea party ends with gracious "thank you"s and appropriate compliments.
- Be silly enough to be fun and correct enough to make your point about what you expect. Whatever you exaggerate in play will come out looking normal in real life.
- At your own dinner table, you can remind him of his manners by referring to him in that same silly overstated voice or by signaling him affectionately when you call him "my dear young prince."

Throwing a Real Pretend Dinner Party

It can also be good practice to let your child "throw a dinner party" just for his friends; no adults allowed. Kids love to *playact* being grown-up, and it is far more effective than scolding them, "Act grown-up!" The dinner can be around a celebration, like New Year's Eve.

- If he is older, he can send written invitations to his friends.
- Tell other parents what you are trying to accomplish and get them in on the fun.
- Have the children dress up in their best clothes. You would be surprised to see how pride in the way he looks can positively affect a child's manners.
- It is especially fun for kids if you do the serving. Parents can pretend to be waiters.
- Candles, flowers, and a special meal will make this memorable and give your child the practice he needs before he goes for the real thing.
- Take a photo, so everyone can have a souvenir (and a reminder) of the bash.

Pretend Games: Who Gets the Job?

My children made up a practice game for manners after I told them about an article in the *Wall Street Journal* that described a study showing the real reasons many people do not get desired jobs: They forfeit them over the lunch table, not at the interview desk. The article went on to describe which etiquette blunders were sure to blow the job offer. The study cited elbows on the table, chewing with an open mouth, and other such bloopers. Soon after we all read the article, my kids started a dinnertime game, "Who Gets the Job?" They watched the table like hawks and hooted at each other (not so politely), "You lost the job!" whenever one of them made a mistake in manners. I credit their "game" with reinforcing their good behavior, and I still get a "Mom, you lost the job" if I talk with food in my mouth.

> ▶ **PYB Words of Wisdom:** *Bear this in mind. No matter how successful you are at getting your child to know what he has to do, he will not be on his best behavior on the home front. Do not get discouraged. You will hear his praises sung by others, because away from home is where all these skills will come to the fore, and that is just what you are hoping to accomplish.*

Winning Practice Tactic #2: Visitation

Have you ever sent your child to day care, nursery school or kindergarten, or college? If you have, you know that before your child actually begins to attend any of these places, it is customary that she is invited to make a visit or two in advance of her enrollment. For younger children, a home visit is frequently part of the transition process as well. This allows the children to become accustomed to unfamiliar territory, making them less skittish about venturing out, whether it is the "big world" of the playground or the college campus.

When you do your advance work, you may see something that indicates your child is not developmentally ready for an undertaking, or that there is not a good fit between his temperament and the new venture. A sports league may be full of boys more competitive and bigger than your child, and your visit can help you make the wise decision to postpone enrollment for a while, saving you both from countless struggles over "I'm not good enough." Electing to delay signing your son on to a sports team until he is ready can transform a failure into a triumph. Visitation helps you make good parenting decisions.

Encouraging Cooperation on a First Visit to a Doctor/Dentist Through Visitation

- **Make a get-acquainted appointment.** Before you go for a first visit, call the dentist and ask him if you can stop by with your child for a "get-acquainted" call and if he can take a few moments to introduce himself. If he says no, he's too busy, find another dentist.
- **Read a book in preparation.** The night before your outing to meet him or her, read one of the many books about first visits to the dentist, and tell your child that the next afternoon you are going to meet Dr. Kaplan, who will be "Your own tooth doctor."
- **Use positive reframing.** To minimize anxiety, do not say, "He will fill any cavities that hurt you." Let your son know that the tooth doctor will help him keep his teeth strong and healthy, making the doctor an ally, not a scary monster.
- **Develop familiarity with the office.** If it is feasible, when you go to the office, spend a few minutes letting your child play in the waiting room, and make sure to introduce your child to the staff.
- **Pay attention to rapport.** Listen to the dentist talk with your child to see if there is a rapport. This is the time to evaluate if you want to use this professional. If your child is not hitting it off when all is calm, it might be far worse when he starts medical procedures. Listen carefully and do not be shy about finding another professional if you sense there is no good chemistry. A mature professional understands that he will not be right for every child.
- **Make your visit relaxed.** Don't hurry. When you leave, have your child say good-bye to the dentist and tell him, "We will see you next week for a checkup."
- **Tune into your child's reactions.** On the way home, stop for a few minutes of talk time to ask your child what he liked best about his visit to Dr. Kaplan. If you sense a strong objection, you may need more visits or another doctor.
- **Reinforce your good work.** The following week, reread the book you introduced earlier. The groundwork that you are laying is especially helpful if your child has to undergo any procedures. It does take time to make this extra visit, but it is far better than having to drag an unhappy child to an unfamiliar place that frightens him.

Encouraging Adjustment to Summer Camp Through Visitation

If you want to avoid heart-wrenching calls from a homesick camper, consider using this visitation strategy for your grade-schooler.

- **Visit the idea of camp early.** Discuss the prospect of camp **one year** in advance.
- **Gather information.** Ask him to get a list of names from friends who love their camps. Give your child a share in the decision-making; after all, he will be the one living at camp. Let him have input, but reserve the right to veto. Mom and Dad need to listen, but they also need to have the final say in such a big and costly venture.
- **Visit camps virtually.** Harness the Internet for a virtual introduction to camps. Suggest that he and you both look online at these and other camps that might be of interest.
- **Visit camps actually.** If possible, during the summer prior to camp, take a few days of your summer vacation to make camp visits with your child. When you have chosen one, return to revisit the Web site together. Most camps will also send a video.
- **Visit with former campers.** Ask for the names of other campers with whom you and your child can speak. Schedule a personal visit with one of these campers. *Do not rely on the phone or e-mail.* A face-to-face visit is paramount and will tell you and your child much more about what he might expect. Spending time with an unfriendly child who talks about how his team trounced everyone in color war might make you wonder about how friendly and welcoming this camp may be to a newcomer like your child.
- **Arrange for a home visit.** A camp staff member may be available for a home visit. This is customary for many camps and especially important if you have been unable to visit the campgrounds.

This visitation strategy sounds like a lot of work, and it is. Children spend many summers at camp, so this is an investment in making the right choice over the long term. If you handle this strategy well, you will only be going through this process once. Using this strategy also saves on phone bills from unhappy campers, and, at worst, it saves you from money lost when a miserable child must come home, and from the sense of defeat the child will inevitably feel over this disaster.

Here are some other visitation suggestions for different situations.

- Look at online previews with your child to see which movies might be too much for him and which are appropriate.
- Let your son visit the soccer team before signing him up; you might discover the kids are too big or too rough in advance.

Winning Practice Tactic #3: Rehearsing

This strategy is a very close relative to *visitation*, but it adds another dimension. It is not just about scouting out a place and collecting information. Rehearsing involves creating an opportunity for your child to go through an experience *similar* to the one they will be venturing on, as a trial run. It is often best to start rehearsals with a situation that shares some of the same features of the "real thing." It is then possible to upgrade the experience until it becomes very much like the new venture.

Encouraging a Resistant or Anxious Child

To illustrate this approach, let's look at a child who is anxious about swimming and water.

- **Start gently introducing things related to the fear.** Read a book about the seaside. Look through magazines and have your child cut out pretty pictures of different bodies of water. Put them up on her walls and the refrigerator. Get her a guppie and point out to her that he, like all of his fish friends, is not afraid of the water.
- **Help establish pleasant associations to the new experience.** At night, when you put her to bed, speak in a quiet, measured voice. Tell her to close her eyes and think of the prettiest of all the pictures of the sea that she has cut out. Encourage her to imagine the warm sand under her feet, the breeze on her face, the cool water lapping at her toes. As you do this, encourage her to relax, breathe, and let the good feelings wash over her.
- **Rehearse an "almost" try.** Buy her water wings and let her wear them around the house. Let her wear the water wings in the bathtub and give her goggles, too. In a kiddie pool or tub, encourage a splashing game. Let friends join her. Help her learn to lie back and "float" with

only a bit of water, so it does not get in her nose and mouth when she is on her back.

- **Stage a "dress rehearsal."** Take her to a pool. Find lessons specifically designed for the fearful child.

Rehearsing to Overcome Social Anxiety in School

By fourth grade, children perform publicly in school. It may mean that they read a book report aloud, present a science project, play an instrument in the school band concert, or act in a class play. Going public is a misery for most grade-schoolers, because developmentally they are acutely self-conscious and self-critical. By age eight and nine, just when your child is asked to go public, this feeling intensifies, perfect timing! For your grade-schooler, try this. Have your child:

- Read aloud privately into a tape recorder.
- Read aloud in front of an imaginary audience in his room.
- Rehearse his presentation—if he is willing—in front of his parents. As long as the work is done, respect his right of refusal.
- If going public causes him undue stress, *do not force him to perform.* Ask his teacher if there is another option, like making copies for the class to read, having her read his paper aloud, or having children switch papers so that they read one another's aloud and do not feel under so much pressure and scrutiny.

Rehearsing for a New Baby-sitter

1. **Read stories as preparation.** At bedtime, read a book on baby-sitting or make up your own story about going out.
2. **Make a "play date" with a baby-sitter.** Invite a baby-sitter over for a play date with your child and stay close by. At this time, you can evaluate if there will be a good rapport between the two of them.
3. **Have a *dress rehearsal*.** Let the baby-sitter come when you have errands to run and will be back in a short while, or while you are working at home. Get your child and the sitter involved in an activity like a board game, or arts and crafts. When you return home or finish your work, tell your child she will have a chance to continue the project on the coming Saturday night, when the sitter will return.
4. **Positively reframe your night out.** With some advanced warning, tell your child you will be going out but make a point to be upbeat.

Do not say, "We will be leaving you with the baby-sitter." Give this a *positive spin*; "Mom and Dad think you are grown-up enough to have a special evening with your baby-sitter when we go out to the theater on Saturday."

5. **Share your night out.** Let your daughter pick out your clothes and play a part in your evening out, which also models enthusiasm for doing different and new things and makes her feel included. You can also add this positive note: "Mom and Dad are having a special night, and so are you. Maybe having an ice cream with your baby-sitter can make it even more special for you."

6. **Allow transition time.** The evening you are going out, have the baby-sitter come at least a half-hour before you leave. Let your child and the sitter resume the activity they were doing the last time they met.

7. **Leave with a formal good-bye.** Never sneak out of the house, even if your child protests. She will calm down, because she has a lot of rehearsal time under her belt. She will also trust you, which will make *all* nights out to follow even smoother.

Winning Practice Tactic #4: Role-playing

Encourage a child to playact an upcoming encounter. In a role-play, your child can assume any part. It is often most helpful when she acts the part of whom-or whatever is anxiously anticipated. This switching makes your child feel powerful instead of helpless, which has a soothing effect, making her feel braver and in charge. Role-playing allows her to become familiar with the activities she will encounter, and the feelings it evokes as well, but it makes her the "boss."

• **Role-playing a visit to the doctor/dentist.** Before a doctor or dentist visit, encourage your child to play "doctor." An appropriate costume helps. An old white shirt works as a "doctor's coat." Buy a toy doctor's kit. Bring your child a "sick doll" who needs her help with a fever. Let her give the doll shots and medicine. Give her positive spin and empathetic words of healing. "I know that you are going to do everything you can to make your doll get better. Tell your doll that you are sorry the shot you are giving her will cause pain but that you are going to give her a lollipop for being so brave."

- **Role-playing the first day of school.** Playing school with siblings and friends is an excellent way to prepare for the "big day." Each child can take turns being the teacher. Give your child the equipment. A chalkboard, books, and paper can make it feel like the real thing. Volunteer to join in and be a student, too. Encourage your child/teacher to role-play appropriate classroom manners, such as raising hands, speaking in turn, and asking permission to leave seats. In this way, she becomes familiar with class rules and feels in charge. Volunteer to be a pupil. Try being a silly pupil who misbehaves, and encourage your child to help this child get good at school.
- **Role-playing a new behavioral milestone, e.g., moving from crib to big boy/girl bed.** Let your child role-play being the daddy to his teddy bear who will be moving into his new bed. Encourage your child to explain the situation to the teddy. If you listen carefully, you will hear your child's own concern expressed, and you can then have an empathetic "talk" with the teddy bear. Though you are empathizing with a stuffed animal, your son is really the target of your compassion. He hears it and feels understood, along with his stuffed friend.

ROLE REVERSAL WITH AN ANXIOUS CHILD*

If you have a small child who is afraid of animals, e.g., she whines or cries when a dog comes near, to encourage her bravery, try one of these role reversals:

1. Tell her that the dog is jumping because it is afraid of her. In an exaggerated way, ask her to "please stop scaring the dog." Suggest that your child try to stay near the dog until it calms down and knows that she is not scary.
2. If you want to get a family pet, arrange a trip to the pound and together find a dog that is scared of her. Visit this animal, "so the puppy can get used to" your child before you bring it home.

---

*These techniques are inspired by the work of my friend and colleague, the founder of family therapy, Dr. Salvatore Minuchin.

Role-Playing to Help a Child Handle Teasing

The sting of rejection that a grade-schooler often feels can be a reason for a child's irritability at home; it makes kids cranky, sullen, and uncooperative. At its worst, a child may refuse to go to school. Role-playing can help social interactions, enabling him to get along with his peers more effectively. Start by being empathetic about his problem: "I know you are having a rough time with all the teasing and being picked on at school." Ask your open-ended question, "What is it like? Tell me about it. How does it make you feel when it happens?" Then make this offer:

- "I would like to help you make things work better for you at school. Let's play that we are in the lunchroom. I will be you. You be Daniel, who is the worst tease. Show me how he behaves toward you." Then switch roles.
- Evaluate the situation as you role-play. Perhaps you see that your sensitive son reacts so strongly to teasing that he makes a good target. Kids love to taunt someone whom they can "get to."
- If you sense overreacting is part of the problem, you can role-play a person who is nonreactive and stays calm in the face of the teasing. Show him the facial expression and the body language of someone who does not let a tease get under his skin.
- Have your child look at his face in the mirror and be aware of his body language when the teasing gets to him, and see what he looks like when he is perturbed and provoked.
- Encourage him to role-play expressions that communicate a stern "I do not tolerate this behavior"—and words to go with that expression. Make no-nonsense, stern faces together.
- Once he knows the limit-setting moves, let him role-play the new, improved version of himself, and you become the tease.
- Make a game of it: "Betcha I can make you mad!" The point of this "game" is for your child to set clear limits conveyed through his words and baby language in response to taunting.

The idea here is to help your child feel sturdier and stand up for his right to be treated with respect by his peers. This is good for him and a good model for his friends. However, if you sense he is being bullied, take appropriate action. Kids need adult help to stop bullying.

Role-playing gives your child *alternate responses* that he might not have had naturally. This new repertoire allows him to navigate the choppy waters of social interactions at school without coming home a wreck and then displacing his anger on you.

PARENT FOR A DAY: LET YOUR CHILD ROLE-PLAY YOU

Have your child take on your job for the day. This change of perspective can help reduce friction, because it gives your child a sense that he is important and in charge. It also helps him develop an appreciation for the work you do for him and the family, making him less resistant to your requests to share the family workload.

A Few Last Words

....

Dear Fellow Parents,

   In these pages, I have tried to share with you every last thing I know about raising cooperative and decent kids. I have tried to do it in a way that I find helpful and that I think helps other parents, too. I have taken everything I bring from my personal and professional experience and have offered it here to you, so that you could look over my shoulder, and the shoulders of the many parents with whom I work, to see good parenting in action. I feel certain that, after reading this volume, you know many things that will make your family life smoother, your parenting life easier, and your children more responsive. I think you will raise better children more easily, from the wisdom you have absorbed in these pages.

   I will leave you with a last thought, which, of course, takes us back to the beginning. Mother Nature had it right when she came up with her container for raising kids: safe, warm, sturdy, and with room to grow. She was smart enough to know that her relationship to her developing young was one marked by loving care but also by change, growth, and development. She knew what all parents know: we need to both hold on to and to let go of our children. That balance is not always an easy one to strike, but it is, nevertheless, one to aim for. With children, our goal is to make a delivery, to deliver them as they become increasingly able, into the world beyond home and family. This is the thrill of parenting: to get up in the morning each day and see your children expand into their universe. Good parenting makes this happen. It is a glorious trip. I trust that what I have shared with you in these pages from my knowledge and my heart will make this glorious trip smooth and filled with joy.

Bonnie Maslin

BODY LANGUAGE FOR PARENTING

To raise a well-behaved child use your mind *and* body.
Use your Legs to take a stand

Arms to take hold of your child, to embrace her, to raise her up

Eyes to see what your child is all about

Ears to listen to what she has to say

Mouth to communicate, to put your feelings into words
and encourage her to do the same

And heart to love her, always